Francis Hopkinson Smith

Caleb West

Master Diver

Francis Hopkinson Smith

Caleb West
Master Diver

ISBN/EAN: 9783743350403

Manufactured in Europe, USA, Canada, Australia, Japa

Cover: Foto ©ninafisch / pixelio.de

Manufactured and distributed by brebook publishing software (www.brebook.com)

Francis Hopkinson Smith

Caleb West

CALEB WEST
MASTER DIVER

BY

F. HOPKINSON SMITH

Illustrated

NEW YORK
GROSSET & DUNLAP
PUBLISHERS

COPYRIGHT, 1897 AND 1898, BY HOUGHTON, MIFFLIN AND CO.
COPYRIGHT, 1898, BY F. HOPKINSON SMITH
ALL RIGHTS RESERVED

ONE HUNDRED AND TWENTIETH THOUSAND

CONTENTS

CHAPTER		PAGE
I.	THE CAPE ANN SLOOP	1
II.	A MORNING'S MAIL	12
III.	CAPTAIN BRANDT AT THE THROTTLE	24
IV.	AMONG THE BLACKFISH AND TOMCODS	42
V.	AUNTY BELL'S KITCHEN	60
VI.	A LITTLE DINNER FOR FIVE	76
VII.	BETTY'S FIRST PATIENT	103
VIII.	THE "HEAVE HO" OF LONNY BOWLES	122
IX.	WHAT THE BUTCHER SAW	139
X.	STRAINS FROM BOCK'S 'CELLO	162
XI.	CAPTAIN JOE'S TELEGRAM	181
XII.	CAPTAIN JOE'S CREED	194
XIII.	A SHANTY DOOR	210
XIV.	TWO ENVELOPES	225
XV.	A NARROW PATH	236
XVI.	UNDER THE WILLOWS	259
XVII.	THE SONG OF THE FIRE	269
XVIII.	THE EQUINOCTIAL GALE	275
XIX.	FROM THE LANTERN DECK	284
XX.	AT THE PINES	300
XXI.	THE RECORD OF NICKLES, THE COOK	319
XXII.	AFTER THE BATTLE	334
XXIII.	A BROKEN DRAW	341
XXIV.	THE SWINGING GATE	351
XXV.	UNDER THE PITILESS STARS	359
XXVI.	CALEB TRIMS HIS LIGHTS	373

CALEB WEST, MASTER DIVER

CHAPTER I

THE CAPE ANN SLOOP

THE rising sun burned its way through a low-lying mist that hid the river, and flashed its search-light rays over the sleeping city. The blackened tops of the tall stacks caught the signal, and answered in belching clouds of gray steam that turned to gold as they floated upwards in the morning air. The long rows of the many-eyed tenements cresting the hill blinked in the dazzling light, threw wide their shutters, and waved curling smoke flags from countless chimneys.

Narrow, silent alleys awoke. Doors opened and shut. Single figures swinging dinner-pails, and groups of girls with baskets, hurried to and fro. The rumbling of carts was heard and shrill street cries.

Suddenly the molten ball swung clear of the purple haze and flooded the city with tremulous light. The vanes of the steeples flashed and blazed. The slanting roofs, wet with the night dew, glistened like silver. The budding trees, filling the great squares, flamed pink and yellow, their tender branches quivering in the rosy light.

Now long, deep-toned whistles — reveille of forge, spindle, and press — startled the air. Surging crowds filled the thoroughfares; panting horses tugged at the surface cars; cabs rattled over the cobblestones, and loaded trucks began to block the crossings.

The great city was astir.

At the sun's first gleam, Henry Sanford had waked with joyous start. Young, alert, full of health and courage as he was, the touch of its rays never came too early for him. To-day they had been like the hand of a friend, rousing him with promises of good fortune.

Dressing with eager haste, he had hurried into the room adjoining his private apartments, which served as his uptown business office. Important matters awaited him. Within a few hours a question of vital moment had to be decided, — one upon which the present success of his work depended.

As he entered, the sunshine, pouring through the wide windows, fell across a drawing-table covered with the plans of the lighthouse he was then building; illumined a desk piled high with correspondence, and patterned a wall upon which were hung photographs and sketches of the various structures which had marked the progress of his engineering career.

But it was toward a telegram lying open on his desk that Sanford turned. He took it in his hand and read it with the quiet satisfaction of one who knows by heart every line he studies. It was headed Keyport, and ran as follows: —

To Henry Sanford, C. E., Washington Square, New York.

Cape Ann sloop arrived and is a corker. Will be at your uptown office in the morning.

Joseph Bell.

"Dear old Captain Joe, he's found her at last!" he said to himself, and laughed aloud.

With a joyous enthusiasm that lent a spring and vitality to every movement, he stepped to the window and raised the sash to let in the morning air.

It was a gala-day for the young engineer. For months Captain Joe had been in search of a sloop of peculiar construction, — one of so light a draught that she could work in a rolling surf, and yet so stanch that she could sustain the strain of a derrick-boom rigged to her mast. Without such a sloop the building of the light-house Sanford was then constructing for the government on Shark Ledge, lying eight miles from Keyport, and breasting a tide running six miles an hour, could not go on. With such a sloop its early completion was assured.

The specifications for this lighthouse provided that the island which formed its base — an artificial one made by dumping rough stones over the sunken rock known as Shark's Ledge — should be protected not only from sea action, but from the thrust of floating ice. This Sanford was to accomplish by paving its under-water slopes with huge granite blocks, to form an enrockment, — each block to be bedded by a diver.

The engineer-in-chief of the Lighthouse Board at Washington had expressed grave doubts as to the practicability of the working methods submitted by Sanford for handling these blocks, questioning whether a stone weighing twelve tons could be swung overboard, as suggested by him, from the deck of a vessel and lowered to a diver while the boat was moored in a six-mile current. As, however, the selection of the means to be employed lay with the contracting engineer, and not with the Board, Sanford's working plans had finally been approved. He had lacked only a sloop to carry them out. This sloop Captain Joe had now found.

No wonder, then, that the splendor of the early sunshine had seemed a harbinger of success, nor that as the minutes flew his eagerness increased to grasp the captain's hand.

At the first sound of his heavy step in the hall outside, Sanford sprang from his desk and threw the door wide open to welcome the big, burly fellow, — comrade and friend for years, as well as foreman and assistant engineer on his force.

"Are you sure she'll handle the stones?" were the first words he addressed to the captain, — there were no formalities between these men. "Nothing but a ten-horse engine, remember, will lift them from the dock. What's the sloop's beam?"

"Thirty foot over all, an' she's stiff as a church," answered Captain Joe, all out of breath with his run up the stairs, — pushing his Derby hat back from his forehead as he spoke. "An' her cap'n ain't no slouch, nuther. I see him yesterday 'fore I come down. Looks 's ef he hed th' right stuff in him. Says he ain't afeard o' th' Ledge, an' don't mind layin' her broadside on, even ef she does git a leetle mite scraped."

"How's her boiler?" Sanford asked, with sudden earnestness.

"I ain't looked her b'iler over yit, but her cylinders is big enough. If her steam gives out, I'll put one of our own aboard. She'll do, sir. Don't worry a mite; we'll spank that baby when we git to 't," — and his leathery, weather-tanned face cracked into smiles.

Sanford laughed again. The cheerful humor

of this man, whose judgment of men never failed him, and whose knowledge of sea-things made him invaluable, was always a tonic to him.

"I'm glad you like her skipper," he said, taking from a pigeonhole in his perfectly appointed desk, as he spoke, the charter-party of the sloop. "I see his name is Brandt, and the sloop's name is the Screamer. Hope she'll live up to her name. The charter-party, I think, ought to contain some allusion to the coast-chart, in case of any protest Brandt may make afterwards about the shoaliness of the water. Better have him put his initials on the chart," he added, with the instinctive habit of caution which always distinguished his business methods. "Do you think the shallow water round the Ledge *will* scare him?" he continued, as he crossed the room to a row of shelves filled with mechanical drawings, in search of a round tin case holding the various charts of Long Island Sound.

Captain Joe did not answer Sanford's question at once. His mind was on something else. He took off his hat and pea-jacket, hung them on a hook, moved back the pile of books from the middle of the table, with as little consideration as he would have shown to so many bricks, corked a bottle of liquid ink for safety, flattened with his big hands the chart which Sanford had unrolled, weighted its four corners with a

T square and some color-pans, and then, bending his massive head, began studying its details with all the easy confidence of a first officer on a Cunarder.

As he leaned over the chart the sunlight played about his face and brought into stronger relief the few gray hairs which silvered the short brown curls crisped about his neck and temples. These hairs betrayed the only change seen in him since the memorable winter's day when he had saved the lives of the passengers on the sinking ferry-boat near Hoboken by calking with his own body the gash left in her side by a colliding tug. But time had touched him nowhere else. He was still the same broad-as-he-was-long old sea-dog; tough, sturdy, tender-eyed, and fearless. His teeth were as white, his mouth was as firm, his jaw as strong and determined.

The captain placed his horn-tipped finger on a dot marked "Shark's Ledge Spindle," obliterating in the act some forty miles of sea-space; repeated to himself in a low voice, "Six fathoms — four — one and a half — hum, 't ain't nothin'; that Cape Ann sloop can do it;" and then suddenly remembering Sanford's question, he answered, with quick lifting of his head and with a cheery laugh, "Skeer him? Wait till ye see him, sir. And he won't make no *pro*-test, nuther. He ain't that kind."

When the coast-chart had been rolled up

and replaced in the tin case, to be taken to Keyport for the skipper's initials, both men resumed their seats by Sanford's desk. By this time some of the young engineer's enthusiasm over the finding of the sloop had begun to cool. He seemed, as he sat there, a different man, as with businesslike address he turned to the discussion of various important details connected with the work.

"Anything left of the old house, captain?" he asked, taking from the table a rough sketch of the new shanty to be built on the Ledge, — the one used while the artificial island was being built having been injured by the winter storms.

"Not much, sir: one side's stove in an' the roof's smashed. Some o' the men are in it now, gittin' things in shape, but it's purty rickety. I'm a-goin' to put the new one here," — his finger on the drawing, — "an' I'm goin' to make it o' tongue-an'-grooved stuff an' tar the roof to git it water-tight. Then I'll hev some iron bands made with turnbuckles to go over the top timbers an' fasten it all down in the stone-pile. Oh, we'll git her so she'll stay put when hell breaks loose some night down Montauk way!" and another hearty laugh rang out, shaking the captain's brawny chest, as he rolled up the drawing and tucked it in the case for safety.

"There's no doubt we'll have plenty of

that," said Sanford, with a slight touch of anxiety in his tones. "And now about the working force. Will you make many changes?" he asked.

"No, sir. We'll put Caleb West in charge of the divin'; ain't no better man 'n Caleb in er out a dress. Them enrockments is mighty ugly things to set under water, an' I won't trust nobody but Caleb to do it. Lonny Bowles 'll help tend derricks; an' there's our regular gang, — George Nickles an' the rest of 'em. I only got one new man so far: that's a young feller named Bill Lacey. He looks like a skylarkin' chap, but I kin take that out o' him. He kin climb like a cat, an' we want a man like that to shin the derricks. He's tended divers, too, he says, an' he'll do to look after Caleb's life-line an' hose when I can't. By the way, sir, I forgot to ask ye about them derricks. We got to hev four whackin' big sticks to set them big stone on top o' the concrete when we git it finished, an' there ain't no time to lose on 'em. I thought maybe ye'd order 'em to-day from Medford?"

While Sanford was writing a telegram to a shipbuilder at Medford ordering "four clean, straight, white pine masts not less than twenty inches at the butt," and delivering it to his negro servant, Sam, whom he called from the adjoining room, Captain Joe had arisen from his chair and had taken down his pea-jacket and

Derby hat, without which he never came to New York,— it was his one concession to metropolitan exactions : the incongruity between the pea-jacket and the Derby hat always delighted Sanford.

"But, Captain Joe," said Sanford, looking up, "you must n't go ; breakfast will be ready in a minute. Young Mr. Hardy is coming, whom you met here once before. He wants to meet you again."

"Not this mornin', sir. I've got a lot o' things to look after 'fore I catch the three-ten. I'm obleeged to ye all the same," and he humped his arms and shoulders into his weather-beaten pea-jacket and picked up the tin case.

"Well, I wish you would," said Sanford, with a hand on the captain's shoulder, and real disappointment in his tone, "but you know best, I suppose."

With the big brown hand of the captain in his own he followed him to the top of the stairs, where he stood watching the burly figure descending the spiral staircase, the tin case under his arm, spy-glass fashion.

"You 'll see me in the morning, captain," Sanford called out, not wanting him to go without another word. "I 'll come by the midnight train."

The captain looked up and waved his hand cheerily in lieu of a reply.

Sanford waited until the turn of the staircase hid him from view, then turned, and, drawing the heavy curtains of the vestibule, passed through it to his private apartments, flooded with the morning light.

CHAPTER II

A MORNING'S MAIL

SANFORD dropped into a brown leather chair, and Sam, with the fawning droop of a water-spaniel, placed the morning paper before him, moved a small table nearer, on which his master could lay the morning's mail as it was opened, adjusted the curtains so as to keep the glare from his paper, and with noiseless tread withdrew to the kitchen. Whatever the faults of this product of reconstruction might have been, — and Sam had many, — neglect of Sanford's comfort was not one of them.

According to his lights he was scrupulously honest. Although he dressed with more care on Sunday afternoons than his master, — generally in that gentleman's cast-off clothes, and always in his discarded neckties and gloves, — smoked his tobacco, purloined his cigars, and occasionally drank his wine, whenever the demands of his social life made such inroads on Sanford's private stock necessary to maintain a certain prestige among his ebonized brethren, he invariably drew the line at his master's loose change and his shirt-studs. This was due, doubtless, to some drops of blood, trickling through his veins and inherited from an old family butler of an ancestor, which, while they permitted him the free use of everything his master ate, drank, and wore, — a common privilege of the slave days, — debarred him completely from greater crimes.

His delinquencies — all of them perfectly well known to Sanford — never lost him his master's confidence: he knew the race, and never expected the impossible. Not only did he place Sam in charge of his household expenditures, but he gave him entire supervision as well of his rooms and their contents.

In these apartments Sam took the greatest pride. They were at the top of one of those old-fashioned, hip-roofed, dormer-windowed houses still to be found on Washington Square, and consisted of five rooms, with dining-room and salon.

Against the walls of the salon stood low bookcases, their tops covered with curios and the hundred and one knickknacks that encumber a bachelor's apartment. Above these again hung a collection of etchings and sketches in and out of frames, many of them signed by fellow members of the Buzzards, a small Bohemian club of ten who often held their meetings here.

Under a broad frieze ran a continuous shelf, holding samples of half the pots of the universe, from a Heidelberg beer-mug to an East

Indian water-jar; and over the doors were grouped bunches of African arrows, spears, and clubs, and curious barbaric shields; while the centre of the room was occupied by a square table covered with books and magazines, ash-trays, Japanese ivories, and the like. Set in among them was an umbrella-lamp with a shade of sealing-wax red. At intervals about the room were smaller tables, convenient for decanters and crushed ice, and against the walls, facing the piano, were wide divans piled high with silk cushions, and near the window which opened on a balcony overlooking the square stood a carved Venetian wedding-chest, which Sanford had picked up on one of his trips abroad.

Within easy reach of reading-lamp and chair rested a four-sided bookcase on rollers, filled with works on engineering and books of reference; while a high, narrow case between two doors was packed with photographs and engravings of the principal marine structures of our own and other coasts. It was at once the room of a man of leisure and a man of work.

Late as was the season, a little wood fire smouldered in the open fireplace, — one of the sentiments to which Sanford clung, — while before it stood the brown leather chair in which he sat.

"I forgot to say that Captain Bell will not be here to breakfast, Sam, but Mr. Hardy is coming," said Sanford, suddenly recollecting himself.

"Yaas, sah; everything's ready, sah," replied Sam, who, now that the telegram had been dispatched and the morning papers and letters delivered, had slipped into his white jacket again.

Sanford picked up the package of letters, a dozen or more, and began cutting the envelopes. Most of them were read rapidly, marked in the margin, and laid in a pile beside him. There were two which he had placed by themselves without opening: one from his friend Mrs. Morgan Leroy, and the other from Major Tom Slocomb, of Pocomoke, Maryland.

Major Slocomb wrote to inform him of his approaching visit to New York, accompanied by his niece, Miss Helen Shirley, of Kent County, — "a daughter, sir, of Colonel Talbot Shirley, one of our foremost citizens, whom I believe you had the honor of meeting during your never-to-be-forgotten visit among us."

The never-to-be-forgotten visit was one that Sanford had made the major the winter before, when he was inspecting the site for a stone and brush jetty he was about to build for the government, in the Chesapeake, near those famous estates which the Pocomokian inherited from his wife, "the widow of Major Talbot, suh."

During this visit the major had greatly endeared himself to the young engineer. Under all the Pocomokian's veneer of delightful mendacity, utter shiftlessness, and luxurious extravagance, Sanford had discovered certain qualities of true loyalty to those whom he loved, and a very tender sympathy for the many in the world worse off than himself. He had become convinced too that the major's conversion from a vagabond with gentlemanly instincts to a gentleman with strong Bohemian tendencies might easily be accomplished were a little more money placed at the Pocomokian's disposal. With an endless check-book and unlimited overdrafts, settlements to be made every hundred years, the major would be a prince among men.

The niece to whom the major referred in his letter lived in an adjoining county with a relative much nearer of kin. Like many other possessions of this acclimated Marylander, she was really not his niece at all, but another heritage from his deceased wife. The major first saw her on horseback, in a neat-fitting riding-habit which she had made out of some blue army kersey bought at the country store. One glance at her lovely face, the poise of her head, the easy grace of her seat, and her admirable horsemanship decided him at once. Henceforward her name was to be emblazoned on the scroll of his family tree!

A MORNING'S MAIL

It was not until Sanford had finished the major's letter that he turned to that from Mrs. Leroy. He looked first at the circular postmark to see the exact hour at which it had been mailed; then he rose from the big chair, threw himself on the divan, tucked a pillow under his head, and slowly broke the seal. The envelope was large and square, decorated with the crest of the Leroys in violet wax, and addressed in a clear, round, almost masculine hand. "My dear Henry," it began, "if you are going to the Ledge, please stop at Medford and see how my new dining-room is getting on. Be sure to come to luncheon to-morrow, so we can talk it over," etc., and ended with the hope that he had not taken cold when he left her house the night before.

It had contained but half a dozen lines, and was as direct as most of her communications; yet Sanford held it for a long time in his hands, read and re-read it, looked at the heading, examined the signature, turned it over carefully, and, placing it in its envelope, thrust it under the sofa-pillow. With his hands behind his head he lay for some time in thought. Then taking Mrs. Leroy's letter from under the pillow, he read it again, put it in his pocket, and began pacing the room.

The letter had evidently made him restless. He threw wide the sashes of the French window which opened on the iron balcony, and looked for a moment over the square below, where the hard, pen-line drawing of its trees was blurred by the yellow-green bloom of the early spring. He turned back into the room, rearranged a photograph or two on the mantel, and, picking up a vase filled with roses, inhaled their fragrance and placed them in the centre of the dainty breakfast-table, with its snowy linen and polished silver, that Sam had just been setting near him. Reseating himself in his chair, he called again to the ever watchful darky, who had been following his movements through the crack of the pantry door.

"Sam."

"Yaas, 'r," came a voice apparently from the far end of the pantry; "comin', sah."

"Look over the balcony again and see if Mr. Hardy is on his way across the square. Why! what's become of the fellow?" he said to himself, consulting the empire clock with broken columns which decorated the mantel. "It's after ten now. I'll wager Helen wrote him by the same mail. No wonder he's late. Let me see! She gets here in three days. Jack will be out of his head." And Sanford sighed.

"I 'spec's dat's him a-comin' up now, sah," Sam called. "I yeared de downstairs do' click a minute ago. Here he is, sah," drawing aside the curtain that hid the entrance to the outer hall.

"Sorry, old man," came a voice increasing

in distinctness as the speaker approached, "but I couldn't help it. I had a lot of letters to answer this morning, or I should have been on time. It don't make any difference to you; it's your day off."

"My day off, is it? I was out of bed this morning at six o'clock. Captain Joe stopped here on his way from the train; he has just left; and if you had stayed away a minute more, I'd have breakfasted without you. And that isn't all. That sloop I've been looking for has arrived, and I go to Keyport to-night."

"The devil you do!" said Jack, a shade of disappointment crossing his face. "That means, I suppose, you won't be back this spring. How long are you going to be building that lighthouse, anyhow, Henry?"

"Two years more, I'm afraid," said Sanford thoughtfully. "Breakfast right away, Sam. Take the seat by the window, Jack. I thought we'd breakfast here instead of in the dining-room; the air's fresher."

Jack opened his coat, took a rose from the vase, adjusted it in his buttonhole, and spread his napkin over his knees.

He was much the younger of the two men, and his lot in life had been far easier. Junior partner in a large banking-house down town, founded and still sustained by the energy and business tact of his father, with plenty of time for all the sports and pastimes popular with men of his class, he had not found it a difficult task to sail easily through life without a jar.

"What do you hear from Crab Island, Jack?" asked Sanford, a sly twinkle in his eye, as he passed him the muffins.

"They've started the new club-house," said Jack, with absolute composure. "We are going to run out that extension you suggested when you were down there last winter." He clipped his egg lightly, without a change of countenance.

"Anything from Helen Shirley?"

"Just a line, thanking me for the magazines," Jack answered in a casual tone, not the faintest interest betraying itself in the inflections of his voice. Sanford thought he detected a slight increase of color on his young friend's always rosy cheeks, but he said nothing.

"Did she say anything about coming to New York?" Sanford asked, looking at Jack quizzically out of the corner of his eye.

"Yes; now I come to think of it, I believe she did say something about the major's coming, but nothing very definite."

Jack spoke as if he had been aroused from some reverie entirely foreign to the subject under discussion. He continued to play with his egg, flecking off the broken bits of shell with the point of his spoon. With all his pretended composure, however, he could not raise his eyes to those of his host.

"What a first-class fraud you are, Jack!" said Sanford, laughing at last. He leaned back in his chair and looked at Hardy good-humoredly from under his eyebrows. "I would have read you Slocomb's letter, lying right before you, if I hadn't been sure you knew everything in it. Helen and the major will be here next week, and you know the very hour she'll arrive, and you have staked out every moment of her time. Now don't try any of your high-daddy tricks on me. What are you going to do next Tuesday night?"

Jack laughed, but made no attempt to parry a word of Sanford's thrust. He looked up at last inquiringly over his plate and said, "Why?"

"Because I want you to dine here with them. I'll ask Mrs. Leroy to chaperon Helen. Leroy is still abroad, and she can come. We'll get Bock, too, with his 'cello. What other ladies are in town?"

Jack's face was aglow in an instant. The possibility of dining in Sanford's room, with its background of rich color and with all its pretty things that Helen he knew would love so well, lent instant interest to Sanford's proposition. He looked about him. He made up his mind just where he would seat her after dinner: the divan nearest the curtains was the best. How happy she would be, and how new it would all be to her! He could have planned nothing more delightful. Then remembering that Sanford had asked him a question, he recovered himself and nonchalantly gave the names of several young women he knew who might be agreeable guests. But after a moment's reflection he suggested as a second thought that Sanford leave these details to Mrs. Leroy. Jack knew her tact, and he knew to a nicety just how many young girls Mrs. Leroy would bring. The success of bachelor dinners, from Hardy's present standpoint, was not dependent upon the attendance of half a dozen extra young women and *two* men; quite the reverse.

The date for the dinner arranged, and the wisdom of leaving the list of guests to Mrs. Leroy agreed upon, the talk drifted into other channels: the Whistler pastels at Klein's; the garden-party to be given at Mrs. Leroy's country-seat near Medford when the new dining-room was finished and the roses were in bloom; the opportunity Sanford might now enjoy of combining business with pleasure, Medford being a short run from Shark Ledge; the success of Smearly's last portrait at the Academy, a photograph of which lay on the table; the probable change in Slocomb's fortunes, now that, with the consent of the insurance company who held the mortgage, he had rented what was left of the Widow Talbot's estate to a strawberry planter from the North, in order to live in New York; and finally, under Jack's guidance, back to Helen Shirley's visit.

When the two men, an hour later, passed into the corridor, Sanford held two letters in his hand ready to mail: one addressed to Major Slocomb, with an inclosure to Miss Shirley, the other to Mrs. Morgan Leroy.

Sam watched them over the balcony until they crossed the square, cut a double shuffle with both feet, admired his black grinning face in the mirror, took a corncob pipe from the shelf in the pantry, filled it with some of Sanford's best tobacco, and began packing his master's bag for the night train to Keyport.

CHAPTER III

CAPTAIN BRANDT AT THE THROTTLE

THE sun was an hour high when Sanford arrived at Keyport and turned quickly toward the road leading from the station to Captain Joe's cottage, a spring and lightness in his step which indicated not only robust health, but an eagerness to reach at once the work absorbing his mind. When he gained the high ground overlooking the cottage and dock, he paused for a view that always charmed him with its play of light and color over sea and shore, and which seemed never so beautiful as in the early morning light.

Below him lay Keyport Village, built about a rocky half-moon of a harbor, its old wharves piled high with rotting oil-barrels and flanked by empty warehouses, behind which crouched low, gray-roofed cabins, squatting in a tangle of streets, with here and there a white church spire tipped with a restless weather-vane. Higher, on the hills, were nestled some old homesteads with sloping roofs and wide porches, and away up on the crest of the heights, overlooking the sea, stood the more costly structures with well-shaved lawns spotted with homesick trees from a warmer clime, their arms stretched appealingly toward the sea.

At his feet lay the brimming harbor itself, dotted with motionless yachts and various fishing-craft, all reflected upside down in the still sea, its glassy surface rippled now and then by the dipping buckets of men washing down the decks, or by the quick water-spider strokes of some lobster-fisherman, — the click of the rowlocks pulsating in the breathless morning air.

On the near point of the half-moon stood Keyport Light, — an old-fashioned factory chimney of a Light, — built of brick, but painted snow-white with a black cigar band around its middle, its top surmounted by a copper lantern. This flashed red and white at night, over a radius of twenty miles. Braced up against its base, for a better hold, was a little building hiding a great fog-horn, which on thick days and nights bellowed out its welcome to Keyport's best.

On the far point of the moon — the one opposite the Light, and some two miles away — stretched sea-meadows broken with clumps of rock and shelter-houses for cattle, and between these two points, almost athwart the mouth of the harbor, like a huge motionless whale lay Crotch Island, its backbone knotted with summer cottages. Beyond the island away out under the white glare of the risen sun could be seen a speck of purplish-gray fringed with bright splashes of spray glinting in the dazzling light. This was Shark's Ledge.

As Sanford looked toward the site of the new Light a strange sensation came over him There lay the work on which his reputation would rest and by which he would hereafter be judged. Everything else he had so far accomplished was, he knew, but a preparation for this his greatest undertaking. Not only were the engineering problems involved new to his experience, but in his attitude in regard to them he had gone against all precedents as well as against the judgments of older heads, and had relied almost exclusively upon Captain Joe's personal skill and pluck. While it was true that he never doubted his ultimate success, there always came a tugging at his heartstrings and a tightening of his throat whenever he looked toward the site of the lighthouse.

Turning from the scene with a long drawn breath, he walked with slackened step down the slope that led to the long dock fronting the captain's cottage. As he drew nearer he saw that the Screamer had been moored between the captain's dock (always lumbered with paraphernalia required for sea-work) and the great granite-wharf, which was piled high with enormous cubes of stone, each as big as two pianos.

On her forward deck was bolted a hoisting-engine, and thrust up through the hatch of the forecastle was the smoke-stack of the boiler, already puffing trial feathers of white steam into the morning air. She had, too, the heavy boom and stout mast used as a derrick. Captain Joe had evidently seen no reason to change his mind about her, for he was at the moment on her after-deck, overhauling a heavy coil of manilla rope, and reeving it in the block himself, the men standing by to catch the end of the line.

When Sanford joined the group there was no general touching of hats, — outward sign of deference that a group of laborers on land would have paid their employer. In a certain sense, each man here was chief. Each man knew his duty and did it, quietly, effectually, and cheerfully. The day's work had no limit of hours. The pay was never fixed by a board of delegates, one half of whom could not tell a marlinespike from a monkey-wrench. These men had enlisted for a war with winds and storms and changing seas, and victory meant something more to them than pay once a month and plum duff once a week. It meant hours of battling with the sea, of tugging at the lines, waist-deep in the boiling surf that rolled in from Montauk. It meant constant, unceasing vigilance day and night, in order that some exposed site necessary for a bedstone might be captured and held before a southeaster could wreck it, and thus a vantage-point be lost in the laying of the masonry.

Each man took his share of wet and cold

and exposure without grumbling. When, by some accident, a cowardly and selfish spirit joined the force, Captain Joe, on the first word of complaint, handed the man his money and put him ashore. The severity of the work was never resented. It was only against their common enemies, the winds and the seas, that murmurs were heard. "Drat that wind!" one would say. "Here she's a-haulin' to the east'rd agin, an' we ain't got them j'ints [in the masonry] p'inted." Or, "It makes a man sick to see th' way this month's been a-goin' on, — not a decent day since las' Tuesday."

Sanford liked these men. He was always at home with them. He loved their courage, their grit, their loyalty to one another and to the work itself. The absence of ceremony among them never offended him. His cheery "Good-morning" as he stepped aboard was as cheerily answered, but no other demonstration took place.

Captain Joe stopped work only long enough to shake Sanford's hand and to present him to the newcomer, Captain Bob Brandt of the Screamer.

"Cap'n Bob!" he called, waving his hand.

"Ay, ay, sir!" came the ready response of his early training.

"Come aft, sir. Mr. Sanford wants ye." The "sir" was merely a recognition of the captain's rank.

A tall, straight, blue-eyed young fellow of twenty-two, with a face like an open book, walked down the deck, — one of those perfectly simple, absolutely fearless, alert men found so often on the New England coast, with legs and arms of steel, body of hickory, and hands of whalebone: cabin-boy at twelve, common sailor at sixteen, first mate at twenty, and full captain the year he voted.

Sanford looked him all over, from his shoes to his cap. He knew a round full man when he saw him. This one seemed to be without a flaw. Sanford saw too that he possessed that yeast of good nature without which the best of men are heavy and dull.

"Can you lift these blocks, Captain Brandt?" he asked in a hearty tone, more like that of a comrade than an employer, his hand extended in greeting.

"Well, I can try, sir," came the modest reply, the young man's face lighting up as he looked into Sanford's eyes, where he read with equal quickness a ready appreciation, so encouraging to every man who intends to do his best.

Captain Brandt and every member of the gang knew that it was not the mere weight of these enrockment blocks which made the handling of them so serious a matter; twelve tons is a light lift for many boat-derricks. It was the fact that they must be loaded aboard a vessel not only small enough to be easily handled in any reasonable weather, but with a water-draught shoal enough to permit her lying safely in a running tide alongside the Ledge while the individual blocks were being lowered over her side.

The hangers-on about the dock questioned whether any sloop could do this work. All winter, in fact, they had discussed it about the tavern stoves.

"Billy," said old Marrows, an assumed authority on stone-sloops, but not in Sanford's employ, although a constant applicant, "I ain't sayin' nothin' agin her beam, mind, but she's too peaked forrud. 'Nother thing, when she's got them stones slung, them chain-plates won't hold 'er shrouds. I wouldn't be s'prised to see that mast jerked clean out'er her."

Bill Lacey, the handsome young rigger to whom the remark was addressed, leaned over the sloop's rail, scanned every bolt in her plates, glanced up at the standing rigging, tried it with his hand as if it were a tight-rope, and with a satisfied air answered, "Them plates is all right, Marrows, — it's her b'iler that's a-worryin' me. What do you say, Caleb?" turning to Caleb West, a broad-shouldered, grizzled man in a sou'wester, who was mending a leak in a diving-dress, the odor of the burning cement in a pan beside him mingling with the savory smell of frying pork coming up from the galley.

"Wall, I ain't said, Billy," replied Caleb in a cheery voice, stroking his bushy gray beard. "Them as don't know better keep shet."

There was a loud laugh at the young rigger's expense, in which everybody except Lacey and Caleb joined. Lacey's face hardened under the thrust, while Caleb still smiled, a quaint expression overspreading his features, — one that often came when something pleased him, and which by its sweetness showed how little venom lay behind his reproofs.

"These 'ere sloops is jes' like women," said George Nickles, the cook, a big, oily man, with his sleeves rolled up above his elbows, a greasy apron about his waist. He was dipping a bucket overboard. "Ye can't tell nothin' about 'em till ye tries 'em."

The application of the simile not being immediately apparent, — few of Nickles' similes ever were, — nobody answered. Lacey stole a look at Nickles and then at Caleb, to see if the shot had been meant for him, and meeting the diver's unconscious clear blue eyes, looked seaward again.

Lonny Bowles, a big derrickman from Noank quarries, in a red shirt, discolored on the back with a pink Y where his suspenders had crossed, now moved nearer and joined in the discussion.

"She kin h'ist any two on 'em, an' never wet 'er deck combin's. I seen these Cape Ann sloops afore, when we wuz buildin' Stonin'ton breakwater. Ye would n't believe they had it in 'em till ye see 'em work. Her b'iler's all right."

"Don't you like the sloop, Caleb?" said Sanford, who had been listening. "Don't you think she 'll do her work?" he continued, moving a rebellious leg of the rubber dress to sit the closer.

"Well, of course, sir, I ain't knowed 'er long 'nough to swear by yit. She's fittin' for loadin' 'em on land, maybe, but she may have some trouble gittin' rid of 'em at the Ledge. Her b'iler looks kind o' weak to me," and the master diver bent over the pan, stirring the boiling cement with his sheath-knife, the rubber suit sprawled out over his knees, the awkward, stiff, empty legs and arms of the dress flopping about as he patched its many leaks. Then he added with a quaint smile, "But if Cap'n Joe says she's all right, ye can pin to her."

Sanford moved a little closer to Caleb, holding the pan of cement for him, and watching him at work. He had known him for years as a fearless diver of marvelous pluck and endurance; one capable of working seven consecutive hours under water. When an English bark had run on top of Big Spindle Reef and backed off into one hundred and ten feet of water, the captain and six of the crew were saved, but the captain's wife, helpless in the cabin, had been drowned. Caleb had gone below, cleared away the broken deck that pinned her down, and had brought her body up in his arms. His helmet was spattered inside with the blood that trickled from his ears, owing to the enormous pressure of the sea. This had been not a twelvemonth since.

The constant facing of dangers had made of the diver a quiet, reticent man. There was, too, a gentleness and restful patience about him that always appealed to Sanford, and next to Captain Joe he was the one man on the working force whom he trusted most. Of late his pale blue eyes had shone with a softer light, as if he were perpetually hugging some happiness to himself. Those who knew him best said that all this happy gentleness had come with the girl wife. Since he had entered Sanford's employment he had married a second and a younger wife, — a mere child, the men said, young enough to be his daughter, too young for a man of forty-five.

And yet Caleb was not an old man, if the possession of vigor and energy meant anything. His cheeks had the rosy hue of perfect health, and his step was lighter and more agile than that of many men half his years. Only his beard was gray. Yet he was called by his shipmates old, for in the hard working world in which he lived none but the earlier years of a man's life counted as youth.

His cabin, a small, two-story affair, bought with the money he had saved during his fifteen years on the Lightship and after his first wife's death, lay a short distance up the shore above that of Captain Joe, and in plain sight of the Screamer.

When Caleb rose to wash his hands, he caught sight of a blue apron tossing on its distant porch. Bill Lacey saw the apron too, and had answered it a moment later with a little wave of his own. Caleb did not notice Billy's signal, but Captain Joe did, and a peculiar look filled his eye that the men did not often see. In his confusion Lacey flushed scarlet, and upset the pan of cement.

When Nickles announced breakfast, Captain Joe soused a bucket overboard, rested it on the rail and plunged in his hands, the splashing drops glistening in the sunlight, and called out:—

"Come, Mr. Sanford,—breakfast's ready, men." Then, waving his hand to Caleb and the others who had been discussing the Screamer, he said, laughing, "All you men what's gittin' skeery 'bout this sloop kin step ashore. I'm a-goin' to load three o' them stone aboard here after breakfast, if I roll her over bottom side up."

Sanford sat at the head of the table, his back to the companionway, the crew's bunks within reach of his hand. He was the only man who wore a coat. Set out before him were fried eggs sizzling in squares of pork; hashed potatoes, browned in what was left of the sizzle; saleratus biscuit, full of dark spots; and coffee in tin cups. There was also a small jug of molasses, protected by a pewter top, and there was, too, a bottle of tomato catsup, whose contents were indiscriminately spattered over every plate.

Long years of association had familiarized Sanford with certain rules of etiquette to be observed at a meal like this. Whoever finished first, he knew, must push back his stool out of the way and instantly mount to the deck. In confined quarters, elbow-room is a luxury, and its free gift a courtesy. He also knew that to leave anything on his plate would have been regarded as an evidence of extreme bad manners, suggesting moreover a reflection upon the skill of the cook. It was also a part of the code to wipe one's knife carefully on the last piece of bread, which was to be swallowed immediately, thus obliterating all traces of the repast, except, of course, the bones, which must be picked clean and piled on one side of the plate. Captain Joe himself never neglected any of these little amenities.

Sanford forgot none of them. He wiped his knife and cleared his plate as carefully as any of his men. He drank from his tin cup, and ate his eggs and fried pork too with the same zest that he would have felt before one of Sam's choicest breakfasts. He really enjoyed these repasts. To him there was something wonderfully inspiring in watching a group of big, strong, broad-breasted, horny-handed laboring men intent on satisfying a hunger born of fresh air and hard work. There was an eagerness about their movements, a relish as each mouthful disappeared, attended by a good humor and sound digestion that would have given a sallow-faced dyspeptic a new view of life, and gone far toward converting a dilettante to the belief that although forks and napkins were perhaps indispensable luxuries, existence might not be wholly desolate with plain fingers and shirt-cuffs.

Breakfast over, Captain Joe was the first man on deck. He had left his pea-jacket in the cabin, and now wore his every-day outfit — the blue flannel shirt, long since stretched out of shape in its efforts to accommodate itself to the spread of his shoulders, and a pair of trousers in which each corrugated wrinkle outlined a knotted muscle twisted up and down a pair of legs sturdy as rudder-posts.

"Come, men!" he called in a commanding voice, with none of the gentler tones heard at the breakfast-table. "Pull yourselves together. . . . Bill Lacey, lower away that hook and git them chains ready. . . . Fire up, Cap'n Brandt, and give 'er every pound o' steam she'll carry. . . . Here,—one or two of ye, run this 'ere line ashore and make her bow fast. . . . Drop that divin'-suit, Caleb; this ain't no time to patch things."

These orders were volleyed at the men as he stepped from the sloop to the wharf, each man springing to his place with an alacrity seldom seen among men of other crews. Close association with Captain Joe always inspired a peculiar confidence and loyalty not only among his own men, but in all the others who heard his voice. His personal magnetism, his enthusiasm, his seeming reckless fearlessness, and yet extreme caution and watchful care for the safety of his men, had created among his employees a blind confidence in his judgment that always resulted in immediate and unquestioned obedience to his orders, no matter what the risk might seem.

The sloop was now lying alongside the wharf, with beam and stern lines made fast to the outlying water-spiles to steady her. When the tackle was shaken clear, the boom was lowered at the proper angle; the heavy chain terminating in an enormous S-hook, which hung directly over the centre of one of the big enrockment blocks.

Captain Joe moved down the dock and adjusted with his own hands the steel "Lewis" that was to be driven into the big trial stone. Important details he never left to others. If this Lewis should slip, with the stone suspended over the sloop's deck, the huge block would crush through her timbers, sinking her instantly.

The Screamer's captain was at the throttle, watching the steadily rising steam-gauge.

"Give 'er a turn and take up the slack!" shouted Captain Joe.

"Ay, ay, sir!" answered the skipper quickly, as the cogs of the hoisting-engine began to move, winding all the loose slackened "fall" around the drum, until it straightened out like a telegraph wire.

"What's she carryin' now, Cap'n Bob?" again shouted Captain Joe.

"Seventy-six pounds, sir."

"Give 'er time — don't push 'er."

A crowd began to gather on the dock: fishermen and workmen on their way to the village, idlers along the shore road, and others. They all understood that the trial of the sloop was to be made this morning, and great interest was felt. The huge stones had rested all winter on this wharf, and had been discussed and rediscussed until each one outweighed the Pyramids. Loading such pieces on board a vessel like the Screamer had never been done in Keyport before.

Old Marrows whispered certain misgivings, as he made fast a line far up on the wharf. Some of the listeners moved back across the road, yielding to the vague fear of the inexperienced. Bets were offered that "her mast would be tore clean out of her;" or that "she'd put her starboard rail under water afore she'd start 'em;" and that "she'd sink where she lay."

The needle of the gauge on the sloop's boiler revolved slowly until it registered ninety pounds. Little puffs of blue vaporless steam hissed from the safety-valve. The boiler was getting ready to do its duty.

Captain Joe looked aloft, ordered the boom topped a few inches, so that the lift would be plumb, sprang upon the sloop's deck, scrutinized the steam-gauge, saw that the rope was evenly wound on the drum, emptied an oil-can into the sunken wooden saddle in which the butt of the boom rested, followed with his eye every foot of the manilla fall from the drum through the double blocks to the chain hanging over the big stone, called to the people on the dock to get out of harm's way, saw that every man was in his place, and shouted the order, clear and sharp, —

"Go ahead!"

The cogs of the drum of the hoisting-engine spun around until the great weight began to tell; then the strokes of the steam-pistons slowed down. The outboard mooring-lines were now tight as standing rigging. The butt of the boom in the sunken saddle was creaking as it turned, a pungent odor from the friction-heated oil filling the air. The strain increased, and the sloop careened toward the wharf until her bilge struck the water, drawing taut as bars of steel her outboard shrouds. Ominous clicks came from the new manilla as its twists were straightened out.

Captain Bob Brandt still stood by the throttle, one of his crew firing,—sometimes with refuse cotton waste soaked in kerosene. He was watching every part of his sloop then under strain to see how she stood the test.

The slow movement of the pistons continued.

The strain on the outboard shroud became intense. A dead silence prevailed, broken only by the clicking fall and the creak of the roller blocks.

Twice the safety-valve blew a hoarse note of warning.

Slowly, inch by inch, the sloop settled in the water, stopped suddenly, and quivered her entire length. Another turn of the drum on her deck and the huge stone canted a point, slid the width of a dock plank, and with a hoarse, scraping sound turned half round and swung clear of the wharf!

A cheer went up from the motley crowd on the dock.

Not a word escaped the men at work. The worst was yet to come.

The swinging stone must yet be lowered on deck.

"Tighten up that guy," said Captain Joe quietly, between his teeth, never taking his eyes from the stone; his hand meanwhile on the fall, to test its strain.

Bill Lacey and Caleb ran to the end of the dock, whipped one end of a line around a mooring-post, and with their knees bent to the ground held on with all their strength. The other end of the guy was fastened to the steel S-hook that held the Lewis now securely in the stone.

"Easy — ea-s-y!" said Captain Joe, a momentary shadow of anxiety on his face. The guy held by Caleb and Lacey gradually slackened. The great stone, now free to swing clear, moved slowly in mid-air over the edge of the wharf, passed above the water, cleared the rail of the sloop, and settled on her deck as gently as a grounding balloon.

The cheer that broke from all hands brought the fishwives to their porches.

CHAPTER IV

AMONG THE BLACKFISH AND TOMCODS

HARDLY had the men ceased cheering when the boom was swung back, another huge stone was lifted from the wharf, and loaded aboard the sloop. A third followed, was lowered upon rollers on the deck and warped amidships, to trim the boat. The mooring-lines were cast off, and the sloop's sail partly hoisted for better steering, and a nervous, sputtering little tug tightened a tow-line over the Screamer's bow.

The flotilla now moved slowly out of the harbor toward the Ledge. Captain Brandt stood at the wheel. His face was radiant. His boat had met the test, just as he knew she would. She had stood by him too many times before for him to doubt her now.

There had been one night at Rockport when she lay till morning, bow on to a gale, within a cable's length of the breakwater. This saw-toothed ledge, with the new floating buoys of Captain Joe's, could not frighten him after that.

Yet not a word of boasting passed his lips. He spun his wheel and held his peace.

When the open harbor was reached, the men overhauled the boom-tackle, getting ready for the real work of the day. Bill Lacey and Caleb West lifted the air-pump from its case, and oiled the plunger. Caleb was to dive that day himself, — work like this required an experienced hand, — and find a bed for these first three stones as they were lowered under water. Lacey was to tend the life-line.

As the tug and sloop passed into the broad water, Medford Village could be seen toward the southeast. Sanford adjusted his marine-glass, and focused its lens on Mrs. Leroy's country-house. It lay near the water, and was surmounted by a cupola he had often occupied as a lookout when he had been Mrs. Leroy's guest, and the weather had been too rough for him to land at the Ledge. He saw that the bricklayers were really at work, and that the dining-room extension was already well under way, the scaffolding being above the roof. He meant, if the weather permitted, to stop there on his way home.

Soon the Ledge itself loomed up. The concrete men were evidently busy, for the white steam from the mixers rose straight into the still air.

An hour more and the windows on the lee side of the shanty could be distinguished, and a little later, the men on the platform as they gathered to await the approaching flotilla.

When they caught sight of the big blocks stored on the Screamer's deck, they broke into a cheer that was followed by a shrill saluting whistle from the big hoisting-engine on the Ledge, answered as cheerily by the approaching tug. Work on the Ledge could now begin in earnest.

If Crotch Island was like the back of a motionless whale, Shark's Ledge was like that of a turtle,—a turtle say one hundred and fifty feet long by a hundred wide, lying in a moving sea, and always fringed by a ruffling of surf curls, or swept by great waves that rolled in from Montauk. No landing could ever be made here except in the eddy formed by the turtle itself, and then only in the stillest weather.

The shell of this rock-incrusted turtle had been formed by dumping on the original Ledge, and completely covering it, thousands of tons of rough stone, each piece as big as a cart-body. Upon this stony shell, which rose above high-water mark, a wooden platform had been erected for the proper storage of gravel, sand, barrels of cement, hoisting-engines, concrete mixers, tools, and a shanty for the men. It was down by the turtle's side — down below the slop of the surf — that the big enrockment blocks were to be placed, one on the other, their sides touching close as those on a street pavement. The lowest stone of all was to be laid on the bottom of the sea in thirty feet of water; the top one was to be placed where its upper edges would be thrust above its splash. In this way the loose rough stones of the turtle's shell would have an even covering and the finished structure be protected from the crush of floating ice and the fury of winter gales.

By a change of plan the year before, a deep hole nearly sixty feet in diameter had been made in the back of this turtle by lifting out these rough stones. This hole was now being filled with concrete up to low-water level and retained in form by circular iron bands. On top of this enormous artificial bedstone was to be placed the tower of the lighthouse itself, constructed of dressed stone, many of the single pieces to be larger than those now on the Screamer's deck. The four great derrick-masts with "twenty-inch butts" which had been ordered by telegraph the day before in Sanford's office were to be used to place these dressed stones in position.

The situation was more than usually exposed. The nearest land to the Ledge was Crotch Island, two miles away, while to the east stretched the wide sea, hungry for fresh victims, and losing no chance to worst the men on the Ledge. For two years it had fought the captain and his men without avail. The Old Man of the Sea hates the warning voice of the fog-horn and the cheery light in the tall tower — they rob him of his prey.

The tug continued on her course for half a mile, steered closer, the sloop following, and gained the eddy of the Ledge out of the racing tide. Four men from the platform now sprang into a whaleboat and pulled out to meet the sloop, carrying one end of a heavy hawser which was being paid out by the men on the Ledge. The hawser was made fast to the sloop's cleats and hauled tight. The tug was cast loose and sent back to Keyport. Outboard hawsers were run by the crew of the whaleboat to the floating anchor-buoys, to keep the sloop off the stone-pile when the enrockment blocks were being swung clear of her sides.

Caleb and Lacey began at once to overhaul the diving-gear. The air-pump was set close to the sloop's rail; and a short ladder was lashed to her side, to enable the diver to reach the water easily. The air-hose and life-lines were then uncoiled.

Caleb threw off his coat and trousers, that he might move the more freely in his diving-dress, and with Lonny Bowles's assistance twisted himself into his rubber suit, — body, arms, and legs being made of one piece of air-tight and water-tight rubber cloth.

By the time the sloop had been securely moored, and the boom-tackle made ready to lift the stone, Caleb stood on the ladder completely equipped, except for his copper helmet, tne last thing done to a diver before he sinks under water. Captain Joe always adjusted Caleb's himself. On Caleb's breast and between his shoulders hung two lead plates weighing twenty-five pounds each, and on his feet were two iron-shod shoes of equal weight. These were needed as ballast, to overbalance the buoyancy of his inflated dress, and enable him to sink or rise at his pleasure. Firmly tied to his wrist was a stout cord, — his life-line, — and attached to the back of the copper helmet was a long rubber hose, through which a constant stream of fresh air was to be pumped inside his helmet and suit.

In addition to these necessary appointments there was hung over one shoulder a canvas haversack, containing a small cord, a chisel, a water-compass, and a sheath-knife. The sheath-knife is the last desperate resource of the diver when his air-hose becomes tangled or clogged, his signals are misunderstood, and he must either cut his hose in the effort to free himself and reach the surface, or suffocate where he is.

Captain Joe adjusted the copper helmet, and stood with Caleb's glass face-plate in his hand, thus leaving his helmet open for a final order in his ear, before he lowered him overboard. The cogs of the Screamer's drum began turning, followed by the same creaking and snapping of manilla and straining of boom that had been heard when she was loaded.

Meanwhile between the sea and the sloop a fight had already begun. The current which swept by within ten feet of her bilge curled and eddied about the buoy-floats, tugging at their chains, while wave after wave tried to reach her bow, only to fall back beaten and snapping like hungry wolves.

The Cape Ann sloop had fought these fights before: all along her timber rail were the scars of similar battles. She had only to keep her bow-cheeks from the teeth of these murderous rocks, and she could laugh all day at their open jaws.

With the starting of the hoisting-engine the steam began to hiss through the safety-valve, and the bow-lines of the sloop straightened like strands of steel. Then there came a slight, staggering movement as she adjusted herself to the shifting weight. Without a sound, the stone rose from the deck, cleared the rail, and hung over the sea. Another cheer went up — this time from both the men on board the sloop and those on the Ledge. Captain Brandt smiled with closed lips. Life was easy for him now.

"Lower away," said Captain Joe in the same tone he would have used in asking for the butter, as he turned to screw on Caleb's face-plate, shutting out the fresh air, and giving the diver only pumped air to breathe.

The stone sank slowly into the sea, the dust and dirt of its long outdoor storage discoloring the clear water.

"Hold her," continued Captain Joe, his hand still on Caleb's face-plate, as he stood erect on the ladder. "Stand by, Billy. Go on with that pump, men, — give him plenty of air."

Two men began turning the handles of the pump. Caleb's dress filled out like a balloon; Lacey took his place near the small ladder, the other end of Caleb's life-line having been made fast to his wrist, and the diver sank slowly out of sight, his hammer in his hand, the air bubbles from his exhaust-valve marking his downward course.

As Caleb sank, he hugged his arms close to his body, pressed his knees together, forcing the surplus air from his dress, and dropped rapidly toward the bottom. The thick lead soles of his shoes kept his feet down and his head up, and the breast-plates steadied him.

At the depth of twenty feet he touched the tops of the sea-kelp growing on the rocks below, — he could feel the long tongues of leaves scraping his legs. Then, as he sank deeper, his shoes struck an outlying boulder. Caleb pushed himself off, floated around it, measured it with his arms, and settled to the gravel. He was now between the outlying boulder and the Ledge. Here he raised himself erect on his feet and looked about: the gravel beneath him was white and spangled with starfish; little crabs lay motionless, or scuttled away at his crunching tread; the sides of the isolated boulder were smooth and clean, the top being covered with waving kelp. In the dim, greenish light this boulder looked like a weird head, — a kind of submarine Medusa, with her hair streaming upward. The jagged rock-pile next it, its top also covered with kelp, resembled a hill of purple and brown corn swaying in the ceaseless current.

Caleb thrust his hand into his haversack, grasped his long knife, slashed at the kelp of the rock-pile to see the bottom stones the clearer, and sent a quick signal of "All right — lower away!" through the life-line, to Lacey, who stood on the sloop's deck above him.

Almost instantly a huge square green shadow edged with a brilliant iridescent light sank down towards him, growing larger and larger in its descent. Caleb peered upward through his face-plate, followed the course of the stone, and jerked a second signal to Lacey's wrist. This signal was repeated in words by Lacey to Captain Brandt, who held the throttle, and the shadowy stone was stopped within three feet of the gravel bottom. Here it swayed slowly, half turned, and touched on the boulder.

Caleb watched the stone carefully until it

was perfectly still, crept along, swimming with one hand, and measured carefully with his eye the distance between the boulder and the Ledge. Then he sent a quick signal of "Lower — all gone," up to Lacey's wrist. The great stone dropped a chain's link; slid halfway the boulder, scraping the kelp in its course; careened, and hung over the gravel with one end tilted on a point of the rocky ledge. As it hung suspended, its lower end buried itself in the gravel near the boulder, while the upper lay aslant up the slope of the rock-covered ledge.

Caleb again swam carefully around the stone, opened his arms, and inflating his dress rose five or six feet through the green water, floated over the huge stone, and grasping with his bare hand the lowering chain by which the stone hung, tested its strain. The chain was as rigid as a bar of steel. This showed that the stone was not fully grounded, and therefore dangerous, being likely to slide off at any moment. The diver now sent a telegram of short and long jerks aloft, asking for a crowbar; hooked his legs around the lowering chain and pressed his copper helmet to the chain links to listen to Captain Joe's answer. A series of dull thuds, long and short, struck by a hammer above — a means of communication often possible when the depth of water is not great — told him that the crowbar he had asked for would be sent down at once. While he waited motionless, a blackfish pressed his nose to the glass of his face-plate, and scurried off to tell his fellows living in the kelp how strange a thing he had seen that day.

A quick jerk from Lacey, and the point of the crowbar dangled over Caleb's head. In an instant, to prevent his losing it in the kelp, he had lashed another and smaller cord about its middle, and with the bar firmly in his hand laid himself flat on the stone. The diver now examined carefully the points of contact between the boulder and the hanging stone, inserted one end of the bar under its edge, sent a warning signal above, braced both feet against the lowering chain, threw his whole strength on the bar, and gave a quick, sharp pull. The next instant the chain tightened; the bar, released from the strain, bounded from his hand; there was a headlong surge of the huge shadowy mass through the waving kelp, and the great block slipped into its place, stirring up the bottom silt in a great cloud of water-dust.

The first stone of the system of enrockment had been bedded!

Caleb clung with both hands to the lowering chain, waited until the water cleared, knocked out the Lewis pin that held the S-hook, thus freeing the chain, and signaled "All clear — hoist." Then he hauled the crowbar towards him by the cord, signaled for the next stone, moved away from the reach of falling bodies, and sank into a bed of sea-kelp as comfortably as if it had been a sofa-cushion.

These breathing spells rest the lungs of a diver and lighten his work. Being at rest he can manage his dress the better, inflating it so that he is able to get his air with greater ease and regularity. The relief is sometimes so soothing that in long waits the droning of the air-valve will lull the diver into a sleep, from which he is suddenly awakened by a quick jerk on his wrist. Many divers, while waiting for the movements of those above, play with the fish, watch the crabs, or rake over the gravel in search of the thousand and one things that are lost overboard and that everybody hopes to find on the bottom of the sea.

Caleb did none of these things. He was too expert a diver to allow himself to go to sleep, and he had too much to think about to play with the fish. He sat quietly awaiting his call, his thoughts on the day of the week and how long it would be before Saturday night came again, and whether, when he left that morning, he had arranged everything for the little wife, so that she would be comfortable until his return. Once a lobster moved slowly up and nipped his red fingers with its claw, thinking them some tidbit previously unknown. (The dress terminates at the wrist with a waterproof and air-tight band, leaving the hands bare.) At another time two tomcods came sailing past, side by side, flapped their tails on his helmet, and scampered off. But Caleb, sitting comfortably on his sofa-cushion of seaweed thirty feet under water, paid little heed to outside things. His eyes only saw a tossing apron and a trim little figure on a cabin porch, as she waved him a last good-by.

In the world above, a world of fleecy clouds and shimmering sea, some changes had taken place since Caleb sank out of the sunlight. Hardly had the second stone been made ready to be swung overboard, when there came a sudden uplifting of the sea. One of those tramp waves preceding a heavy storm had strayed in from Montauk and was making straight for the Ledge.

Captain Joe sprang on the sloop's rail and looked seaward, and a shade of disappointment crossed his face.

"Stand by on that outboard ha'sser!" he shouted in a voice that was heard all over the Ledge.

The heavy outboard hawser holding the sloop whipped out of the sea with the sudden strain, thrashed the spray from its twists, and quivered like a fiddle-string. The sloop staggered for an instant, plunged bow under, careened to her rail, and righted herself within oar's touch of the Ledge. Three feet from her bilge streak crouched a grinning rock with its teeth set!

Captain Joe smiled and looked at Captain Brandt.

"Ain't nothin' when ye git used to 't, Cap'n Bob. I ain't a-goin' ter scratch 'er paint. Got to bank yer fires. Them other two stone 'll have to wait till the tide turns."

"Ay, ay, sir," replied the skipper, throwing the furnace door wide open. The danger was passed for the second time, and in the final test his boat had proved herself. Yet again he did not boast. There was only a fearless ready-to-meet-anything air about him as, with shoulders squared and head up, he walked down the deck and said to Captain Joe, in a tone as if he were only asking for information, but without the slightest shade of anxiety, "If that 'ere ha'sser 'd parted, Cap'n Joe, when she give that plunge, it would 'a' been all up with us, — eh?"

"Yes, — 'spec' so," answered the captain, his mind, now that the danger had passed, neither on the question nor on the answer. Then suddenly awakening with a look of intense interest, "That line was a new one, Cap'n Bob. I picked it out a-purpose; them kind don't part."

Sanford, who had been standing by the tiller, anxiously watching the conflict with the sea, walked forward and grasped the skipper's hand.

"I want to congratulate you," he said, "on your sloop and on your pluck. It is not every man can lie around this stone-pile for the first time and keep his head."

Captain Brandt flushed like a bashful girl, and turned away his face. "Well, sir — ye see" — He never finished the sentence. The compliment had upset him more than the escape of the sloop.

All was bustle now on board the Screamer. The boom was swung in aboard, lowered, and laid on the deck. Caleb had been hauled up to the surface, his helmet unscrewed, and his shoes and breast-plate taken off. He still wore his dress, so that he could be ready for the other two stones when the tide turned. Meanwhile he walked about the deck looking like a great bear on his hind legs, his bushy beard puffed out over his copper collar.

During the interval of the change of tide dinner was announced, and the Screamer's crew went below to more sizzle and doughballs, and this time a piece of corned beef, while Sanford, Captain Joe, Caleb, and Lacey sprang into the sloop's yawl and sculled for the shanty and their dinner, keeping close to the hawser still holding the sloop.

The unexpected made half the battle at the

Ledge. It was not unusual to see a southeast roll, three days old, cut down in an hour to the smoothness of a mill-pond by a northwest gale, and before night to find this same dead calm followed by a semi-cyclone. Only an expert could checkmate the consequences of weather manœuvres like these. Before Captain Joe, sitting at the head of the table, had filled each man's plate with his fair proportion of cabbage and pork, a whiff of wind puffed in the bit of calico that served as a curtain for the shanty's pantry window, — the one facing east. Captain Joe sprang from his seat, and, bareheaded as he was, mounted the concrete platforms and looked seaward. Off towards Block Island he saw a little wrinkling line of silver flashing out of the deepening haze, while toward Crotch Island scattered flurries of wind furred the glittering surface of the sea with dull splotches, — as when one breathes upon a mirror. The captain turned quickly, entered the shanty, and examined the barometer. It had fallen two points.

"Finish yer dinner, men," he said quietly. "That's the las' stone to-day, Mr. Sanford. It's beginnin' ter git lumpy. It'll blow a livin' gale o' wind by sundown."

A second and stronger puff now swayed the men's oilskins, hanging against the east door. This time the air was colder and more moist. The sky overhead had thickened. In the southeast lay two sun-dog clouds, their backs shimmering like opals, while about the feverish eye of the sun itself gathered a reddish circle like an inflammation.

Sanford was on the platform, reading the signs of the coming gale. It was important that he should reach Keyport by night, and he had no time to spare. As the men came out one after another, each of them glanced toward the horizon, and quickening his movements fell to work putting the place in order. The loose barrow planks were quickly racked up on the shanty's roof, out of the wash of the expected surf; an extra safety-guy was made fast to the platform holding the hoisting-engine, and a great tarpaulin drawn over the cement and lashed fast. Meanwhile Captain Joe busied himself in examining the turnbuckles of the holding-down rods, which bound the shanty to the Ledge, and giving them another tightening twist, ordering the heavy wooden shutters for the east side of the shanty to be put up, and seeing that the stove-pipe that stuck through the roof was taken down and stored inside.

All this time the Screamer tugged harder at her hawser, her bow surging as the ever-increasing swell raced past her.

Orders to man the yawl were now given and promptly obeyed.

"Keep everything snug, Caleb, while I'm

gone!" Captain Joe shouted, as he stepped into the boat. "It looks soapy, but it may be out to the nor'ard an' clear by daylight. Sit astern, Mr. Sanford. Pull away, men, we ain't got a minute."

When the Screamer, with two unset stones still on her deck, bore away from the Ledge with Sanford, Captain Joe, and Lacey on board, the spray was flying over the shanty roof.

Caleb stood on the platform waving his hand. He was still in his diving-dress. His helmet only had been removed, and his bushy beard was flying in the wind.

"Tell Betty I'll be home for Sunday," the men heard him call out, as they flew by under close reef.

CHAPTER V

AUNTY BELL'S KITCHEN

THE storm was still raging, the wind beating in fierce gusts against the house and rattling the window-panes, when Sanford awoke in the low-ceiled room always reserved for him at Captain Joe's.

"Turrible dirty, ain't it?" the captain called, as he came in with a hearty good-morning and threw open the green blinds. "I guess she'll scale off; it's hauled a leetle s'uth'ard since daylight. The glass is a-risin', too. Aunty Bell says breakfas' 's ready jes' 's soon 's you be."

"All right, captain. Don't wait. I'll come in ten minutes," replied Sanford.

Outside the little windows a wide-armed tree swayed in the storm, its budding branches tapping the panes. Sanford went to the window and looked out. The garden was dripping, and the plank walk that ran to the swinging-gate was glistening in the driving rain.

These changes in the weather did not affect his plans. Bad days were to be expected, and the loss of time at an exposed site like that of the Ledge was always considered in the original estimate of the cost of the structure. If the sea prevented the landing of stone for a day or so, the sloop, as he knew, could load a full cargo of blocks from the wharf across the road, now hidden by the bursting lilacs in the captain's garden; or the men could begin on the iron parts of the new derricks, and if it cleared, as Captain Joe predicted, they could trim the masts and fit the bands. Sanford turned cheerfully from the window, and picked up his big sponge that lay by the tin tub Aunty Bell always filled for him the night before.

The furniture and appointments about him were of the plainest. There were a bed, a wash-stand and a portable tub, three chairs, and a small table littered with drawing materials. Dimity curtains, snow-white, hung at the windows, and the bureau was covered with a freshly laundered white Marseilles cover. On the walls were tacked mechanical drawings, showing cross-sections of the several courses of masonry, — prospective views of the concrete base and details of the cisterns and cellars of the lighthouse. Each of these was labeled "Shark Ledge Lighthouse. Henry Sanford, Contractor," and signed, "W. A. Carleton, Asst. Supt. U. S. L. Estb't." In one corner of the room rested a field transit, and a pole with its red-and-white target.

The cottage itself was on the main shore

road leading from the village to Keyport Light, and a little removed from the highway. It had two stories and a narrow hall with rooms on either side. In the rear were the dining-room and kitchen. Overlooking the road in front was a wide portico with sloping roof.

There were two outside doors belonging to the house. These were always open. They served two purposes, — to let in the air and to let in the neighbors. The neighbors included everybody who happened to be passing, from the doctor to the tramp. This constant stream of visitors always met in the kitchen, — a low-ceiled, old-fashioned interior, full of nooks and angles, that had for years adapted itself to everybody's wants and ministered to everybody's comfort, — and was really the cheeriest and cosiest room in the house.

Its fittings and furnishings were as simple as they were convenient. On one side, opposite the door, were the windows, looking out upon the garden, their sills filled with plants in winter and sou'wester hats in summer. In the far corner stood a pine dresser painted bright green, decorated with rows of plates and saucers set up on edge, besides various dishes and platters, all glistening from the last touch of Aunty Bell's hand polish. Next to the dresser was a broad, low settle, also of pine and also bright green, except where countless pairs of overalls had worn the paint away. Chairs of all kinds stood about, — rockers for winter nights, and more ceremonious straight-backs for meal-times. There was a huge table, too, with always a place for one more, and a mantel-rest for pipes and knickknacks, — never known to be without a box of matches or a nautical almanac. There were rows of hooks nailed to the backs of the doors, especially adapted to rubber coats and oilskins. And tucked away in a corner under the stairs was a fresh, sweet-smelling, brass-hooped cedar bucket with a cocoanut dipper that had helped to cool almost every throat from Keyport Village to Keyport Light.

But it was the stove that made this room unique: not an ordinary, commonplace cooking-machine, but a big, generous, roomy arrangement, pushed far back out of everybody's way, with out-riggers for broiling, and capacious ovens for baking, and shelves for keeping things hot, besides big and little openings on top for pots and kettles and frying-pans, of a pattern unknown to the modern chef; each and every one dearly prized by the cheery little soul who burnt her face to a blazing red in its service. This cast-iron embodiment of all the hospitable virtues was the special pride of Aunty Bell, the captain's wife, a neat, quick, busy little woman, about half the size of the captain in height, width, and thickness. Into its recesses she poured the warmth of her heart, and from out of its capacious receptacles she took the products of her bounty. Every kettle sang and every griddle "sizzed" to please her, and every fire crackled and laughed at her bidding.

When Sanford entered there was hardly room enough to move. A damp, sweet smell of fresh young grass came in at an open window. Through the door could be seen the wet graveled walks, washed clean by the storm, over which hopped one or more venturesome robins in search of the early worm.

Carleton, the government superintendent, sat near the door, his chair tilted back. In the doorway itself stood Miss Mary Peebles, the schoolmistress, an angular, thin, mild-eyed woman, in a rain-varnished waterproof. Even while she was taking it off, she was protesting that she was too wet to come in, and could not stop. Near the stove stooped Bill Lacey, drying his jacket. Around the walls and on the window-sills were other waifs, temporarily homeless, — two from the paraphernalia dock (regular boarders these), and a third, the captain of the tug, whose cook was drunk.

All about the place — now in the pantry, now in the kitchen, now with a big dish, now with a pile of plates or a pitcher of milk — bustled Aunty Bell, with a smile of welcome and a cheery word for every one who came.

Nobody, of course, had come to breakfast, — that was seen from the way in which everybody insisted he had just dropped in for a moment out of the wet to see the captain, hearing he was home from the Ledge, and from the alacrity with which everybody, one after another, as the savory smells of fried fish and soft clams filled the room, forgot his good resolutions and drew up his chair to the hospitable board.

Most of them told the truth about wanting to see the captain. Since his sojourn among them, and without any effort of his own, he had filled the position of adviser, protector, and banker to half the people along the shore. He had fought Miss Peebles's battle, when the school trustees wanted the girl from Norwich to have her place. He had recommended the tug captain to the towing company, and had coached him over-night to insure his getting a license in the morning. He had indorsed Caleb West's note to make up the last payment on the cabin he had bought to put his young wife Betty in; and when the new furniture had come over from Westerly, he had sent two of his men to unload it, and had laid some of the carpets himself on a Saturday when Betty expected Caleb in from the Ledge, and wanted to have the house ready for his first Sunday at home.

When Mrs. Bell announced breakfast, Captain Joe, in his shirt-sleeves, took his seat at the head of the table, and with a hearty, welcoming wave of his hand invited everybody to sit down, — Carleton first, of course, he being the man of authority, and representing to the workingman that mysterious, intangible power known as the "government."

The superintendent generally stopped in at the captain's if the morning were stormy; it was nearer his lodgings than the farmhouse where he took his meals — and then breakfast at the captain's cost nothing. He had come in on this particular day ostensibly to protest about the sloop's having gone to the Ledge without a notification to him. He had begun by saying, with much bluster, that he did n't know about the one stone that Caleb West was "reported" to have set; that nothing would be accepted unless he was satisfied, and nothing paid for by the department without his signature. But he ended in great good humor when the captain invited him to breakfast and placed him at his own right hand. Carleton liked little distinctions when made in his favor; he considered them due to his position.

The superintendent was a type of his class. His appointment at Shark Ledge Light had been secured through the efforts of a brother-in-law who was a custom-house inspector. Before his arrival at Keyport he had never seen a stone laid or a batch of concrete mixed. To this ignorance of the ordinary methods of construction was added an overpowering sense of his own importance coupled with the knowledge that the withholding of a certificate — the superintendent could choose his own time for giving it — might embarrass everybody connected with the work. He was not dishonest, however, and had no faults more serious than those of ignorance, self-importance, and conceit. This last broke out in his person: he wore a dyed mustache, a yellow diamond shirt-pin, and on Sundays patent leather shoes one size too small.

Captain Joe understood the superintendent thoroughly. "Ain't it cur'us," he would sometimes say, "that a man's old 's him is willin' ter set round all day knowin' he don't know nothin', never larnin', an' yit allus afeard some un'll find it out?" Then, as the helplessness of the man rose in his mind, he would add, "Well, poor critter, somebody's got ter support him; guess the guv'ment 's th' best paymaster fur him."

When breakfast was over, the skipper of the Screamer dropped in to make his first visit, shaking the water from his oilskins as he entered.

"Pleased to meet yer, Mis' Bell," he said in his bluff, wholesome way, acknowledging the captain's introduction to Mrs. Bell, then casting his eyes about for a seat, and finally taking an edge of a window-sill among the sou'westers.

"Give me your hat an' coat, and do have breakfast, Captain Brandt," said Mrs. Bell in a tone as hearty as if it were the first meal she had served that day.

"No, thank ye, I had some 'board sloop," replied Captain Brandt.

"Here, cap'n, take my seat," said Captain Joe. "I'm goin' out ter see how the weather looks." He picked up the first hat he came to, — as was his custom, — and disappeared through the open door, followed by nearly all the seafaring men in the room.

As the men passed out, each one reached for his hat and oilskins hanging behind the wooden door, and waddling out stood huddled together in the driving rain like yellow penguins, their eyes turned skyward.

Each man diagnosed the weather for himself. Six doctors over a patient with a hidden disease are never so impressive nor so obstinate as six seafaring men over a probable change of wind. The drift of the cloud-rack scudding in from the sea, the clearness of the air, the current of the upper clouds, were each silently considered. No opinions were given. It was for Captain Joe to say what he thought of the weather. Breaking clouds meant one kind of work for them, — fitting derricks, perhaps, — a continued storm meant another.

If the captain arrived at any conclusion, it was not expressed. He had walked down to the gate and leaned over the palings, looking up at the sky across the harbor, and then behind him toward the west. The rain trickled unheeded down the borrowed sou'wester and fell upon his blue flannel shirt. He looked up and down the road at the passers-by tramping along in the wet: the twice-a-day postman, wearing an old army coat and black rubber cape; the little children crowding together under one umbrella, only the child in the middle keeping dry; and the butcher in the meat wagon with its white canvas cover and swinging scales. Suddenly he gave a quick cry, swung back the gate with the gesture of a rollicking boy, and threw both arms wide open in a mock attempt to catch a young girl who sprang past him and dashed up the broad walk with a merry ringing laugh that brought every one to the outer door.

"Well, if I live!" exclaimed Mrs. Bell. "Mary Peebles, you jes' come here an' see Betty West. Ain't you got no better sense, Betty, than to come down in all this soakin' rain? Caleb 'll be dreadful mad, an' I don't blame him a mite. Come right in this minute and take that shawl off."

"I ain't wet a bit, Aunty Bell," laughed Betty, entering the room. "I got Caleb's high rubber boots on. Look at 'em. Ain't they big!" showing the great soles with all the animation of a child. "An' this shawl don't let no water through nowhere. Oh, but did n't it blow round my porch las' night!" Then turning to the captain, who had followed close behind, "I think you're real mean, Cap'n Joe, to keep

Caleb out all night on the Ledge. I was that dead lonely I could'er cried. Oh, is Mr. Sanford here?" she asked quickly, and with a little shaded tone of deference in her voice, as she caught sight of him in the next room. "I thought he'd gone to New York. How do you do, Mr. Sanford?" with another laugh and a nod of her head, which Sanford as kindly returned.

"We come purty nigh leavin' everybody on the Ledge las' night, Betty, an' the sloop too," said Captain Joe, "cutting" his eye at the skipper as he spoke. Then in a more serious tone, "I lef' Caleb a-purpose, child. We got some stavin' big derricks to set, an' Mr. Sanford wants 'em up week arter next, an' there ain't nobody kin fix the anchor sockets but me an' Caleb. He's at work on 'em now, an' I had to come back to git th' bands on 'em. He'll be home for Sunday, little gal."

"Well, you jes' better, or I'll lock up my place an' come right down here to Aunty Bell. Caleb was n't home but two nights last week, and it's only the beginnin' of summer. I ain't like Aunty Bell, — she can't get lonely. Don't make no difference whether you're home or not, this place is so chuck-full of folks you can't turn round in it; but 'way up where I live, you don't see a soul sometimes all day but a peddler. Oh, I jes' can't stand it, an' I won't. Land sakes, Aunty Bell, what a lot of folks you've had for breakfast!"

With another laugh she turned to the table, picked up a pile of plates, and carried them into the pantry to Miss Peebles, who was there helping in the wash-up.

Lacey, who had stopped to look after his drying coat when the men went out, watched her slender, graceful figure, and bright, cheery, joyous face, full of dimples and color and sparkle, the hair in short curls all over her head, the throat plump and white, the little ears nestling and half hidden.

She had been brought up in the next village, two miles away, and had come over every morning, when she was a girl, to Miss Peebles's school. Almost everybody knew her and loved her; Captain Joe as much as if she had been his own child. She filled a place in his heart of which he seldom spoke, — never to Aunty Bell, — a place empty until Betty came, and always aching since he and his wife had laid away, on the hill back of the village church, the only child that had ever come to them.

When Caleb gave up the lightship Captain Joe had established him with Betty's mother as boarder, and that was how the marriage came about.

When Betty returned to the room again, her arms loaded with plates, Carleton and Lacey were standing.

"Take this seat; you must be tired walking down so far," said Carleton, with a manner never seen in him except when some pretty woman was about.

"No, I'm not a bit tired, but I'll set down till I get these boots off. Aunty Bell, can you lend me a pair of slippers? One of these plaguy boots leaks."

"I'll take 'em off," offered Carleton, with a gesture of gallantry.

"You'll do nothin' of the kind!" she exclaimed, with a toss of her head. "I'll take 'em off myself," and she turned her back, and slipped the boots from under her dress. "But you can take 'em to Aunty Bell an' swap 'em for her slippers," she added, with a merry laugh at the humor of her making the immaculate Carleton carry off Caleb's old boots. The slippers on, she thanked him, with a nod, and, turning her head, caught sight of Lacey.

"What are you doing here, Bill Lacey?" she asked. "Why ain't you at the Ledge?"

Although the young rigger had been but a short time on the captain's force, he had employed every leisure moment of it in making himself agreeable to the wives of the men. To Betty his attentions had been most marked.

He had saved her the best of the long thin shavings that curled from his spoke-shave when he was planing the huge derrick masts on the wharf. And when she came to gather them as kindling for her stove, he had done everything in his power to win her confidence, detaining her in talk long after the other women had departed with their loads.

When he answered her sally to-day, his white teeth gleamed under his curling mustache.

"Captain wants me," he said, "to fit some bands round the new derricks. We expect 'em over from Medford to-day, if it clears up."

"An' there ain't no doubt but what ye'll get yer job, Billy," burst out the captain; "it's breakin' now over Crotch Island," and he bustled again out of the open door, the men who had followed him turning back after him.

Carleton waited until he became convinced that no part of his immaculate personality burdened Betty's mind, and then, a little disconcerted by her evident preference for Lacey, joined Sanford in the next room. There he renewed his complaint about the enrockment block having been placed without a notification to him, and it was not until Sanford invited him on the tug for a run to Medford to inspect Mrs. Leroy's new dining-room that he became pacified.

As Mrs. Bell and the schoolmistress, Miss Peebles, were still in the pantry, a rattling of china marking their progress, the kitchen was empty except for Lacey and Betty. The young rigger, seeing no one within hearing, crossed the room, and, bending over Betty's chair, said in a low tone, "Why did n't you come down to the dock yesterday when we was a-hoistin' the stone on the Screamer? 'Most everybody 'longshore was there. I had some chips saved for ye."

"Oh, I don't know," returned Betty indifferently.

"Ye ought'er seen the old man yesterday," continued Lacey; "me an' him held the guy, and he was a-blowin' like a porpoise."

Betty did not answer. She knew how old Caleb was.

"Had n't been for me it would'er laid him out."

The girl started, and her eyes flashed. "Bill Lacey, Caleb knows more in a minute than you ever will in your whole life. You shan't talk that way about him, neither."

"Well, who 's a-talkin'?" said Lacey, looking down at her, more occupied with the curve of her throat than with his reply.

"You are, an' you know it," she answered sharply.

"I did n't mean nothin', Betty. I ain't got nothin' agin him 'cept his gittin' *you*." Then in a lower tone, "You need n't take my head off, if I did say it."

"I ain't takin' your head off, Billy." She looked into his eyes for the first time, her voice softening. She was never angry with any one for long; besides, she felt older than he, and a certain boyishness in him appealed to her.

"You spoke awful cross," he said, bending

until his lips almost touched her curls, "an' you know, Betty, there ain't a girl, married or single, up 'n' down this shore nor nowheres else, that I think as much of as I do you, an' if" —

"Here, now, Bill Lacey!" some one shouted.

The young rigger stepped back, and turned his head.

Captain Joe was standing in the doorway, with one hand on the frame, an ugly, determined expression filling his eyes.

"They want ye down ter the dock, young feller, jes' 's quick 's ye kin get there."

Lacey's face was scarlet. He looked at Captain Joe, picked up his hat, and walked down the garden path without a word.

Betty ran in to Aunty Bell.

When the two men reached the swinging-gate, Captain Joe laid his hand on Lacey's shoulder, whirled him round suddenly, and said in a calm, decided voice that carried conviction in every tone, "I don't say nothin', an' maybe ye don't mean nothin', but I've been a-watchin' ye lately, an' I don't like yer ways. One thing, howsomever, I'll tell ye, an' I don't want ye ter forgit it: if I ever ketch ye a-foolin' round Caleb West's lobster-pots, I'll break yer damned head. Do ye hear?"

CHAPTER VI

A LITTLE DINNER FOR FIVE

SANFORD's apartments were in gala-dress. Everywhere there was a suggestion of spring in all its brightness and promise. The divans of the salon were gay with new cushions of corn-yellow and pale green. The big table was resplendent in a new cloth, — a piece of richly colored Oriental stuff that had been packed away and forgotten in the Venetian wedding-chest that stood near the window. All the pipes, tobacco pouches, smoking-jackets, slippers, canes, Indian clubs, dumb-bells, and other bachelor belongings scattered about the rooms had been tucked out of sight, while books and magazines that had lain for weeks heaped up on chairs and low shelves, and unframed prints and photographs that had rested on the floor propped up against the wall and furniture, had been hidden in dark corners or hived in their several portfolios.

On the table stood a brown majolica jar taller than the lamp, holding a great mass of dogwood and apple blossoms, their perfume filling the room. Every vase, umbrella jar,

A LITTLE DINNER FOR FIVE   77

jug, and bit of pottery that could be pressed into service, was doing duty as flower-holder, while over the mantel and along the tops of the bookcases, and even over the doors themselves, streamed festoons of blossoms intertwined with smilax and trailing vines.

Against the tapestries covering the walls of the dining-room hung big wreaths of laurel tied with ribbons. One of these was studded with violets, forming the initials H. S. The mantel was a bank of flowers. From the four antique silver church lamps suspended in the four corners of the room swung connecting festoons of smilax and blossoms. The dinner-table itself was set with the best silver, glass, and appointments that Sanford possessed. Some painted shades he had never seen before topped the tall wax candles.

Sanford smiled when he saw that covers had been laid for but five. That clever fellow Jack Hardy had carried his point, — all those delicate questions relating to the number and the selection of the guests had been left to Mrs. Leroy. She had proved her exquisite tact: Bock had been omitted, there were no superfluous women, and Jack could have his tête-à-tête with Helen undisturbed. It was just as well, Sanford thought. With these two young persons happy, the dinner was sure to be a success.

Upon entering his office, he found that the decorative raid had extended even to this his most private domain. The copper helmet of a diving-dress — one he sometimes used himself when necessity required — had been propped up over his desk, the face-plate unscrewed, and the hollow opening filled with blossoms, their leaves curling about the brass buttons of the collar. The very drawing-boards had been pushed against the wall, and the rows of shelves holding his charts and detailed plans had been screened from sight by a piece of Venetian silk exhumed from the capacious interior of the old chest.

The corners of Sam's mouth touched his ears when Sanford looked at him, and every tooth was lined up with a broad grin.

"Doan' ask me who done it, sah. I ain't had nuffin to do wid it, — wid nuffin but de table. I sot dat."

"Has Mrs. Leroy been here?" Sanford asked, coming into the dining-room, and looking again at the initials on the wall. He knew that Jack could never have perfected the delicate touch alone.

"Yaas 'r, an' Major Slocomb an' Mr. Hardy done come too. De gen'lemen bofe gone ober to de club. De major say he comin' back soon 's ever you gets here. But I ain't ter tell nuffin 'bout de flowers, sah. Massa Jack say ef I do he brek my neck, an' I 'spec's he will. But Lord, sah, *dese* ain't no flowers. Look at dis," he added, uncovering a great bunch of

A LITTLE DINNER FOR FIVE

American Beauties, — "dat's ter go 'longside de lady's plate. An' dat ain't ha'f of 'em. I got mos' a peck of dese yer rose-water roses in de pantry. Massa Jack gwine ter ask yer to sprinkle 'em all ober de table-cloth; says dat's de way dey does in de fust famblies South."

"Have the flowers I ordered come?" Sanford asked, as he turned towards the sideboard to fill his best decanter.

"Yaas 'r, got 'em in de ice-chest. But Massa Jack say dese yer rose-water roses on de table-cloth 's a extry touch; don't hab dese high-toned South'n ladies ebery day, he say."

Sanford reëntered the salon and looked about. Every trace of its winter dress too had gone. Even the heavy curtains at the windows had been replaced by some of a thin yellow silk.

"That's so like Kate," he said to himself. "She means that Helen and Jack shall be happy, at any rate. She's missed it herself, poor girl. It's an infernal shame. Bring in the roses, Sam: I'll sprinkle them now before I dress. Any letters except these?" he added, looking through a package on the table, a shade of disappointment crossing his face as he pushed them back unopened.

"Yaas'r, one on yo' bureau dat's jus' come."

Sanford forgot Jack's roses, and with a quick movement of his hand drew the curtains of his bedroom and disappeared inside. The letter was there. He seldom came home from any journey without finding one of these little missives to greet him. He broke the seal and was about to read the contents when the major's cheery, buoyant voice was heard in the outside room. The next instant he had pushed the curtains aside and peered in.

"Where is he, Sam? In here, did you say?"

Not to have been able to violate the seclusion of Sanford's bedroom at all times, night or day, would have grievously wounded the sensibilities of the distinguished Pocomokian; it would have implied a reflection on the closeness of their friendship. It was true he had met Sanford but half a dozen times, and it was equally true that he had never before crossed the threshold of this particular room. But these trifling drawbacks, mere incidental stages in a rapidly growing friendship, were immaterial to him.

"My dear boy," he cried, as he entered the room with arms wide open, "but it does my heart good to see you!" and he hugged Sanford enthusiastically, patting his host's back with his fat hands over the spot where the suspenders crossed. Then he held him at arm's length.

"Let me look at you. Splendid, by gravy! fresh as a rose, suh, handsome as a picture! Just a trace of care under the eyes, though. I see the nights of toil, the hours of suffering. I wonder the brain of man can stand it. But the building of a lighthouse, the illumining of a pathway in the sea for those buffeting with the waves, — it is gloriously humane, suh!"

Suddenly his manner changed, and in a tone as grave and serious as if he were full partner in the enterprise and responsible for its success, the major laid his hand, this time confidingly, on Sanford's shirt-sleeve, and said, "How are we getting on at the Ledge, suh? Last time we talked it over, we were solving the problem of a colossal mass of — of — some stuff or other that" —

"Concrete," suggested Sanford, with an air as serious as that of the major. He loved to humor him.

"That's it, — concrete; the name had for the moment escaped me, — concrete, suh, that was to form the foundation of the lighthouse."

Sanford assured the major that the concrete was being properly amalgamated, and discussed the laying of the mass in the same technical terms he would have used to a brother engineer, smiling meanwhile as the stream of the Pocomokian's questions ran on. He liked the major's glow and sparkle. He enjoyed most of all the never ending enthusiasm of the man, — that spontaneous outpouring which, like a bubbling spring, flows unceasingly, and always with the coolest and freshest water of the heart.

"And how is Miss Shirley?" asked the young engineer, throwing the inquiry into the shallows of the talk as a slight temporary dam.

"Like a moss rosebud, suh, with the dew on it. She and Jack have gone out for a drive in Jack's cyart. He left me at the club, and I went over to his apartments to dress. I am staying with Jack, you know. Helen is with a school friend. I know, of co'se, that yo'r dinner is not until eight o'clock, but I could not wait longer to grasp yo'r hand. Do you know, Sanford," with sudden animation and in a rising voice, "that the more I see of you, the more I"—

"And so you are coming to New York to live, major," said Sanford, dropping another pebble at the right moment into the very middle of the current.

The major recovered, filled, and broke through in a fresh place. The new questions of his host only varied the outlet of his eloquence.

"Coming, suh? I have *come*. I have leased a po'tion of my estate to some capitalists from Philadelphia who are about embarking in a strawberry enterprise of very great magnitude. I want to talk to you about it later." (He had rented one half of it — the dry half, the half a little higher than the salt-marsh — to a huckster from Philadelphia, who was trying to raise early vegetables, and whose cash advances upon the rent had paid the overdue interest on the mortgage, leaving a margin hardly more than sufficient to pay for the suit of clothes he stood in, and his traveling expenses.)

By this time the constantly increasing pressure of his caller's enthusiasm had seriously endangered the possibility of Sanford's dressing for dinner. He glanced several times uneasily at his watch, lying open on the bureau before him, and at last, with a hurried "Excuse me, major," disappeared into his bathroom, and closed its flood-gate of a door, thus effectually shutting off the major's overflow, now perilously near the danger-line.

The Pocomokian paused for a moment, looked wistfully at the blank door, and, recognizing the impossible, called to Sam and suggested a cocktail as a surprise for his master when he appeared again. Sam brought the ingredients on a tray, and stood by admiringly (Sam always regarded him as a superior being) while the major mixed two comforting concoctions, — the one already mentioned for Sanford, and the other designed for the especial sustenance and delectation of the distinguished Pocomokian himself.

This done he took his leave, having infused into the apartment, in ten short minutes, more sparkle, freshness, and life than it had known since his last visit.

Sanford saw the cocktail on his bureau when he entered the room again, but forgot it in his search for the letter he had laid aside on the major's entrance. Sam found the invigorating compound when dinner was over, and immediately emptied it into his own person.

"Please don't be cross, Henry, if you can't find all your things," the letter read. "Jack Hardy wanted me to come over and help him arrange the rooms as a surprise for the Maryland girl. He says there's nothing between them, but I don't believe him. The blossoms came from Newport. I hope you had time to go to Medford and find out about my dining-room, and that everything is going on well at the Ledge. I will see you to-night at eight.
               K. P. L."

Sanford, with a smile of pleasure, shut the letter in his bureau drawer, and entering the dining-room, picked up the basket of roses and began those little final touches about the room and table which he never neglected. He lighted the tapers in the antique lamps that hung from the ceiling, readjusting the ruby glass holders; he kindled the wicks in some quaint brackets over the sideboard; he moved the Venetian flagons and decanters nearer the centrepiece of flowers, — those he had himself ordered for his guests and their chaperon, — and cutting the stems from the rose-water roses sprinkled them over the snowy linen.

With the soft glow of the candles the room took on a mellow, subdued tone; the pink roses on the cloth, the rosebuds on the candle-shades, and the mass of Mermets in the centre being the distinctive features, and giving the key-note of color to the feast. To Sanford a dinner-table with its encircling guests was always a palette. He knew just where the stronger tones of black coats and white shirt-fronts placed beside the softer tints of fair shoulders and bright faces must be relieved by blossoms in perfect harmony, and he understood to a nicety the exact values of the minor shades in linen, glass, and silver, in the making of the picture.

The guests arrived within a few minutes of one another. Mrs. Leroy, in yellow satin with big black bows caught up on her shoulder, a string of pearls about her throat, came first: she generally did when dining at Sanford's; it gave her an opportunity to have a chance word with him before the arrival of the other guests, and to give a supervising glance over the appointments of his table. And then Sanford always deferred to her in questions of taste. It was one of the nights when she looked barely twenty-five, and seemed the fresh, joyous girl Sanford had known before her marriage. The ever present sadness which her friends often read in her face had gone. To-night she was all gayety and happiness, and her eyes, under their long lashes, were purple as the violets which she wore. Helen Shirley was arrayed in white muslin,—not a jewel,—her fair cheeks rosy with excitement. Jack was immaculate in white tie and high collar, while the self-installed, presiding genial of the feast, the major, appeared in a costume that by its ill-fitting wrinkles betrayed its pedigree, — a velvet-collared swallow-tail coat that had lost its one-time freshness in the former service of some friend, a skin-tight pair of trousers, and a shoe-string cravat that looked as if it had belonged to Major Talbot himself (his dead wife's first husband), and that was now so loosely tied it had all it could do to keep its place.

"No one would have thought of all this but you, Kate," said Sanford, lifting Mrs. Leroy's cloak from her shoulders.

"Don't thank me, Henry. All I did," she answered, laughing, "was to put a few flowers about, and to have my maid poke a lot of man-things under the sofas and behind the chairs, and take away those horrid old covers and curtains. I know you'll never forgive me when you want something to-morrow you can't find, but Jack begged so hard I couldn't help it. How did you like the candle-shades? I made them myself," she added, tipping her head on one side like a wren.

"I knew you did, and I recognized your handiwork somewhere else," Sanford answered, with a significant shrug of his shoulders towards the dining-room, where the initial wreath was hung.

"It is a bower of beauty, my dear madam!" exclaimed the major, bowing like a French dancing-master of the old school when Sanford presented him, one hand on his waistcoat

"*Helen . . . in white muslin — not a jewel*"

buttons, the right foot turned slightly out. "I did not know when I walked through these rooms this afternoon whose fair hands had wrought the wondrous change. Madam, I salute you," and he raised her hand to his lips.

Mrs. Leroy looked first in astonishment as she drew back her fingers. Then as she saw his evident sincerity, she made him an equally old-fashioned curtsy, and broke into a peal of laughter.

While this bit of comedy was being enacted, Jack, eager to show Helen some of Sanford's choicest bits, led her to the mantelpiece, over which hung a sketch by Smearly, — the original of his Academy picture; pointed out the famous wedding-chest and some of the accoutrements over the door; and led her into the private office, now lighted by half a dozen candles, one illuminating the copper diving-helmet with its face-plate of flowers. Helen, who had never been in a bachelor's apartment before, thought it another and an enchanted world. Everything suggested a surprise and a mystery.

But it was when she entered the dining-room on Sanford's arm that she gave way completely. "I never saw anything so charming!" she exclaimed. "And H. S. all in a lovely wreath — why, these are *your* initials, Mr. Sanford," looking up innocently into his eyes.

Sanford smiled quizzically, and a shade of cruel disappointment crossed Jack's face. Mrs.

Leroy broke into another happy, contagious laugh, and her eyes, often so impenetrable in their sadness, danced with merriment.

The major watched them all with ill-disguised delight, and, beginning to understand the varying expressions flitting over his niece's face, said, with genuine emotion, emphasizing his outburst by kissing her rapturously on the cheek, "You dear little girl, you, don't you know your own name? H. S. stands for Helen Shirley, not Henry Sanford."

Helen gave a little start, avoiding Jack's gaze, and blushed scarlet. She might have known, she said to herself, that Jack would do something lovely, just to surprise her. Why did she betray herself so easily?

When, a moment later, in removing her glove, she brushed Jack's hand, lying on the table-cloth beside her own, the slightest possible pressure of her little finger against his own conveyed her thanks.

Everybody was brimful of happiness: Helen radiant with the inspiration of new surroundings so unlike those of the simple home she had left the day before; Jack riding in a chariot of soap-bubbles, with butterflies for leaders, and drinking in every word that fell from Helen's lips; the major suave and unctuous, with an old-time gallantry that delighted his admirers, boasting now of his ancestry, now of his horses, now of his rare old wines at home;

Sanford leading the distinguished Pocomokian into still more airy flights, or engaging him in assumed serious conversation whenever that obtuse gentleman insisted on dragging Jack down from his butterfly heights with Helen, to discuss with him some prosaic features of the club-house at Crab Island; while Mrs. Leroy, happier than she had been in weeks, watched Helen and Jack with undisguised pleasure, or laughed at the major's good-natured egotism, his wonderful reminiscences and harmless pretensions, listening between pauses to the young engineer by her side, whose heart was to her an open book.

Coffee was served on the balcony, the guests seating themselves in the easy-chairs. Mrs. Leroy selected a low camp-stool, resting her back against the railing, where the warm tones of the lamp fell upon her dainty figure. She was at her best to-night. Her prematurely gray hair, piled in fluffy waves upon her head and held in place by a long jewel-tipped pin, gave an indescribable softness and charm to the rosy tints of her skin. Her blue-gray eyes, now deep violet, flashed and dimmed under the moving shutters of the lids, as the light of her varying emotions stirred their depths. About her every movement was that air of distinction, and repose, and a certain exquisite grace which never left her, and which never ceased to have its fascination for her friends. Added to this were a sprightliness and a vivacity which, although often used as a mask to hide a heavy heart, were to-night inspired by her sincere enjoyment of the pleasure she and the others had given to the young Maryland girl and her lover.

When Sam brought the coffee-tray she insisted on filling the cups herself, dropping in the sugar with a dainty movement of her fingers that was bewitching, laughing as merrily as if there had never been a sorrow in her life. At no time was she more fascinating to her admirers than when at a task like this. The very cup she handled was instantly invested with a certain preciousness, and became a thing to be touched as delicately and as lightly as the fingers that had prepared it.

The only one who for the time was outside the spell of her influence was Jack Hardy. He had taken a seat on the floor of the balcony, next the wall — and Helen.

"Jack, you lazy fellow," said Mrs. Leroy, with mock indignation, as she rose to her feet, "get out of my way, or I'll spill the coffee. Miss Shirley, why don't you make him go inside? He's awfully in the way here."

One of Jack's favorite positions, when Helen was near, was at her feet. He had learned this one the summer before at her house on Crab Island, when they would sit for hours on the beach.

"I'm not in anybody's way, my dear Mrs. Leroy. My feet are tied in a Chinese knot under me, and my back has grown fast to the rain-spout. Major, will you please say something nice to Mrs. Leroy and coax her inside?"

Sam had rolled a small table, holding a flagon of cognac and some crushed ice, beside the major, who sat half buried in the cushions of one of Sanford's divans. The Pocomokian struggled to his feet.

"You mustn't move, major," Mrs. Leroy called. "I'm not coming in. I'm going to stay out here in this lovely moonlight, if one of these very polite young gentlemen will bring me an armchair." With a look of pretended dignity at Jack and Sanford.

"Take *my* seat," said Jack, with a laugh, springing to his feet, suddenly realizing Mrs. Leroy's delicate but pointed rebuke. "Come, Miss Helen," a better and more retired corner having at this moment suggested itself to him, "we won't stay where we are abused. Let us join the major." And with an arm to Miss Shirley and a sweeping bow to Mrs. Leroy, Jack walked straight to the divan nearest the curtains.

When Helen and Jack were out of hearing, Mrs. Leroy looked toward the major, and, reassured of his entire absorption in his own personal comfort, turned to Sanford, and said in low, earnest tones, in which there was not a trace of the gayety of a moment before, "Can the new sloop lay the stones, Henry? You have n't told me a word yet of what you have been doing for the last few days at the Ledge."

"I think so, Kate," replied Sanford in an equally serious voice. "We laid one yesterday before the easterly gale caught us. You got my telegram, did n't you?"

"Of course! but I was anxious for all that. Ever since I had that talk with General Barton I 've felt nervous over the laying of those stones. He frightened me when he said no one of the Board at Washington believed you could do it. It would be so awful if your plan should fail."

"But it 's not going to fail, Kate. I can do it, and will." There was a decided tone in his voice, and his eyebrows were knitted in the way she loved: she read his determination in every word and look. "All I wanted was a proper boat, and I 've got that. I watched her day before yesterday. I was a little nervous until I saw her lower the first stone. Her captain is a plucky fellow, — Captain Joe likes him immensely. I wish you could have been there to see how cool he was, — not a bit flustered when he saw the rocks under the bow of his sloop."

Kate handed him her empty coffee-cup, and going to the edge of the balcony rested her elbows on the railing, a favorite gesture of hers, and looked down on the treetops of the square.

"Caleb West, of course, went down with the first stone, did n't he?" she asked when he joined her again. She knew Caleb's name as she did those of all the men in Sanford's employ. There was no detail of the work he had not explained to her.

"And was the sea-bottom as you expected to find it?" she added.

"Even better," he answered, eager to discuss his plans with her. "Caleb reports that as soon as he gets the first row of enrockment stones set, the others will lie up like bricks. And it.'s all coming out exactly as we have planned it, too, Kate."

He went over with her again, as he had done so many times before, all of his plans for carrying on the work and the difficulties that had threatened him. He talked of his hopes and fears, of his confidence in his men, his admiration for them, and his love for the work itself. To Sanford, as to many men, there were times when the sympathy and understanding of a woman, the generous faith and ready belief of one who listens only to encourage, became a necessity. To have talked to a man as he did to Kate would not only have bored his listener, but might have aroused a suspicion of his own professional ability.

"I wonder what General Barton will think

when he finds your plan succeeds? He says everywhere that you cannot do it," Kate continued, with a certain pride in her voice, after listening to some further details of Sanford's plans for placing the enrockment blocks.

"I don't know and I don't care. It's hard to get these old-time engineers to believe in anything new, and this foundation is new. But all the same, I'd rather pin my faith to Captain Joe than to any one of them. What we are doing at the Ledge, Kate, requires mental pluck and brute grit, — nothing else. Scientific engineering won't help us a bit."

Sanford now stood erect, with face aglow and kindling eyes, his back to the balcony rail. Every inflection of his voice showed a keen interest in the subject.

"And yet, after all, Kate, I realize that my work is mere child's play. Just see what other men have had to face. At Minot's Ledge, you know, — the light off Boston, — they had to chisel down a submerged rock into steps, to get a footing for the tower. But three or four men could work at a time, and then at dead low water. They got only one hundred and thirty hours' work the first year. The whole Atlantic rolled in on top of them, and there was no shelter from the wind. Until they got the bottom courses of their tower bolted to the steps they had cut in the rock, they had no footing at all, and had to do their work from a small boat.

A LITTLE DINNER FOR FIVE 95

Our artificial island helps us immensely; we have something to stand on. And it was even worse at Tillamook Rock, on the Pacific coast. There the men were landed on a precipitous crag sticking up out of the sea, from breeches buoys slung to the masthead of a vessel. For weeks at a time the sea was so rough that no one could reach them. They were given up for dead once. All that time they were lying in canvas tents lashed down to the sides of the crag to keep them from being blown into rags. All they had to eat and drink for days was raw salt pork and the rain-water they caught from the tent covers. And yet those fellows stuck to it day and night until they had blasted off a place large enough to put a shanty on. Every bit of the material for that lighthouse, excepting in the stillest weather, was landed from the vessel that brought it, by a line rigged from the masthead to the top of the crag; and all this time, Kate, she was thrashing around under steam, keeping as close to the edge as she dared. Oh, I tell you, there is something stunning to me in such a battle with the elements!"

Kate's cheeks burned as Sanford talked on. She was no longer the dainty woman over the coffee-cups, nor the woman of the world she had been a few moments before, eager for the pleasure of assembled guests.

Her eyes flashed with the intensity of her feelings. "When you tell me such things,

Henry, I am all on fire," she cried. Then she stopped as suddenly as if some unseen hand had been laid upon her, chilling and shriveling the hot burning words. "The world is full of such great things to be done," she sighed, "and I lead such a mean little life."

Sanford looked at her in undisguised admiration. Then, as he watched her, his heart smote him. He had not intended to wound her by his enthusiasm over his own work, nor to awaken in her any sense of her own disappointments; he had only tried to allay her anxieties over his affairs. He knew by the force of her outburst that he had unconsciously stirred those deeper emotions, the strength of which really made her the help she was to him. But he never wanted them to cause her suffering.

These sudden transitions in her moods were not new to him. She was an April day in her temperament, and would often laugh the sunniest of laughs when the rain of her tears was falling. These were really moods he loved.

It was the present frame of mind, however, that he dreaded, and from which he always tried to save her. It did not often show itself. She was too much a woman of the world to wear her heart upon her sleeve, and too good and tactful a friend to burden even Sanford with sorrows he could not lighten. He knew what had inspired the outburst, for he had known her for years. He had witnessed the long years of silent suffering which she had borne so sweetly,—even cheerfully at times,—had seen with what restraint and self-control she had cauterized by silence and patient endurance every fresh wound, and had watched day by day the slow coming of the scars that drew all the tighter the outside covering of her heart.

As he looked at her out of the corner of his eye,—she leaning over the balcony at his side,—he could see that the tears had gathered under her lashes. It was best to say nothing when she felt like this. He recognized that to have made her the more dissatisfied, even by that sympathy which he longed to give, would have hurt in her that which he loved and honored most,—her silence, and her patient loyalty to the man whose name she bore. "She's had a letter from Leroy," he said to himself, "and he's done some other disgraceful thing, I suppose;" but to Kate he said nothing.

Gradually he led the talk back to Keyport, this time telling her of his men and their peculiarities and humors; of Caleb and his young and pretty wife; and of Aunty Bell's watchful care over his comfort whenever he spent the night at Captain Joe's.

Nothing had disturbed the other guests. The clink of the major's glass and the intermittent gurgle of the rapidly ebbing decanter as Sam supplied his wants could still be heard from the softly lighted room. On the fore-ordained divan, half hidden by a curtain, sat Jack and Helen, their shoulders touching, studying the contents of a portfolio, — some of the drawings upside down, their low talk broken now and then by a happy, irrelevant laugh.

By this time the moon had risen over the treetops, the tall buildings far across the quadrangle breaking the sky-line. Below could be seen the night life of the Park: miniature figures strolling about under the trees, flashing in brilliant light or swallowed up in dense shadow, as they passed through the glare of the many lamps scattered among the budding foliage; a child romping with a dog, or a belated woman wheeling a baby carriage home. The night was still, the air soft and balmy; only the hum of the busy street a block away could be heard where they stood.

Suddenly the figure of a boy darted across the white patch of pavement below them. Sanford leaned far over the railing, a strange, unreasoning dread in his heart.

"What is it, Henry?" asked Mrs. Leroy.

"Looks like a messenger," Sanford answered.

Mrs. Leroy bent over the railing, and watched the boy spring up the low steps of the street door, ring the bell violently, and beat an impatient tattoo with his foot.

A LITTLE DINNER FOR FIVE

"Whom do you want?" Sanford called gently.

The boy looked up, and, seeing the two figures on the balcony, answered, "Mr. Henry Sanford. Got a death message."

"A death message, did he say?" gasped Mrs. Leroy. Her voice was almost a whisper.

"Yes; don't move." He laid a hand on her arm and pointed toward the group inside. A quick, sharp contraction rose in his throat. "Sam," he called in a lowered tone.

"Yaas 'r, — comin' direc'ly."

"Sam, there's a boy at the outside door with a telegram. He says it's a death message. Get it, and tell the boy to wait. Go quietly, now, and let no one know. You will find me here."

Mrs. Leroy sank into a chair, her face in her hands. Sanford bent over her, his voice still calm.

"Don't give way, Kate; we shall know in a moment."

She grasped his hand and held on. "Oh, who do you suppose it is, Henry? Will Sam *never* come?"

While he was comforting her, urging her to be patient and not to let Helen hear, Sam re-entered the room, — his breath gone with the dash down and up three flights of stairs, — walked slowly toward the balcony, and handed Sanford a yellow envelope. Its contents were as follows : —

Screamer's boiler exploded 7.40 to-night. Mate killed; Lacey and three men injured.

JOSEPH BELL.

Sanford looked hurriedly at his watch, forgetting, in the shock, to hand Mrs. Leroy the telegram.

Mrs. Leroy caught his arm. "Tell me quick! Who is it?"

"Forgive me, dear Kate, but I was so knocked out. It is no one who belongs to you. It is the boiler of the Screamer that has burst. Three men are hurt," reading the dispatch again mechanically. "I wonder who they are?" as if he expected to see their names added to its brief lines.

For a moment he leaned back against the balcony, absorbed in deep thought.

"Twenty-three minutes left," he said to himself, consulting his watch again. "I must go at once; they will need me."

She took the telegram from his hand. "Oh, Henry, I am so sorry, — and the boat, too, you counted upon. Oh, how much trouble you have had over this work! I wish you had never touched it!" she exclaimed, with the momentary weakness of the woman. "But look! read it again." Her voice rose with a new hope in it. "Do you see? Captain Joe signs it, — he's not hurt!"

Sanford patted her hand abstractedly, and

A LITTLE DINNER FOR FIVE

said, "Dear Kate," but without looking at her or replying further. He was calculating whether it would be possible for him to catch the midnight train and go to the relief of the men.

"Yes, I can just make it," he said, half aloud, to himself. Then he turned to Sam, who stood trembling before him, looking first at Mrs. Leroy and then at his master, and said in an undertone, "Sam, send that boy for a cab, and get my bag ready. I will change these clothes on the train. Ask Mr. Hardy to step here; not a word, remember, about this telegram."

Jack came out laughing, and was about to break into some raillery, when he saw Mrs. Leroy's face.

Sanford touched his shoulder, and drew him one side out of sight of the inmates of the room. "Jack, there has been an explosion at the work, and some of the men are badly hurt. Say nothing to Helen until she gets home. I leave immediately for Keyport. Will you and the major please look after Mrs. Leroy?"

Sanford's guests followed him to the door of the corridor: Helen radiant, her eyes still dancing; the major bland and courteous, his face without a ruffle; Jack and Mrs. Leroy apparently unmoved.

"Oh, I'm so sorry you must go!" exclaimed Helen, holding out her hands. "Mr. Hardy says you do nothing but live on the train. Thank you ever so much, dear Mr. Sanford; I've had *such* a lovely time."

"My dear suh," said the major, "this is positively cruel! This Hennessy"—he was holding his glass—"is like a nosegay; I hoped you would enjoy it with me. Let me go back and pour you out a drop before you go."

"Why not wait until to-morrow?" said Jack in perfunctory tones, the sympathetic pressure of his hand in Sanford's belying their sincerity. "This night traveling will kill you, old man."

Sanford smiled as he returned the pressure, and, with his eyes resting on Helen's joyous face, replied meaningly, "Thank you, Jack; it's all right, I see. Not a word until she gets home."

Helen's evening had not been spoiled, at all events.

Once outside in the corridor,—Sam down one flight of steps with Sanford's bag and coat,—Mrs. Leroy half closed the door, and laying her hand on Sanford's shoulder said, with a force and an earnestness that carried the keenest comfort straight to his heart, "I've seen you in worse places than this, Henry; you always get through, and you will now. I shall not worry, and neither will you. I know it looks dark to you, but it will be brighter when you reach Keyport and get all the facts. I will come up myself on the early morning train, and see what can be done for the men."

CHAPTER VII

BETTY'S FIRST PATIENT

THE wounded men lay in an empty warehouse which in the whaling-days had been used for the storing of oil, and was now owned by an old whaler living back of the village.

Captain Joe had not waited for permission and a key when the accident occurred and the wounded men lay about him. He and Captain Brandt had broken the locks with a crowbar, improvised an operating-table for the doctors out of old barrels and planks, and dispatched messengers up and down the shore to pull mattresses from the nearest beds.

The room he had selected for the temporary hospital was on the ground floor of the building. It was lighted by four big windows, and protected by solid wooden shutters, now slightly ajar. Through these openings timid rays of sunlight, strangers here for years, stole down slanting ladders of floating dust to the grimy floor, where they lay trembling, with eyes alert, ready for instant retreat. From the overhead beams hung long strings of abandoned cobwebs encrusted with black soot, which the bolder breeze from the open door and windows swayed back and forth, the startled soot falling upon the white cots below. In one corner was a heap of rusty hoops and mouldy staves,— unburied skeletons of old whaling-days. But for the accumulation of years of dust and mould the room was well adapted to its present use.

Lacey's cot was nearest the door. His head was bound with bandages; only one eye was free. He lay on his side, breathing heavily. The young rigger had been blown against the shrouds, and the iron foot-rest had laid open his cheek and forehead. The doctor said that if he recovered he would carry the scar the rest of his life. It was feared, too, that he had been injured internally.

Next to his cot were those of two of the sloop's crew, — one man with ribs and ankle broken, the other with dislocated hip. Lonny Bowles, the quarryman, came next. He was sitting up in bed, his arm in a sling, — Captain Brandt was beside him; he had escaped with a gash in his arm.

Captain Joe was without coat or waistcoat. His sleeves were rolled up above the elbows, his big brawny arms black with dirt. He had been up all night; now bending over one of the crew, lifting him in his arms as if he had been a baby, to ease the pain of his position, now helping Aunty Bell with the beds.

Betty sat beside Lacey, fanning him. Her

eyes were red and heavy, her pretty curls matted about her head. She and Aunty Bell had not had their clothes off. Their faces were smudged with the soot and grime that kept falling from the ceiling. Aunty Bell had taken charge of the improvised stove, heating the water, and Betty had assisted the doctors — there were two — with the bandages and lint.

"It ain't as bad as I thought when I wired ye," said Captain Joe to Sanford, stopping him as he edged a way through the group of men outside. "It's turrible hard on th' poor mate, jes' been married. Never died till he reached th' dock. There warn't a square inch o' flesh onto him, the doctor said, that warn't scalded clean off. Poor feller," and his voice broke, "he ain't been married but three months; she's a-comin' down on the express. Telling her's the wust thing we 've got to do to-day. Cap'n Bob's goin' ter meet 'er. The other boys is tore up some," he went on, "but we'll have 'em crawlin' 'round in a week or so. Lacey's got th' worst crack. Doctor sez he kin save his eye if he pulls through, but ye kin lay yer three fingers in th' hole in his face. He won't be as purty as he was," with an effort at a smile, "but maybe that'll do him good."

Sanford crossed at once to Lacey's bed, and laid his hand tenderly on that of the sufferer. The young fellow opened his well eye, and a smile played for an instant about his mouth, the white teeth gleaming. Then it faded with the pain. Betty bent over him still closer and adjusted the covering about his chest.

"Has he suffered much during the night, Betty?" asked Sanford.

"He didn't know a thing at first, sir. He didn't come to himself till the doctor got through. He's been easier since daylight." Then, with her head turned toward Sanford, and with a significant gesture, pointing to her own forehead and cheek, she noiselessly described the terrible wounds, burying her face in her hands as the awful memory rose before her. "Oh, Mr. Sanford, I never dreamed anybody could suffer so."

"Where does he suffer most?" asked Sanford in a whisper.

Lacey opened his eye. "In my back, Mr. Sanford."

Betty laid her fingers on his hand. "Don't talk, Billy; doctor said ye weren't to talk."

The eye shut again wearily, and the brown, rough, scarred hand with the blue tattoo marks under the skin closed over the little fingers and held on.

Betty sat fanning him gently, looking down upon his bruised face. As each successive pain racked his helpless body she would hold her breath until it passed, tightening her fingers that he might steady himself the better: all her heart went out to him in his pain.

Aunty Bell watched her for a moment; then going to her side, she drew her hand with a caressing stroke under the girl's chin, a favorite love-touch of hers, and said:—

"Cap'n says we got to go home, child, both of us. You're tuckered out, an' I got some chores to do. We can't do no more good here. You come 'long an' get washed up 'fore Caleb comes. You don't want to let him see ye bunged up like this, an' all smudged and dirty with th' soot a-droppin' down. He'll be here in half an hour. They've sent the tug to the Ledge for him an' the men. Come, Betty, that's a good child."

"I ain't a-goin' a step, Aunty Bell. I ain't sleepy a bit. There ain't nobody to change these cloths but me. Caleb knows how to get along," she answered, her eyes watching the quick, labored breathing of the injured man.

The mention of Caleb's name brought her back to herself. Since the moment when she had left her cottage, the night before, and in all her varying moods since, she had not once thought of her husband. At the sound of the explosion she had run out of her house bareheaded, and had kept on down the road, overtaking Mrs. Bell and the neighbors. She had not stopped even to lock her door. She only knew that the men were hurt, and that she had seen Captain Joe and the others working on the sloop's deck but an hour before. She still saw Lacey's ghastly face as the lantern's light fell upon it, and his limp body carried on the barrow plank and laid outside the warehouse door, and could still hear the crash of Captain Joe's iron bar when he forced off the lock. She would not leave the sufferer, now that he had crawled back to life and needed her, — not, at least, until he was out of all danger. When Captain Joe passed a few minutes later with a cup of coffee for one of the sufferers, she was still by Lacey's side, fanning gently. He seemed to be asleep.

"Now, little gal," the captain called out, "you git along home. You done fust-rate, an' the men won't forgit ye for it. Caleb'll be mighty proud when I tell 'im how you stood by las' night when they all piled in on top o' me. You run 'long now after Aunty Bell, an' git some sleep. I'm goin' 'board the sloop to see how badly she's hurted."

Betty only shook her head. Then she rested her face against Captain Joe's strong arm and said, "No, please don't, Captain Joe. I can't go now."

She was still there, the fan moving noiselessly, when Mrs. Leroy, her maid, and Major Slocomb entered the hospital. The major had escorted Mrs. Leroy from New York, greatly to Sanford's surprise, and greatly to Mrs. Leroy's visible annoyance. All her protests the night before had only confirmed him in his determination to meet her at the train in the morning.

"Did you suppose, my dear suh," he said, in answer to Sanford's astonished look, as he handed that dainty woman from the train on its arrival at Keyport, "that I would permit a lady to come off alone into a God-forsaken country like this, that raises nothin' but rocks and scrub pines?"

Mrs. Leroy seemed stunned when she saw the four cots upon which the men lay. She advanced a step toward Lacey's bed, and then, as she caught sight of the bandages and the ghastly face upon the blood-stained pillow, she stopped short and grasped Sanford's arm, and said in a tremulous whisper, "Oh, Henry, is that his poor wife sitting by him?"

"No; that's the wife of Caleb West, the master diver. That's Lacey lying there. He looks to be worse hurt than he is, Kate," anxious to make the case as light as possible.

Her eyes wandered over the room, up at the cobwebbed ceiling and down to the blackened floor.

"What an awfully dirty place! Are you going to keep them here?"

"Yes, until they can get to work again. The building is perfectly dry and healthy, with plenty of ventilation. We will have it cleaned up,—it needs that."

Betty merely glanced at the group as she

sat fanning the sleeping man. Their entrance had made but little impression upon her; she was too tired to move, and too much absorbed in her charge to offer the fine lady a chair.

Something in the girl's face touched the visitor.

"Have you been here all the morning?" she asked, crossing to Betty's side of the cot, and laying a hand on her shoulder. With the passing of the first shock the natural tenderness of her heart had overcome her. She wanted to help.

Betty raised her eyes, the rims red with her long vigil, and the whites all the whiter because of the fine black dust that had sifted down and discolored her pale cheeks.

"I've been here all night, ma'am," she said sweetly and gently, drawn instinctively by Mrs. Leroy's sympathetic face.

"How tired you must be! Can I do anything to help you? Let me fan him while you rest a little."

Betty shook her head.

The major crossed over to the cot occupied by Lonny Bowles, the big Noank quarryman, whose arm was in a sling, and sat down on the edge of the bed. No one had yet thought of bringing in chairs, except for those nursing the wounded. As the Pocomokian looked into Bowles's bronzed, ruddy face, at the wrinkles about his neck, as seamy as those of a young bull, the great broad hairy chest, and the arms and hands big and strong, he was filled with astonishment. Everything about the quarryman seemed to be the exact opposite of what he himself possessed. This almost racial distinction was made clearer when, in the kindness of his heart, he tried to comfort the unfortunate man.

"I'm ve'y sorry," the major began, with an embarrassment entirely new to him, and which he could not account for in himself, "at finding you injured in this way, suh. Has the night been a ve'y painful one? You seem better off than the others. How did you feel at the time?"

Bowles looked him all over with a curious expression of countenance. He was trying to decide in his mind, from the major's white tie, whether he was a minister, whose next remark would be a request to kneel down and pray with him, or whether he were a quack doctor who had come to do a little business on his own account. The evident sincerity and tenderness of the speaker disconcerted him for the moment. He hesitated for a while, and finally formulated a reply in his mind that would cover the case if his first surmise as to his being a minister were correct, and might at the same time result in his being let alone if the second proved to be the case.

"Wall, it was so damn sudden. Fust thing

I knowed I wuz in the water with th' wind knocked out'er me, an' the next wuz when I come to an' they hed me in here an' the doctor a-fixin' me up. I'm all right, ye see, only I'm drier 'n a lime-kiln. Say, cap," — he looked over toward the water-bucket, and called to one of the men standing near the door, — "fetch me a dipper."

To call a landsman "cap" around Keyport is to dignify him with a title which he probably does not possess, but which you think would please him if he did.

"Let me get you a drink," said the major, rising from the bed with a quick spring indicative of his hearty desire to serve him. He dipped the floating tin in the bucket and brought it to the thirsty man.

Bowles drained the contents to its last drop. "He ain't no preach an' he ain't no sawbones," he said to himself, as he returned the empty tin to Slocomb with a "Thank ye, — much obleeged."

Somehow the reply satisfied the major far more than the most elaborately prepared speech of thanks which he remembered ever to have received.

Then the two men continued to talk freely with each other, the one act of kindness having broken down the barrier between them. The Pocomokian, completely forgetting himself, told of his home on the Chesapeake, of his acquaintance with Sanford, of his coming up to look after Mrs. Leroy. The major's tone of voice was as natural and commonplace as if he had been conversing with himself alone. "Could n't leave a woman without protection, you know," to which code of etiquette Bowles bobbed his head in reply; the genuine, unaffected sympathy of the rough man before him seemed to have knocked every fictitious prop from under his own personality.

The quarryman, in turn, talked about the Ledge, and what a rotten season it had been, — nothing but southeasters since work opened; last week the men only got three days' work. It was terrible rough on the boss (the boss was Sanford), paying out wages to the men and getting so little back; but it was n't the men's fault, — they were standing by day and night, catching the lulls when they came; they 'd make it up before the season was over; he and Caleb West had been up all the night before getting ready for the big derricks that Captain Joe was going to set up as soon as they were ready; did n't know what they were going to do now with that Screamer all tore up: a record of danger, unselfishness, loyalty, pluck, hard work, and a sense of duty that was a complete revelation to Slocomb, whose whole life had been one prolonged loaf, and whose ideas of the higher type of man had heretofore been somehow inseparably interwoven with a veranda, a splint-bottomed chair, a palm-leaf fan, and somebody within call to administer to his personal wants.

When Captain Joe returned from an inspection of the sloop's injuries, — strange to say, they were very slight compared to the force of the explosion, — Mrs. Leroy was still talking to Sanford, suggesting comforts for the men, and planning for mosquito nettings to be placed over their cots. The maid, a severe-looking woman in black, who had never relaxed her grasp of the dressing-case, had taken a seat on an empty nail-keg which somebody had brought in, and which she had carefully dusted with her handkerchief before occupying. It was evident from her manner that there was absolutely nothing she could do for anybody.

Captain Joe looked at the party for a moment, noted Mrs. Leroy's traveling costume of blue foulard and dainty bonnet, ran his eye over the maid, glanced at the major, in an alpaca coat, with white waistcoat and necktie and gray slouch hat, and said in his calm, forceful, yet gentle way to Mrs. Leroy, "It was very nice of ye to come an' bring yer friend," pointing to the maid, "an' any o' Mr. Sanford's folks is allers welcome at any time; but we be a rough lot, an' the men's rough, and ye kin see for yerself we ain't fixed up fur company. They'll be all right in a week or so. Ef ye don't mind now, ma'am, I'm goin' to shet them shetters to keep the sun out o' their eyes an' git th' men quiet, — some on 'em ain't slep' any too much. The tug 'll be here to take ye all over to Medford whenever ye 're ready; she 's been to th' Ledge fur th' men. Mr. Sanford said ye 'd be goin' over soon." He glanced about the room as he spoke, until his eye rested on Sanford. "Ye 're goin' 'long, did n't I hear ye say, sir?" Then addressing Slocomb, whose title he tried to remember, "We 've done th' best we could, colonel. It ain't like what ye 're accustomed to, mebbe, — kind'er ragged place, — but we got th' men handy here where we kin take care on 'em, an' still look after th' work, an' we ain't got no time to lose this season; it 's been back-'ard, blowin' a gale half the time. There 's the tug whistle now, ma'am," turning again to Mrs. Leroy.

Mrs. Leroy did not answer. She felt the justice of the captain's evident want of confidence in her, and realized at once that all of her best impulses could not save her from being an intrusion at this time. None of her former experience had equipped her for a situation of such gravity as this. With a curious feeling of half contempt for herself, she thought, as she looked around upon the great strong men suffering there silently, how little she had known of what physical pain must be. She had once read to a young blind girl in a hospital, during a winter, and she had sent delicacies for years to a poor man with some affliction of the spine. She remembered that she had been quite satisfied with herself and her work at the time; and so had the pretty nurses in their caps, and the young doctors whom she met, the head surgeon even escorting her to her carriage. But what had she done to prepare herself for a situation like this? Here was the reality of suffering, and yet with all her sympathy she felt within herself a fierce repugnance to it. After all her aspirations, how weak she was, and how heartily she despised herself!

As she turned to leave the building, holding her skirts in her hand to avoid the dirt, the light of the open door was shut out, and eight or ten great strong fellows in rough jackets and boots, headed by Caleb West, just landed by a tug from the Ledge, walked hurriedly into the room, with an air as if they belonged there and knew they had work to do, and at once.

Caleb strode straight to Lacey's bed. His cap was off, his hands were clasped behind his back. He felt his eyes filling, and a great lump rose in his throat as he stood looking down at him. He never could see suffering unmoved.

The young rigger opened his well eye, and the pale cheek flushed scarlet as he saw Caleb's face bending over him.

"Where did it hit ye, sonny?" asked Caleb, bending closer, and slipping one hand into Betty's as he spoke.

Betty pointed to her own cheek. Lacey, she said, was too weak to answer for himself.

"I've been afeard o' that b'iler," Caleb said, turning to one of the men, "ever sence I see it work."

Betty shook her head warningly, holding a finger to her lips. Caleb and the men stopped talking.

"You been here all night, Betty?" whispered Caleb, putting his mouth close to her ear, and one big hand on her rounded shoulder.

Betty nodded her head.

"Ye ought'er be mighty proud o' her, Caleb," said Captain Joe, joining the group, and speaking in a lowered tone. "Ain't many older women 'longshore would'er done any better. I tried ter git 'er to go home with Aunty Bell two hours ago, but she sez she won't."

Caleb's face glowed and his heart gave a quick bound as he listened to Captain Joe's praise of the girl wife that was all his own. His rough hand pressed Betty's shoulder the closer. He had always known that the first great sorrow or anxiety that came into her life would develop all her nature and make a woman of her. Now the men about him would see the strong womanly qualities which had attracted him.

"Lemme take hold now, Betty," said Caleb, still whispering, and stooping over her again. "Ye're nigh beat out, little woman."

He slipped his arm around her slender waist as if to lift her from the chair. Betty caught his fingers and loosened his hand from its hold.

"I'm all right, Caleb. You go home. I'll be 'long in a little while to get supper."

Caleb looked at her curiously. Her tone of voice was new to him. She had never loosened his arm before, not when she was tired and sick. She had always crept into his lap, and put her pretty white arms around his neck, and tucked her head down on his big beard.

"What's the matter, little one?" he asked anxiously. "Maybe it's hungry ye be?"

"Yes, I guess I'm hungry, Caleb," said Betty wearily.

"I'll go out, Betty, an' git ye some soup or somethin'. I'll be back right away, little woman." He tiptoed past the cot, putting on his cap as he went.

Two of the men followed him with their eyes and smiled. One looked significantly at Lacey and then toward the retreating figure, and shook his head in a knowing way.

Betty had not answered Caleb. She did not even turn her head to follow his movements. She saw only the bruised, pale face before her as she listened to the heavy breathing of the sufferer. She would have dropped from her chair with fatigue and exhaustion but for some new spirit within her which seemed to hold her up, and to keep the fan still in her hand.

BETTY'S FIRST PATIENT 119

When Sanford, after escorting Mrs. Leroy to her home, returned to the improvised hospital, he found the lanterns lighted, and learned that the doctor had dressed the men's wounds, and had reported everybody on the mend, especially Lacey; at Betty's urgent request he had made a careful examination of the young rigger's wounds, and had pronounced him positively out of danger. Only then had she left her post and gone to her own cottage with Caleb.

Captain Joe had followed Aunty Bell home for a few hours' rest, and all the watchers had been changed.

There was but one exception. Beside the cot upon which lay the sailor with the dislocated hip sat the major, with hat and coat off, his shirt-cuffs rolled up. He was feeding the sufferer from a bowl of soup which he held in his hand. He seemed to enjoy every phase of his new experience. It might have been that his sympathies were more than usually aroused, or it might have been that the spirit of vagabondage within him, which fitted him for every condition in life, making him equally at home among rich and poor, and equally agreeable to both, had speedily brought him into harmony with the men about him. Certainly no newly appointed young surgeon in a charity hospital could have been more entirely absorbed in the proper running of the establishment than was Slocomb in the care of these rough men. He had refused point-blank Mrs. Leroy's pressing invitation to spend the night at her house, his refusal causing much astonishment to those who misunderstood his reasons.

"I'm going to take charge here to-night, major," said Sanford, walking toward him, realizing for the first time that he had neglected his friend all day, and with a sudden anxiety as to where he should send him for the night. "Will you go to the hotel and get a room, or will you go to Captain Joe's cottage? You can have my bed. Mrs. Bell will make you very comfortable for the night."

The major turned to Sanford with an expression of profound sympathy in his face, hesitated for a moment, and said firmly, with a slight suggestion of wounded dignity in his manner, and in a voice which was sincerity itself, "By gravy, suh, you would n't talk about going to bed if you'd been yere 'most all day, as I have, and seen what these po' men suffer. My place is yere, suh, an' yere I'm going to stay."

Sanford had to look twice before he could trust his own eyes and ears. What was the matter with the Pocomokian?

"But, major," he continued in protest, determining finally in his mind that some quixotic whim had taken possession of him, "there is n't a place for you to lie down. You had better get a good night's rest, and come back in the morning. There's nothing you can do here. I'm going to sit up with the men myself to-night."

The major did not even wait for Sanford's reply. He placed the hot soup carefully on the floor, slipped one hand under the wounded man's head that he might swallow more easily, and then raised another spoonful to the sufferer's lips.

CHAPTER VIII

THE "HEAVE HO" OF LONNY BOWLES

THE accident to the Screamer had delayed work at the Ledge but a few days. Other men had taken the place of those injured, and renewed efforts had been made by Sanford and Captain Joe to complete to low-water mark the huge concrete disk, forming a bedstone sixty feet in diameter and twelve feet thick, on which the superstructure was to rest. This had been accomplished after three weeks of work, and the men stood in readiness to begin the masonry of the superstructure itself so soon as the four great derricks required in lifting and setting the cut stone of the masonry could be erected. They were only waiting for Mr. Carleton's acceptance of the concrete disk, the first section of the contract. The superintendent's certificate of approval was important, one rule of the Department being that no new section of the work should begin until the preceding section was officially approved.

Carleton, however, declined to give it. His ostensible reason was that the engineer-in-chief was expected daily at Keyport, and should therefore pass upon the work himself. His real reason was a desire to settle a score with Captain Joe by impeding the progress of the work.

This animosity to Captain Joe had been aroused by an article very flattering to the superintendent, published in the "Medford Journal," in which great credit had been given to Carleton for his "heroism and his prompt efficiency in providing a hospital for the wounded men." The day after its publication, the "Noank Times," a political rival, sent to make an investigation of its own, in the course of which the reporter encountered Captain Joe. The captain had not seen the Medford article until it was shown him by the reporter. He thereupon gave the exact facts in regard to the accident and the subsequent care of the wounded men, generously exonerating the government superintendent from all responsibility for the notice; adding with decided emphasis that "Mr. Carleton could n't 'a' said no such thing 'bout havin' provided the hospital himself, 'cause he was over to Medford to a circus the night the accident happened, and did n't git home till daylight next mornin', when everything was over an' the men was in their beds." The result of this interview was a double-leaded column in the next issue of the "Noank Times," which not only ridiculed its rival for the manufactured news, but read a lesson on veracity to Carleton himself.

The denial made by the "Times" was the thrust that had rankled deepest; for Carleton, unfortunately for himself, had inclosed the eulogistic article from the "Medford Journal" in his official report of the accident to the Department, and had become the proud possessor of a letter from the engineer-in-chief commending his "promptness and efficiency."

So far the captain had kept his temper, ignoring both the obstacles Carleton had thrown in his way and the ill-natured speeches the superintendent was constantly making. No open rupture had taken place. Those, however, who knew the captain's explosive temperament confidently expected that he would break out upon the superintendent, in answer to some brutal thrust, in a dialect so impregnated with fulminates that the effect on Carleton would be disastrous. But they were never gratified. "'T ain't no use answerin' back," was all he said. "He don't know no better, poor critter."

Indeed, it was only when a great personal danger threatened his men that the captain's every-day, conventional English seemed inadequate. On such occasions, when the slightest error on the part of his working force might result in the instant death or the maiming of one of them, certain and it is to be hoped unrecorded outbursts of profanity, soaring into crescendos and ending in fortissimos, would often escape from the captain's lips with a vim and rush that would have raised the hair of his Puritan ancestors, — rockets of oaths, that kindled with splutters of dissatisfaction, flamed into showers of abuse, and burst into blasphemies which cleared the atmosphere like a thunderclap. For these transgressions he never made any apology. In the roar of the sea they seemed sometimes the only ammunition he could depend upon. "Somebody'll git hurted round here, if ye ain't careful; somehow I can't make ye understand no other way," he would say. This was as near as he ever came to apologizing for his sinfulness. But he never wasted any of these explosives on such men as Carleton.

As the superintendent persisted in his refusal to give the certificate of acceptance, and as each day was precious, Sanford, whose confidence in the stability and correctness of the work which he and Captain Joe had done was unshaken, determined to begin the erection of the four derricks at once. He accordingly gave orders to clear away the mixing-boards and tools; thus burning his bridges behind him, should the inspection of the engineer-in-chief necessitate any additional work on the concrete disk.

These derricks, with their winches and chain guys, were now lying on the jagged rocks of the Ledge, where they had been landed the day before by Captain Brandt with the boom of the Screamer, — now stanch and sound as ever, a new engine and boiler on her deck. They were designed to lift and set the cut-stone masonry of the superstructure, — the top course at a height of fifty-eight feet above the water-line. These stones weighed from six to thirteen tons each.

During the delay that followed the accident the weather had been unusually fine. Day after day the sun had risen on a sea of silver reflecting the blue of a cloudless sky, with wavy tide-lines engraved on its polished surface. At dawn Crotch Island had been an emerald, and at sunset an amethyst.

With the beginning of the dog-days, however, the weather had changed. Dull leaden fog-banks dimming the distant horizon had blended into a pearly-white sky. Restless, wandering winds sulked in dead calms, or broke in fitful, peevish blasts. Opal-tinted clouds showed at sunrise, and prismatic rings of light surrounded the moon, — all sure signs of a coming storm.

Captain Joe watched the changing sky where hour by hour were placarded the bulletins of the impending outbreak, and redoubled his efforts on the lines of the watch-tackles at which the men were tugging, pulling the derricks to their places.

By ten o'clock on the 15th of August, three of the four derricks, their tops connected by heavy wire rope, had been stepped in their sockets and raised erect, and their seaward guys had been made fast, Caleb securing the ends himself. By noon, the last derrick — the fourth leg of the chair, as it were — was also nearly perpendicular, the men tugging ten deep on the line of the watch-tackles. This derrick, being the last of the whole system and the most difficult to handle, was under the immediate charge of Captain Joe. On account of its position, which necessitated the bearing of its own strain and that of the other three derricks as well, its outboard seaward guy was as heavy as that of a ship's anchor-chain. The final drawing taut of this chain, some sixty feet in length, stretching, as did the smaller ones, from the top of the derrick-mast down to the enrockment block, and the fastening of its sea end in the block, would not only complete the system of the four erected derricks, but would make them permanent and strong enough to resist either sea action or any weight that they might be required to lift. The failure to secure this chain guy into the anchoring enrockment block, or any sudden break in the other guys, would result not only in instantly toppling over the fourth derrick itself, but in dragging the three erect derricks with it. This might mean, too, the crushing to death of some of the men; for the slimy, ooze-covered rocks and concrete disk on which they had to stand and work made hurried escape impossible.

To insure an easier connection between this last chain and the enrockment block, Caleb had fastened below water, into the Lewis hole of the block, a long iron hook. Captain Joe's problem, which he was now about to solve, was to catch this hook into a steel ring which was attached to the end of the chain guy. The drawing together of this hook and ring was to be done by means of a watch-tackle, which tightened the chain guy inch by inch, the gang of men standing in line while Captain Joe, ring in hand, waited to slip it into the hook. A stage manager stretching a tight-rope supported on saw-horses, with a similar tackle, solves, on a smaller scale, just such a problem every night.

Carleton, who never ran any personal risks, sat on the platform, out of harm's way, sneering at the men's struggles, and protesting that it was impossible to put up the four derricks at once. Sanford was across the disk, some fifty feet from Captain Joe, studying the effect of the increased strain on the outboard guys of the three derricks already placed.

The steady rhythmic movement of the men, ankle-deep in the water, swaying in unison, close-stepped, tugging at the tackle-line, like a file of soldiers, keeping time to Lonny Bowles's "Heave ho," had brought the hook and ring within six feet of each other, when the foot of one of the men slipped on the slimy ooze and tripped up the man next him. In an instant the whole gang were floundering among the rocks and in the water, the big fourth derrick swaying uneasily, like a tree that was doomed.

"Every man o' ye as ye were!" shouted Captain Joe, without even a look at the superintendent, who had laughed outright at their fall. While he was shouting he had twisted a safety-line around a projecting rock to hold the strain until the men could regain their feet. The great derrick tottered for a moment, steadied itself like a drunken man, and remained still. The other three quivered, their top connecting guys sagging loose.

"Now make fast, an' two 'r three of ye come here!" cried the captain again. In the easing of the strain caused by the slipping of the men, the six feet of space between hook and ring had gone back to ten.

Two men scrambled like huge crabs over the slippery rocks, and relieved Captain Joe of the end of the safety-line. The others stood firm and held taut the tug-lines of the watch-tackle. The slow, rhythmic movement of the gang to the steady "Heave ho" began again. The slack of the tackle was taken up, and the ten feet between the hook and the ring were reduced to five. Half an hour more, and the four great derricks would be anchored safe against any contingency.

The strain on the whole system became once more intense. The seaward guy of the opposite derrick — the one across the concrete disk — shook ominously under the enormous tension. Loud creaks could be heard as the links of the chain untwisted and the derricks turned on their rusty pintles.

Then a sound like a pistol-shot rang out clear and sharp.

Captain Joe heard Sanford's warning cry, but before the men could ease the strain one of the seaward guys that fastened the top of its derrick to its enrockment-block anchorage snapped with a springing jerk, writhed like a snake in the air, and fell in a swirl across the disk of concrete, barely missing the men.

The gang at the tug-line turned their heads, and the bravest of them grew pale. The opposite derrick, fifty feet away, was held upright by but a single safety-rope. If this should break, the whole system of four derricks, with its tons of chain guys and wire rope, would be down upon their heads.

Carleton ran to the end of the platform, ready to leap. Sanford ordered him back. Two of the men, in the uncertainty of the moment, slackened their hold. A third, a newcomer, turned to run towards the concrete, as the safer place, when Caleb's viselike hand grasped his shoulder and threw him back in line.

There was but one chance left, — to steady the imperiled derrick with a temporary guy strong enough to stand the strain.

"Stand by on that watch-tackle, every —— —— man o' ye! Don't one o' ye move!" shouted Captain Joe in a voice that drowned all other sounds.

The men sprang into line and stood together in dogged determination.

"Take a man, Caleb, as quick 's God 'll let ye, an' run a wire guy out on that derrick." The order was given in a low voice that showed the gravity of the situation.

Caleb and Lonny Bowles stepped from the line, leaped over the slippery rocks, splashed across the concrete disk, now a shallow lake with the rising tide, and picked up another tackle as they plunged along to where Sanford stood, the water over his rubber boots. They dragged a new guy towards the imperiled derrick. Lonny Bowles, in his eagerness to catch the dangling end of the parted guy, began to scale the derrick-mast itself, climbing by the foot-rests, when Captain Joe's crescendo voice overhauled him. He knew the danger better than Bowles.

"Come down out'er that, Lonny!" (Gentle oaths.) "Come down, I tell ye!" (Oaths crescendo.) "Don't ye know no better 'n to" — (Oaths fortissimo.) "Do ye want to pull that derrick clean over?" (Oaths fortissimisso.)

Bowles slid from the mast just as Sanford's warning cry scattered the men below him. There came a sudden jerk; the opposite derrick trembled, staggered for a moment, and swooped through the air towards the men, dragging in its fall the two side derricks with all their chains and guys.

"Down between the rocks, heads under, every man o' ye!" shouted the captain.

The captain sprang last, crouching up to his neck in the sea, his head below the jagged points of two rough stones, just as the huge fourth derrick, under which he had stood, lunged wildly, and with a ringing blow struck a stone within three feet of his head, — the great anchor-chain guy twisting like a cobra over the slimy rocks.

When all was still, Sanford's anxious face rose cautiously from behind a protecting rock near where the first derrick had struck. There came a cheer of safety from Caleb and Bowles, answered by another from Captain Joe, and Sanford and the men crawled out of their holes, and clambered upon the rocks, the water dripping from their clothing.

Not a man had been hurt!

"What did I tell you?" called out Carleton sneeringly, more to hide his alarm than anything else.

"That's too bad, Mr. Sanford, but we can't help it," said Captain Joe in his customary voice, paying no more attention to Carleton's talk than if it had been the slop of the waves at his feet. "All hands, now, on these derricks. We got'er git 'em up, boys, if it takes all night."

Again the men sprang to his orders, and again and again the crescendos of oaths culminated in fortissimos of profanity as the risks for the men increased.

For five consecutive hours they worked without a pause.

Slowly and surely the whole system, beginning with the two side derricks, whose guys still held their anchorage, was raised upright, Sanford still watching the opposite derrick, a new outward guy having replaced the broken one.

It was six o'clock when the four derricks were again fairly erect. The same gang was tugging at the watch-tackle, and the distance between the hook and the ring was once more reduced to five feet. The hook gained inch by inch towards its anchorage. Captain Joe's eyes gleamed with suppressed satisfaction.

All this time the tide had been rising. Most of the rough, above-water rocks were submerged, and fully three feet of water washed over the concrete disk. Only the tops of the rough stones where Sanford stood, and the platform where Carleton sat, out of all danger from derricks or sea, were clear of the incoming wash.

Meanwhile the Screamer's life-boat — the only means the men had that day of leaving the Ledge and boarding the sloop, moored in the lee of the Ledge — had broken from her moorings, and lay dangerously near the rocks. The wind too had changed to the east. With it came a long, rolling swell that broke on the eastern derrick, — the fourth one, the key-note of the system, the one Captain Joe and the men were tightening up.

Suddenly a window was opened somewhere in the heavens, and a blast of wet air heaped the sea into white caps, and sent it bowling along towards the Ledge and the Screamer lying in the eddy.

Captain Joe, as he stood with the hook in his hand, watched the sea's carefully planned attack, and calculated how many minutes were left before it would smother the Ledge in a froth and end all work. He could see, too, the Screamer's mast rocking ominously in the rising sea. If the wind and tide increased, she must soon shift her position to the eddy on the other side of the Ledge. But no shade of anxiety betrayed him.

The steady movement of the tugging men continued, Lonny's "Heave ho" ringing out cheerily in perfect time. Four of the gang, for better foothold, stood on the concrete, their feet braced to the iron mould band, the water up to their pockets. The others clung with their feet to the slippery rocks.

The hook was now within two feet of the

steel ring, Captain Joe standing on a rock at a lower level than the others, nearly waist-deep in the sea, getting ready for the final clinch.

Sanford from his rock had also been watching the sea. As he scanned the horizon, his quick eye caught to the eastward a huge roller pushed ahead of the increasing wind, piling higher as it swept on.

"Look out for that sea, Captain Joe! Hold fast, men,—hold fast!" he shouted, springing to a higher rock.

Hardly had his voice ceased, when a huge green curler threw itself headlong on the Ledge, wetting the men to their arm-pits. Captain Joe had raised his eyes for an instant, grasped the chain as a brace, and taken its full force on his broad back. When his head emerged, his cap was gone, his shirt clung to the muscles of his big chest, and the water streamed from his hair and mouth.

Shaking his head like a big water-dog, he waved his hand, with a laugh, to Sanford, volleyed out another rattling fire of orders, and then held on with the clutch of a devil-fish as the next green roller raced over him. It made no more impression upon him than if he had been an offshore buoy.

The fight now lay between the rising sea and the men tugging at the watch-tackle. After each wave ran by the men gained an inch on the tightening line. Every moment the wind blew harder, and every moment the sea rose higher. Bowles was twice washed from the rock on which he stood, and the newcomer, who was unused to the slime and ooze, had been thrown bodily into a water-hole. Sanford held to a rock a few feet above Captain Joe, watching his every movement. His anxiety for the safe erection of the system had been forgotten in his admiration for the superb pluck and masterful skill of the surf-drenched sea-titan below him.

Captain Joe now moved to the edge of the anchor enrockment block, standing waist-deep in the sea, one hand holding the hook, the other the ring. Six inches more and the closure would be complete.

In heavy strains like these the last six inches gain slowly.

"Give it to 'er, men— all hands now— give it to 'er! Pull, Caleb! Pull, you——— ———!" (Air full of Greek fire.) "Once more— all together——— ———!" (Sky-bombs bursting.) "All to—"

Again the sea buried him out of sight, quenching the explosives struggling to escape from his throat.

The wind and tide increased. The water swirled about the men, the spray flew over their heads, but the steady pull went on.

A voice from the platform now called out,—

it was that of Nickles, the cook: "Life-boat's a-poundin' bad, sir! She can't stan' it much longer."

Carleton's voice shouting to Sanford from the platform came next: "I'm not going to stay here all night and get wet. I'm going to Keyport in the Screamer. Send some men to catch this life-boat."

The captain raised his head and looked at Nickles; Carleton he never saw.

"Let 'r pound an' be damned to 'er! Go on, Caleb, with that tackle. Pull, ye" — Another wave went over him, and another red-hot explosive lost its life.

With the breaking of the next roller the captain uttered no sound. The situation was too grave for explosives. Whenever his profanity stopped short the men grew nervous: they knew then that a crisis had arrived, one that even Captain Joe feared.

The captain bent over the chain, one arm clinging to the anchorage, his feet braced against a rock, the hook in his hand within an inch of the ring.

"*Hold hard!*" he shouted.

Caleb raised his hand in warning, and the rhythmic movement ceased. The men stood still. Every eye was fixed on the captain.

"LET GO!"

The big derrick quivered for an instant as the line slackened, stood still, and a slight shiver ran through the guys. The hook had slipped into the ring!

The system of four derricks, with all their guys and chains, stood as taut and firm as a suspension bridge!

Captain Joe turned his head calmly towards the platform, and said quietly, "There, Mr. Carleton, they'll stand now till hell freezes over."

As the cheering of the men subsided, the captain, squeezing the water from his hair and beard with a quick rasp of his fingers, sprang to Sanford's rock, grasped his outstretched hand, shook it heartily, and called to Caleb, in a firm, cheery voice that had not a trace of fatigue in it after twelve hours of battling with sea and derricks, "All o' you men what's goin' in the Screamer with Mr. Carleton to Keyport for Sunday 'd better look out for that life-boat. Come, Lonny Bowles, pick up them tackles an' git to the shanty. It'll be awful soapy round here 'fore mornin'."

CHAPTER IX

WHAT THE BUTCHER SAW

CALEB sat on the deck of the Screamer on her homeward run, his face turned toward Keyport Light, beyond which his little cabin lay. His eyes glistened, and there came a choking in his throat as he thought of meeting Betty. He could even feel her hand slipped into his, and could hear the very tones of her cheery welcome, when she met him at the gate and they walked together up the garden path to the porch.

Most of the men who had stood to the watch-tackles in the rolling surf sat beside him on the sloop. Those who were still wet, including Sanford, had gone below into the cabin, out of the cutting wind. Those who, like Caleb, had changed their clothes, sat on the after deck. Captain Joe, against Sanford's earnest protest, had remained on the Ledge for the night. He wanted, he said, to see how the derricks would stand the coming storm.

It had been a busy month for the diver. Since the explosion he had been almost constantly in his rubber dress, working not only his regular four hours under water, — all that an ordinary man could stand, — but taking another's place for an hour or two when some piece of submarine work at the Ledge required his more skillful eye and hand. He had set some fifty or more of the big enrockment blocks in thirty feet of water, each block being lowered into position by the Screamer's boom, and he had prepared the anchor sockets in which to step the four great derricks. Twice he had been swept from his hold by the racing current, and once his helmet had struck a projecting rock with such force that he was deaf for days. His hands, too, had begun to blister from the salt water and hot sun. Betty, on his last Sunday at home, had split up one of her own little gloves for plasters, and tried to heal his blisters with some salve. But it had not done his bruises much good, he thought, as he probed with his stub of a thumb the deeper cracks in his tough, leathery palms.

Now that the men were convalescent he gloried more and more in his wife's energy and capacity. To relieve a wounded man, serve him night and day, and by skill, tenderness, and self-sacrifice get him once more well and sound and on his legs, able to do a day's work and earn a day's pay, — this, to Caleb, was something to be proud of and to glory in. But for her nursing, he would often say, poor Billy would now be among the tombstones on the hill back of Keyport Light.

Caleb's estimate of Betty's efforts was not exaggerated. Her patient had been the most severely injured, and her task had therefore been longer and more severe. The cut on Lacey's cheek and frontal bone, dividing his eyebrow like a sabre slash, had been deep and ugly and slow to heal; and the bruise on his back had developed into a wound that in its progress had sapped his youthful strength. He had been her patient from the first, and she had never neglected him an hour since the fatal night when she helped the doctor wind his bandages. When on the third day fever set in, she had taken her seat by his bedside until the delirium had passed. Mrs. Bell and Miss Peebles, the schoolmistress, had relieved each other in the care of the other wounded men, — all of them, strange to say, were single men, and all of them away from home.

Betty would go to her own cabin for an hour each day, but as soon as her work was done she would pull down the shades, lock the house door, and, with a sunbonnet on her head and some little delicacy in her hand, hurry down the shore road again to the warehouse hospital. This had been the first real responsibility of her life, the first time in which anything had been expected of her apart from the endless cooking of three meals a day, and the washing up and sweeping out that followed.

There were no more lonely hours for her now.

A new tenderness, too, had been aroused in her nature because of the helplessness of the boy whose feeble, hot fingers clutched her own. The love which this curly-headed young rigger had once avowed for her when there were strength and ruggedness in every sinew of his body, when his red lips were parted over the white teeth and his eyes shone with pride, had been quite forgotten as she watched by his bed. It was this helplessness of his which was ever present in her mind, his suffering. She realized that the prostrate young fellow before her was dependent on her for his very life and sustenance, as a child might have been. It was for her he waited in the morning, refusing to touch his breakfast until she gave it to him, — unable at first, reluctant afterward. It was for her last touch on his pillow that he waited at night before he went to sleep. It was she alone who brought the smiles to his face, or inspired him with a courage he had almost lost when the pain racked him and he thought he might never be able to do a day's work again.

The long confinement had left its mark on Lacey. He was a mere outline of himself the first day he was able to sit in the sunshine at the warehouse door. His hands were white, and his face was bleached. When he gained a little strength, Captain Joe gave him light duties about the wharf, the doctor refusing to let him go to the Ledge. But even after he was walking about, Betty felt him still under her care, and prepared dainty dishes for him. When she took them to him, she saw, with a strange sinking of her heart, that he gained but slowly, and was still weak and ill enough to need a woman's care.

The story of her nursing and of the doctor's constant tribute to her skill was well known, and Caleb, usually so reticent, would talk of it again and again. Most of the men liked to humor his pride in her, for Betty's blithesome, cheery nature made her a favorite wherever she was known.

"I kind'er wish Cap'n Joe had come ashore to-night," Caleb said, turning to Captain Brandt, who stood beside him, his hand on the tiller. "He's been soakin' wet all day, an' he won't put nothin' dry on ef I ain't with him. 'T warn't for Betty I'd 'a' stayed, but the little gal's so lonesome 't ain't right to leave her. I don' know what Lacey 'd done but for Betty. Did ye see 'er, Lonny, when she come in that night?" All the little by-paths of Caleb's talk led to Betty.

It was the same old question, but Lonny, seated on the other side of the deck, fell in willingly with Caleb's mood.

"See 'er? Wall, I guess! I thought she 'd keel over when the doctor washed Billy's face. He did look ragged, an' no mistake, Caleb; but she held on an' never give in a mite."

Carleton sat close enough to overhear the remark.

"Why shouldn't she?" he sneered, behind his hand, to the man next him. "Lacey's a blamed sight better looking fellow than what she's got. The girl knows a good thing when she sees it. If it was me, I'd" —

He never finished the sentence. Caleb overheard the remark, and rose from his seat, with an expression in his eyes that could not be misunderstood. Sanford, watching the group through the cabin window, and not knowing the cause of Caleb's sudden anger, said afterwards that the diver looked like an old gray wolf gathering himself for a spring, as he stood over Carleton with hands tightly clinched.

The superintendent made some sort of half apology to Caleb, and the diver took his seat again, but did not forgive him; neither did the older men, who had seen Betty grow up, and who always spoke of her somehow as if she belonged to them.

"T ain't decent," said Lonny Bowles to Sanford when he had joined him later in the cabin of the Screamer and had repeated Carleton's remark, "for a man to speak agin a woman; such fellers ain't no better 'n rattlesnakes an' ought'er be trompled on, if they is in guv'ment pay."

When the sloop reached Keyport harbor, the men were landed as near as possible to their several homes. Caleb, in his kindly voice, bade good-night to Sanford, to Captain Brandt, to the crew, and to the working gang. To Carleton he said nothing. He would have overlooked and forgotten an affront put upon himself, but never one upon Betty.

"She ain't got nobody but an ol' feller like me," he often said to Captain Joe,—"no chillen nor nothin', poor little gal. I got to make it up to her some way."

As he walked up the path he was so engrossed with Carleton's flippant remark, conning it over in his mind to tell Betty,—he knew she did not like him,—that he forgot for the moment that she was not at the garden gate.

He looked up at the house and noticed that the shades were pulled down on the garden side of the house.

"She ain't sick, is she?" he said to himself. "I guess nussin' Lacey's been too much for her. I ought'er knowed she'd break down. 'Pears to me she did look peaked when I bid her good-by las' Monday."

"Ye ain't sick, little woman, be ye?" he called out as he opened the door.

There was no response. He walked quickly through the kitchen, passed into the small hall, calling her as he went, mounted the narrow stairs, and opened the bedroom door softly, thinking she might be asleep. The shutters were closed, the room was in perfect order. The bed was empty. The sheet and covering were turned neatly on his side, and the bedding was clean and had not been slept in. At its foot, within reach of his hand, lay his big carpet slippers that she had made for him. He stooped mechanically, gazing at the untouched pillow, still wondering why she had turned the sheet, his mind relieved now that she was not ill.

Then he remembered that it was not yet dark, and that, on account of the coming storm, he was an hour earlier than usual in getting home. His face lightened. He saw it all now: Betty had not expected him so soon, and would be home in a little while.

When he entered the kitchen again he saw the table. There was but one plate laid, with the knife and fork beside it. This was covered by a big china bowl. Under it was some cold meat with the bread and butter. Near the table, by the stove, a freshly ironed shirt hung over a chair.

He understood it all now. She had put his supper and his shirt where he would find them, and was not coming home till late. He would "clean up" right away, so as to be ready for her.

When he had washed, dressed himself in his house clothes, and combed his big beard, he dragged a chair out on the front porch, to watch for her up and down the road.

The men going home, carrying their dinner

pails, nodded to him as they passed, and one stopped and leaned over the gate long enough to wonder whether the big August storm would break that night, adding, "We generally has a blow 'bout this time."

While he sat waiting the butcher stopped to leave the weekly piece of meat for Sunday, — the itinerant country butcher, with his shop in one of the neighboring villages, and his customers up and down all the roads that led out of it; supplies for every household in his wagon, and the gossip of every family on his lips.

His wagon had sides of canvas painted white, with "Fish, Meat and Poultry" in a half-moon of black letters arching over the owner's name, and was drawn by a horse that halted and moved on, not by the touch of the lines, — they were always caught to a hook in the roof of the wagon, — but by a word from the butcher, who stood at the tail-board, where the scales dangled, sorting fish, hacking off pieces of red meat, or weighing scraggly chickens proportionate to the wants and means of his various customers. He was busying himself at this tail-board, the dripping of the ice pock-marking the dusty road below, when he caught sight of Caleb.

"Wall, I kind'er hoped somebody 'd be hum," he said to himself, wrapping the six-pound roast in a piece of yellow paper. With a tuck to his blue over-sleeves, he swung open the gate.

"So ye did n't go 'long, Caleb, with Mis' West? I see it begin to blow heavy, and was wond'rin' whether you 'd get in — best cut, you see," opening the paper for Caleb's inspection, "and I broke them ribs jes' 's Mis' West allers wants 'em. Then I wondered agin how ye could leave the Ledge at all to-day. Mis' Bell tol' me yesterday the cap'n was goin' to set them derricks. I see 'em a-layin' on the dock 'fore that Cape Ann sloop loaded 'em, an' they was monstrous, an' no mistake. Have some butter? She did n't order none this mornin', but I got some come in this forenoon, sweet 's a nut, — four pounds for a dollar, an' " —

Caleb looked at him curiously. "Where did the wife say she was a-goin'?" he interrupted.

"Wall, she did n't say, 'cause I did n't ketch up to her. I was comin' down Nollins Hill over to Noank, when I see her ahead, walkin' down all in her Sunday rig, carryin' a little bag like. I tho't maybe she was over to see the Nollins folks, till I left seven pounds fresh mackerel nex' door to Stubbins's, an' some Delaware eggs. Then I see my stock of ice was nigh gone, so I druv down to the steamboat dock, an' there I catched sight of 'er agin jes' goin' aboard. I knowed then, of course, she was off for Greenport an' New York, an' was jes' sayin' to myself, Wall, I 'll stop an' see if anybody 's ter hum, an' if they 're all gone I won't leave the meat, but " —

"Put the meat in the kitchen," said Caleb, without rising from his chair.

When the butcher drove off, the diver had not moved. His gaze was fixed on the turn of the road. Beads of sweat stood out on his forehead. A faint sickness unnerved him. Had he been cross or impatient with her the last time he was at home, that she should serve him so? Then a surge of anxiety swept over him, as he thought of Betty going without letting him know. Why should she walk all the way to Noank and take the boat across the Sound, twenty miles away, if she wanted to go to New York? The railroad station was nearer and the fare through was cheaper. He would have taken her himself, if he had only known she wanted to go. He could have asked Captain Joe to give him a couple of days off, and would have gone with her. If she had only left some message, or sent some word by the men to the Ledge! Then, as his thoughts traveled in a circle, catching at straws, his brain whirling, his eye fell upon the clump of trees shading Captain Joe's cottage. Aunty Bell would know, of course; why had he not thought of that before? Betty told Aunty Bell everything.

The busy little woman sat on the porch shelling peas, the pods popping about her bright tin pan, as Caleb came up the board walk.

"Why, ye need n't hev give yerself the trouble, Caleb, to come all the way down!" she called out as he came within hearing. "Lonny Bowles's jest been here and told me cap'n ain't comin' home till Monday. I'm 'mazin' glad them derricks is up. He ain't done nothin' but worrit about 'em since spring opened, 'fraid somebody'd get hurted when he set 'em. Took a lantern, here, night 'fore last, jest as we was goin' to bed, after he'd been loadin' 'em aboard the Screamer all day, an' went down to the dock to see if Bill Lacey'd shrunk them collars on tight enough. Guess Betty's glad yer home. I ain't see her to-day, but I don't lay it up agin her. I knowed she was busy cleanin' up 'gin ye come."

Caleb's heart leaped into his throat. If Betty had not told Aunty Bell, there was no one else who would know her movements. It was on his lips to tell her what the butcher had seen, when something in his heart choked his utterance. If Betty had not wanted any one to know, there was no use of his talking about it.

A man of different temperament, a nervous or easily alarmed or suspicious man, would have caught at every clue and followed it to the end. Caleb waited and kept still. She would telegraph or write him and explain it all, he said to himself, or send some one to see him before bedtime. So he merely answered he was glad Aunty Bell knew about Captain Joe, nodded good-night, and passed slowly down the board walk and up the road, his head on his chest, his big beard blowing about his neck in the rising wind. He kept saying to himself that Betty would telegraph or write and explain it all, or send some one to see him before bedtime.

It was dark when he reached home. He lit the kerosene lamp and pulled down the shades. He did not want passers-by to know he was alone. For an hour or more he strode up and down the kitchen, his thumbs in his suspenders, his supper untouched. Now and then he would stop as if listening for a footfall, or fix his eye minutes at a time on some crack in the floor or other object, gazing abstractedly at it, his thoughts far away. Once he drew the lamp close and picked up the evening paper, adjusting his big glasses; reading the same lines over and over, until the paper fell of itself from his hands. Soon, worn out with the hard fight of the day, he fell asleep in his chair, awaking some hours after, his mind torn with anxiety. Then he took off his shoes and crept upstairs in his stocking feet, holding to the balustrade as a tired man will do, entered his bedroom, and dropped into a chair.

All through the night he slept fitfully; waking with sudden starts, roused by the feeling that some horrible shadow had settled upon him, that something he could not name to himself was standing behind him — always there, making him afraid to turn and look. When he was quite awake, and saw the dim outlines of the untouched bed with its smooth white pillows, the undefinable fear would slowly take shape, and he would start up in his chair, and as if to convince himself he would take a long look at the bed, with the relief of one able at last to explain a horror the vagueness of which had tortured him. "Yes, I know, Betty's gone." Then, overcome with fatigue, he would doze again.

With the breaking of the day he sprang from his chair, half dazed, threw up the narrow sash to feel the touch of the cool, real world, and peered between the slats of the shutters, listening to the wind outside, now blowing a gale and dashing against the blinds.

None of the other houses were open yet. He was glad of that, glad of their bare, cold, indifferent exteriors, blind to the outside world. It was as though he felt his secret still safe from prying eyes, and he meant to guard it always from them; to let none of them know what his night had been, or that Betty had been away for so long without telling him. When she came home again she would help, he knew, to smooth away the marks of it all, the record of his pain. Her bright face would look up into his, her little hands pat his cheeks, and he would then know all about it, why she went and where, and he would take the little girl wife in his arms, and comfort her in the suffering that would surely come to her when she discovered that her thoughtlessness had caused him any misery.

No! He would tell no one. He would simply wait, all day if necessary, all day and another night. He could trust her. It was all right, he knew. He did not even mind the waiting.

Then while he was still thinking, still determining to keep silent, still satisfying himself that all was well, he turned rapidly and tiptoed downstairs.

With nervous, trembling fingers he took a suit of tarpaulins and a sou'wester from a hook behind the porch door, and walked down to the dock. Some early lobstermen, bailing a skiff, saw him stand for a moment, look about him, and spring aboard a flat-bottomed sharpie, the only boat near by, — a good harbor boat, but dangerous in rough weather. To their astonishment, he raised the three-cornered sail and headed for the open sea.

"Guess Caleb must be crazy," said one man, resting his scoop for a moment, as he watched the boat dip almost bow under. "Thet sharpie ain't no more fittin' for thet slop sea 'n ever was. What do ye s'pose ails him, anyhow? Gosh A'mighty! see her take them rollers. If it was anybody else but him he wouldn't git to the P'int. Don't make no difference, tho', to him. He kin git along under water jes' 's well 's on top."

As the boat flew past Keyport Light and Caleb laid his course to the Ledge, the keeper, now that the dawn had come, was in the lantern putting out his light and drawing down his shades. Seeing Caleb's boat tossing below him, he took down his glass.

"What blamed fool is that tryin' to get himself measured for a coffin?" he said.

The men were still asleep when Caleb reached the Ledge and threw open the door of the shanty,—all but Nickles, who was preparing breakfast. He looked at Caleb as if he had been an apparition, and followed him to the door of Captain Joe's cabin, a little room by itself. He wanted to hear the dreadful news he brought. Unless some one was dead or dying no man would risk such a sea alone,— not even an old sailor like the diver.

Caleb opened the door of the captain's little room and closed it tight behind him, without a word to the cook. The captain lay asleep in his bunk, one big arm under his head, his short curly hair matted close.

"Cap'n Joe," said Caleb, laying his hand on the sleeping man's shoulder and shaking him gently,—"Cap'n Joe, it 's me,—Caleb."

The captain raised his head and stared at him. Then he sat upright, trying to collect his thoughts.

"Cap'n, I had to come for ye,—I want ye."

"It ain't Aunty Bell, is it?" said Captain

Joe, springing to the floor. The early hour, the sough of the wind and beating of the rain on the roof of the shanty, Caleb dripping wet, with white drawn face, standing over him, told him in a flash the gravity of the visit.

"No, it's my Betty. She's gone,— gone without a word."

"Gone! Who with?"

Caleb sunk on Captain Joe's sea-chest, and buried his face in his blistered hands. For a moment he dared not trust himself to answer.

"I don't know — I don't know"— The broken words came between his rough fingers. Big tears rolled down his beard.

"Who says so? How do you know she's gone?"

"The butcher seen 'er goin' 'board the boat at Noank yesterday mornin'. She fixed everythin' at home 'fore she went. I ain't been to bed all night. I don't know what ye kin do, but I had to come. I thought maybe you'd go home with me."

The captain did not answer. Little scraps of gossip that he had heard now and then among the men floated through his memory. He had never paid any attention to them, except once when he had rebuked Nickles for repeating some slurring remark that Carleton had made one night at table. But even as he thought of them Betty's face rose before him, — her sweet, girlish face with its dimples.

"It's a dirty lie, Caleb, whoever said it. I wouldn't believe it if I see it myself. Ain't no better gal 'n Betty ever breathed. Go with you! Course I will 's soon 's I get my clo'es on." He dressed hurriedly, caught up his oilskins, flung wide the shanty door, and made his way over the platforms towards the wharf.

When they reached the little cove in the rocks below, where the smaller boats were always sheltered, and he saw the sharpie, he stopped short.

"You ain't come out here in that, Caleb?"

"It was all I could get; there warn't nothin' else handy, Cap'n Joe."

The captain looked the frail sharpie over from stem to stern, and then called to Nickles: "Bring down one 'er them empty ker'sene five-gallon cans; we got some bailin' to do, I tell ye, 'fore we make Keyport Light. No, there ain't nothin' up," noticing Nickles's anxious face. "Caleb wants me to Keyport,—that's all. Get breakfast, and tell the men, when they turn out, that I'll be back to-morrow in the Screamer, if it smooths down."

Caleb took his seat on the windward side of the tossing boat, holding the sheet. The captain sat in the stern, one hand on the tiller. The kerosene-can lay at their feet. The knees of the two men touched.

No better sailors ever guided a boat, and none ever realized more clearly the dangers of their position.

The captain settled himself in his seat in silence, his eyes watching every wave that raced by, and laid his course towards the white tower five miles away, blurred gray in the driving rain. Caleb held the sheet, his eyes facing the long, low line of hills where his cabin lay. As he hauled the sheet closer a heavy sigh broke from him. It was the first time since he had known Betty that he had set his face homeward without a thrill of delight filling his heart. Captain Joe heard the smothered sigh, and, without turning his head, laid his great hand with its stiff thole-pin fingers tenderly on Caleb's wrist. These two men knew each other.

"I would n't worry, Caleb," he said, after a little. "That butcher sees too much, an' sometimes he don't know nothin'. He's allers got some cock-an'-bull story 'bout somebody 'r other. Only las' week he come inter Gardiner's drug store with a yarn 'bout the old man bein' pisened, when it warn't nothin' but cramps. Ease a little, Caleb — s-o. Seems to me it's blowin' harder."

As he spoke, a quick slash of the cruel wind cut the top from a pursuing wave and flung it straight in Caleb's face. The diver, with his stiffened fingers, combed the dripping spray from his beard, and without a word drew his tarpaulins closer. Captain Joe continued: —

"Wust 'r them huckster fellers is they ain't

got no better sense 'an to peddle everythin' they know 'long with their stuff. Take in — *take in, Caleb!* That *was* a soaker." The big wave that had broken within a foot of the rail had drenched them from head to foot. "Butcher did n't say nobody was with Betty, did he?" he asked, with a cant of his sou'wester to free it from sea-water.

Caleb shook his head.

"No, and there warn't nobody. I tell ye this thing 'll straighten itself out. Ye can't tell what comes inter women's heads sometimes. She might'er gone over to Greenport to git some fixin's for Sunday, an' would'er come back in the afternoon boat, but it blowed so. Does she know anybody over there?"

Caleb did not answer. Somehow since he had seen Captain Joe hope had gone out of his heart. He had understood but too clearly the doubting question that had escaped the captain's lips, as he sprang from the bed and looked into his eyes. He was not a coward; he had faced without a quiver many dangers in his time; more than once he had cut his air-hose, the last desperate chance of a diver when his lines are fouled. But his legs had shaken as he listened to Captain Joe. There was something in the tone of his voice that had unmanned him.

For a mile or more the two men did not speak again. Wave after wave pursued them, and tossed its angry spray after them. Captain Joe now managed the sail with one hand, and steered with the other. Caleb bailed incessantly.

When they ran under the lee of the lighthouse the keeper hailed them. He had recognized Captain Joe. Indeed, he had followed the sharpie with his glass until it reached the Ledge, and had watched its return "with two fools instead of one," he said.

"Anybody sick?" he shouted.

Captain Joe shook his head, and the sharpie plunged on and rounded the point into the perfect calm of the protecting shore.

Caleb made fast the boat when land was reached, while the captain sprang out. Then they both hurried up Caleb's garden walk to the cabin door.

There was no change in the house. The white china bowl still lay over the supper, the newspaper on the floor; no one had entered since Caleb had left.

The captain began a close search through the rooms: inside the clock, all over the mantelpiece, and on the sitting-room table. No scrap of writing could he find that shed a ray of light on Betty's movements. Then he walked upstairs, Caleb following him, and opened the bedroom closet door. Her dresses hung in their usual places, — all but the one she wore and her cloak, Caleb said.

"She ain't gone for long," said the captain thoughtfully, looking into the closet. "You wait here, Caleb, and git yerself some breakfast. I may be gone two hours, I may be gone all day. When I find out for sure I'll come back. I'm goin' to Noank fust, to see them hands aboard the boat. It's Sunday, an' she ain't a-runnin'."

Caleb waited by the fireless stove. Hour after hour went by. Now and then he would open the front door and peer down the road, trying to make out the captain's burly, hurrying form. When it grew dark he put a light in the window, and raised one shade on the kitchen side of the house, that the captain might know he was still at home and waiting.

About nine o'clock Caleb heard the whistle of a tug and a voice calling for some one to catch a line. He opened the kitchen door and looked out on the wet gloom, that was broken here and there by the masthead lights rocking in the wind. Then he recognized one of the big Medford tugs lying off the dock below his garden; the hands were making fast to a dock spile. Captain Joe sprang ashore, and the tug steamed off.

The captain walked slowly towards the porch, entered the kitchen without a word, and sank heavily into a chair. Caleb made no sound; he stood beside him, waiting, one hand grasping the table.

"She's gone, ain't she?"

The captain nodded his head.

"Gone! Who with?" asked Caleb, unconsciously repeating the words that had rung all day in his ears.

"Bill Lacey," said the captain, with choking voice.

CHAPTER X

STRAINS FROM BOCK'S 'CELLO

Mrs. Leroy was one of the few women in town who realized what Sanford and his friends had long ago discovered, — the possibilities of New York in summer. To her it had now become its most delightful season, a season of long days and short nights — days and nights of utter idleness, great content, and blessed peace of mind; a season when one could dine where one chose without a waiting cab and a hurried departure at the bidding of somebody else; when the eleven o'clock lecturer is silent, the afternoon tea a memory, and the epidemic of the ten-course dinner a forgotten plague.

She had grown to believe with Sanford that if one could impress the possibility of these truths upon the friends one loved, so that they, and only they, could tiptoe back into their houses, keep their blinds closed and their servants hidden, and so delude the balance of the world — those they did not love, the uncongenial, the tiresome, the bumptious, and the aggressive — into believing that they had fled; if this little trick could be played on the world every June, and for three long happy months only congenial spirits could spread themselves over space and eat their lotus in peace (and with their fingers, if they so pleased), then would each one discover that New York in summer could indeed be made the Eldorado of one's dreams.

Her own front door on Gramercy Park was never barricaded, nor was her house dismantled. She changed its dress in May and put it into charming summer attire of matting and chintz, making it a rare and refreshing retreat; and more than half her time she spent within its walls, running down to Medford whenever the cares of that establishment required attention, or a change of mood made a change of scene desirable.

Since the visit when Captain Joe had dismissed her with his thanks from the warehouse hospital at Keyport she had gone to Medford but once.

The major had been a constant visitor, and Jack Hardy and his fiancée, Helen Shirley, had on more than one occasion hidden themselves, on moonlight nights, in the shadows of the big palms fringing her balcony overlooking the Park. Sanford had not seen her as often as he wished. Work on the Ledge had kept him at Keyport, and allowed him but little time in town.

With the setting of the derricks, however, he felt himself at liberty for a holiday, and he had looked forward with a feeling of almost boyish enthusiasm — which he never quite outgrew — to a few days' leisure in town, and a morning or two with Mrs. Leroy.

When the maid brought up his card, Mrs. Leroy was at her desk in the little boudoir, with its heaps of silk cushions, its disorder of books, and bloom of mignonette and red geraniums filling the windows that looked straight into the trees of the Park. Here the sun shone in winter, and here the moonlight traced the outlines of bare branches upon her window-shades, and here in summer the coolest of cool shadows fell from tree and awning.

"Why, I expected you yesterday, Henry," she said, holding out her hand, seating Sanford upon the divan, and drawing up a chair beside him. "What happened?"

"Nothing more serious than an elopement."

"Not Jack and Helen Shirley?" she said, laughing.

"No; I wish it were; they would go on loving each other. This affair brings misery. It's Caleb West's wife. Captain Joe is half crazy about it, and poor Caleb is heartbroken. She has gone off with that young fellow she was nursing the day you came up with the major."

"Eloped! Pretty doings, I must say. Yes,

I remember her, — a trim, rather pretty little woman with short curly hair. I caught a glimpse of Caleb, too, you know, as he came in from the Ledge. He seemed years older than she. What had he done to her?"

"Nothing, so far as I know, except love her and take care of her. Poor Caleb!"

"What did he let her go for, then? I'm sorry for the old diver, but it was his fault, somewhere. The girl had as good a face as I ever looked into. She never left her husband without some cause, poor child. What else has happened at Keyport?"

"Kate, don't talk so. She's treated him shamefully. They have only been married two years."

Mrs. Leroy bent her head and looked out under the awnings for a moment in a thoughtful way. "Only two years?" she said, with some bitterness. "The poor child was impatient. When she had tried it for fifteen she would have become accustomed to it. It is the same old story, I suppose. We hear it every day. He ugly and old and selfish, never thinking of what she would like and what she longed for, keeping her shut up to sing for him when she wanted now and then to sing for herself, and then she found the door of the cage open, and out she flew. Poor little soul! I pity her. She had better have borne it; it is a poor place outside for a tired foot; and she's nothing but a child." Then musing, patting her slipper impatiently, "What sort of a man has she gone with? I couldn't see him that morning, she hung over him so close, and his head was so bandaged."

"I don't know much about him. I haven't known him long," Sanford answered carelessly.

"Good-looking, isn't he, and alive, and with something human and manlike about him?" she asked, leaning forward eagerly, her hands in her lap.

"Yes, I suppose so. He could climb like a cat, anyway," said Sanford.

"Yes, I know, Henry. I see it all. I knew it was the same old story. She wanted something fresh and young, — some one just to play with, child as she is, some one nearer her own age to love. She was lonely. Nothing for her to do but sit down and wait for him to come home. Poor child," with a sigh, "her misery only begins now. What else have you to tell me?"

"Nothing, except that all of the derricks tumbled. I wired you about it. They are all up now, thank goodness." He knew her interest was only perfunctory. Her mind, evidently, was still on Betty, but he went on with his story: "Everybody got soaking wet. Captain Joe was in the water for hours. But we stuck to it. Narrowest escape the men have had this summer, Kate, since the Screamer's. It's a great mercy nobody was hurt. I expected every minute some one would get crushed. No one but Captain Joe could have got them up that afternoon. It blew a gale for three days. When did you get here? I thought you had gone back to Medford until Sam brought me your note."

"No, I am still here, and shall be here for a week. Now, don't tell me you're going back to-night?"

"No, I'm not, but I can't say how soon; not before the masonry begins, anyhow. Jack Hardy is coming to-morrow night to my rooms. I have asked a few fellows to meet him, — Smearly and Curran, and old Bock with his 'cello, and some others. Since Jack's engagement he's the happiest fellow alive."

"They all are at first, Henry," said Mrs. Leroy, laughing, her head thrown back. The memory of Jack and Helen was still so fresh and happy a one that it instantly changed her mood.

Betty and Caleb for the moment were forgotten, while they talked of Helen's future, of the change in Jack's life, of his new housekeeping, and of the thousand and one things that interested them both, — the kind of talk that two such friends indulge in who have been parted for a week or more, and who, in the first ten minutes, run lightly over their individual experiences, so that both may start fresh again with nothing hidden in either life. When he rose to go, she kept him standing while she pinned in his buttonhole a sprig of mignonette picked from her window-box, and said, with the deepest interest, "I can't get that poor child out of my mind. Don't be too hard on her, Henry; she's the one who will suffer most."

When Sanford reached his rooms again he sank into a chair which Sam had drawn close to the window, and sighed with content. "Oh, these days off!" he exclaimed.

The appointments of his own apartments seemed never so satisfying and so welcome as when he had spent a week with his men, taking his share of the exposure with all the discomforts that it brought. His early life had fitted him for these changes, and a certain cosmopolitan spirit in the man, a sort of underlying stratum of Bohemianism, had made it easy for him to adapt himself to his surroundings, whatever they might be. Not that his restless spirit could long have endured any life, either rough or luxurious, that repeated itself day after day. He could idle with the idlest, but he must also work when the necessity came, and that with all his might.

Sam always made some special preparation for his home-coming. To-day the awnings were hung over window and balcony, and the most delightful of luncheons had been arranged, — cucumbers smothered in ice, soft-shell crabs, and a roll of cream cheese with a dash of Kirsch and sugar. "I know he don't git nuffin fit for a dog to eat when he's away. 'Fo' God I don't know how he stands it," Sam was accustomed to observe to those of his friends who sometimes watched his preparations.

"Major's done been hyar 'mos' ebery day you been gone, sah," he said, drawing out Sanford's chair, when luncheon was served. "How is it, sah,—am I to mix a cocktail *ebery* time he comes? An' dat box ob yo' big cigars am putty nigh gone; ain't no more 'n fo'r 'r five of 'em lef'." The major, Sam forgot to mention, was only partly to blame for these two shrinkages in Sanford's stores.

"What does he come so often for, Sam?" asked Sanford, laughing.

"Dat's mor' 'an I know, sah, 'cept he so anxious to git you back, he says. He come twice a day to see if you're yere. Co'se dere ain't nuffin cooked, an' so he don't git nuffin to eat, but golly! he's powerful on jewlips. I done tole him yesterday you wouldn't be back till to-morrow night. Dat whiskey's all gin out; he saw der empty bottle hisse'f; he ain't been yere agin to-day," with a chuckle.

"Always give the major whatever he wants," said Sanford. "And Sam," he called as that darky was disappearing in the pantry, "a few gentlemen will be here to supper to-morrow night. Remind me to make a list in the morning of what you will want."

The list was made out, and a very toothsome and cooling list it was, — a frozen melon tapped and filled with a pint of Pommery sec, by way of beginning. All the trays and small tables with their pipes and smokables were brought out, a music-stand was opened and set up near a convenient shaded candle, and the lid of the piano was lifted and propped up rabbit-trap fashion.

Just as the moon was rising, silvering the tops of the trees in the square below, Smearly in white flannels and flaming tie arrived fresh from his studio, where he had been at work on a ceiling for some millionaire's salon. Jack followed in correct evening dress, and Curran from his office, in a business suit. The major was arrayed in a nondescript combination of yellow nankeen and black bombazine, that would have made him an admirable model for a poster in two tints. He was still full of his experiences at the warehouse hospital after the accident to the Screamer. His little trip to Keyport as acting escort to Mrs. Leroy had not only opened his eyes to a class of workingmen of whose existence he had never dreamed, but it had also furnished him with a new and inexhaustible topic of conversation. Every visitor at his downtown office had listened to his recital by the hour. To-night, however, the major had a new audience, and a new audience always added fuel to the fire of his eloquence.

When the subject of the work at the Ledge came up, and the sympathy of everybody was expressed to Sanford over the calamity to the Screamer, — they had not seen him since the explosion, — the major broke out : —

"You ought to have gone with us, my dear Smearly." (To have been the only eye-witness at the front, except Sanford himself, gave the major great scope.) "Giants, suh, — every man of 'em ; a race, suh, that would do credit to the Vikings ; bifurcated walruses, suh ; amphibious titans, that can work as well in water as out of it. No wonder our dear Henry" (this term of affection was not unusual with the major) "accomplishes such wonders. I can readily understand why you never see such fellows anywhere else ; they dive under water when the season closes," he continued, laughing, and, leaning over Curran's shoulder, helped himself to one of the cigars Sam was just bringing in.

"And the major outdid himself, that day, in nursing them," interrupted Sanford. "You would have been surprised, Jack, to see him take hold. When I turned in for the night on a cot, he was giving one of the derrickmen a sponge bath."

"Learned it in the army," said Curran, with a sly look at Smearly. Both of them knew the origin of the major's military title.

The major's chin was upturned in the air; his head was wreathed in smoke, the match, still aflame, held aloft with outstretched hand. He always lighted his cigars in this lordly way.

"Many years ago, gentlemen," the major replied, distending his chest, throwing away the match, and accepting the compliment in perfect good faith; "but these are things one never forgets." The major had never seen the inside of a camp hospital in his life.

The guests now distributed themselves, each after the manner of his likes: Curran full length on a divan, the afternoon paper in his hand; Jack on the floor, his back to the wall, a cushion behind his head; Smearly in an armchair; and the major bolt upright on a camp-stool near a table which held a select collection of drinkables, presided over by a bottle of seltzer in a silver holder. Sam moved about like a restless shadow, obedient to the slightest lifting of Sanford's eyebrow, when a glass needed filling or a pipe replenishing.

At ten o'clock, lugging in his great 'cello, Bock came, — short, round, and oily, with a red face that beamed with good humor, and fat puffy hands that wrinkled in pleats when he held his bow. Across a perpetually moist forehead was pasted a lock of black hair. He wore a threadbare coat spattered with spots, baggy black trousers, and a four-button brown holland waistcoat, never clean, — sometimes connected with a collar so much ashamed of the condition of its companion shirt-front that it barely showed its face over a black stock that was held together by a spring. A man who was kindly and loyal; who loved all his kind, spoke six languages, wrote for the Encyclopædia, and made a 'cello sing like an angel.

Despite his frouziness, everybody who knew Bock liked him; those who heard him play loved him. There was a pathos, a tender, sympathetic quality in his touch, that one never forgot: it always seemed as if, somehow, ready tears lingered under his bow. "With a tone like Bock's" was the highest compliment one could pay a musician. To Sanford this man's heart was dearer than his genius.

"Why, Bock, old man," he called, "we did n't expect you till eleven."

"Yes, I know, Henri, but ze first wiolin, he take my place. Zey will not know ze difference." One fat hand was held up deprecatingly, the fingers outspread. "Everybody fan and drink ze beer. Ah, Meester Hardy, I have hear ze news; so you will leave ze brotherhood. And I hear," lowering his voice and laying his other fat hand affectionately on Jack's, "zat she ees most lofely. Ah, it ees ze best zing," his voice rising again. "When ve get old and ugly like old Bock, and so heels over head wiz all sorts of big zings to build like Mr. Sanford, or like poor Smearly paint, paint, all ze time paint, it ees too late to zink of ze settle down. Ees it not so, you man Curran over zere, wiz your newspaper over your head?" This time his voice was flung straight at the recumbent editor as a climax to his breezy salutation.

"Yes, you're right, Bock; you're ugly enough to crowd a dime museum, but I'll forgive you everything if you'll put some life into your strings. I heard your orchestra the other night, and the first and second violins ruined the overture. What the devil do you keep a lot of" —

"What ees ze matter wiz ze overture, Meester Ole Bull?" said Bock, pitching his voice in a high key, squeezing down on the divan and pinching Curran's arm with his fat fingers.

"Everything was the matter. The brass drowned the strings, and Reynier might have had hair-oil on his bow for all the sound you heard. Then the tempo was a beat too slow."

"Henri Sanford, do you hear zis crazy man zat does not know one zing, and lie flat on his back and talk such nonsense? Ze wiolin, Meester Musical Editor Curran, must be pianissimo, — only ze leetle, ze ve'y leetle, you hear. Ze aria is carried by ze reeds."

"Carried by your grandmother!" said Curran, springing from the divan. "Here, Sam, put a light on the piano. Now listen, you pagan. Beethoven would get out of his grave if he could hear you murder his music. The three bars are so," — touching the keys, "not so!" And thus the argument went on.

Out on the balcony, Smearly and Quigley,

the marine painter, who had just come in, were talking about the row at the Academy over the rejection of Morley's picture, while the major was in full swing with Hardy, Sanford, and some of the later arrivals, including old Professor Max Shutters, the biologist, who had been so impressively introduced by Curran to the distinguished Pocomokian that the professor had at once mistaken the major for a brother scientist.

"And you say, Professor Slocomb," said the savant, his hand forming a sounding-board behind his ear, "that the terrapin, now practically extinct, was really plentiful in your day?"

"My learned suh, I have gone down to the edge of my lawn, overlooking the salt-marsh, and seen 'em crawling around like potato bugs. The niggahs could n't walk the shore at night without trampling on 'em. This craze of yo'r millionaire epicures for one of the commonest shell-fish we have is"—

"Amphibia," suggested the professor, as if he had recognized a mere slip of the tongue. "I presume you are referring to the *Malaclemmys palustris*,—the diamond-back species."

"You are right, suh," said the major. "I had forgotten the classification for the moment," with an air of being perfectly at home on the subject. "The craze for the *palustris*, my dear suh, is one of the unaccountable signs of the times; it is the beginning of the fall of our institutions, suh. We cannot forget the dishes of peacock tongues in the old Roman days, — a thousand peacocks at a cou'se, suh."

The major would have continued down through Gibbon and Macaulay if Curran had not shouted out, "Keep still, every soul of you! Bock is going to give us the Serenade."

The men crowded about the piano. Smearly stood ready to turn the leaves of the music for Curran, and Jack drew a chair closer to the 'cellist.

Bock uncovered the 'cello and held it between his knees, his fat hand resting lightly on the strings. As Curran, with his foot on the pedal of the piano, passed his hand rapidly over the keys, Bock's head sank to the level of his shoulders, his straggling hair fell over his coat collar, his raised fingers balanced for a moment the short bow, and then Schubert's masterpiece poured out the very fullness of its heart.

A profound hush, broken only by the music, fell on the room. The old professor leaned forward, both hands cupped behind his ears. Sanford and Jack smoked on, their eyes half closed, and even the major withheld his hand from the well-appointed tray and looked into his empty glass.

At a time when the spell was deepest and the listeners held their breath, the perfect harmony was broken by a discordant ring at the outer door. Curran turned his head angrily, and Sanford looked at Sam, who glided to the door with a catlike tread, opening it without a sound, and closing it gently behind him. The symphony continued, the music rising in interest, and the listeners forgot the threatened interruption.

Then the door opened again, and Sam, making a wide détour, bent over Sanford and whispered in his ear. A woman wanted to see him in the hall. Sanford started, as if annoyed, arose from his seat, and again the knob was noiselessly turned and the door as noiselessly closed, shutting Sanford into the corridor.

"Do you wish to see me, madam?" he asked, crossing to a chair in which the woman sat wrapped in a long cloak, her face buried in her hands.

The woman turned her head towards him without raising her eyelids.

"And you don't know me any more, Mr. Sanford?"

"Betty! You here!" said Sanford, looking in astonishment at the crouching figure before him.

"I had to come, sir. The druggist at the corner showed me the house. I was a-waitin' outside in the street below, hopin' to see you come in. Then I heard the music and knew you were home." The voice shook with every word. The young dimpled face was drawn and pale, the pretty curly hair in disorder about her forehead. She had the air of one who had been hunted and had just found shelter.

"Does Lacey know you are here?" asked Sanford, a dim suspicion rising in his mind.

Betty shivered slightly, as if the name had hurt her. "No, sir. I left him two nights ago. I got away while he was asleep. All I want now is a place for to-night, and then perhaps to-morrow I can get work."

"And you have no money?" asked Sanford.

Betty shook her head. "I had a little of my own, but it's all gone, and I'm so tired, and — the city frightens me so — when the night comes." The head dropped lower, the sobs choking her. After a little she went on, drying her eyes with her handkerchief, rolled tight in one hand; and resting her cheek on the bent fingers, "I did n't know nobody but you, Mr. Sanford. I can pay it back." The voice was scarcely audible.

Sanford stood looking down upon her bowed head. The tired eyelids were half closed, the tears glistening in the light of the overhanging lamp, the shadows of her black curls flecking her face. The cloak hung loosely about her, the curve of her pretty shoulders outlined in its folds. Then she lifted her head, and, looking Sanford in the eyes for the first time, said in a broken, halting voice, "Did you — did you — see — Caleb — Mr. Sanford?"

Sanford nodded slowly in answer. He was trying to make up his mind what he should do with a woman who had broken the heart of a man like Caleb. Through the closed door he heard the strains of Bock's 'cello, the notes vibrating plaintively. They belonged to some other world.

"Betty," he said, leaning over her, "how could you do it?"

The girl covered her face with her hands and shrank within her cloak. Sanford went on, his sense of Caleb's wrongs overpowering him: "What could Lacey do for you? If you could once see Caleb's face you would never forgive yourself. No woman has a right to leave a man who was as good to her as your husband was to you. And now what has it all come to? You've ruined yourself, and broken his heart."

The girl trembled and bent her head, cowering under the pitiless words; then, in a half-dazed way, she rose from her seat, and, without looking at Sanford, said in a tired, hopeless voice, as if every word brought a pain, "I think I'll go, Mr. Sanford."

Sanford watched her silently as she drew her cloak about her and turned to the door. The pathos of the shrinking girlish figure overcame him. He began to wonder if there were something under it all that even Captain Joe did not know of. Then he remembered the tones of compassion in Mrs. Leroy's voice when her heart had gone out to this girl the morning before, as she said, "Poor child, her misery only begins now; it is a poor place for a tired foot."

For an instant he stood irresolute. "Wait," he said. "Wait a moment."

Betty stood still, without raising her head.

Sanford paused in deep thought, with averted eyes.

"Betty," he murmured at last in a softened voice, "you can't go out like this alone. I'll take you, child, where you will be safe for the night."

CHAPTER XI

CAPTAIN JOE'S TELEGRAM

THE morning after Betty's visit to Sanford's apartments, Captain Joe was seen hurrying up the shore road at Keyport toward his cottage. His eyes shone with excitement, and his breath came in short, quick puffs. He wore his rough working-clothes, and held a yellow envelope in his hand. When he reached the garden gate he swung it open with so mighty a jerk that the sound of the dangling ball and chain thumping against the palings brought Aunty Bell running to the porch.

"Sakes alive, Cap'n Joe!" she exclaimed, following him into the kitchen, "whatever's the matter? Ain't nobody hurted, is there?"

"There will be ef I don't git to New York purty quick. Mr. Sanford's got Betty, an' them Leroy folks is a-keepin' on her till I git there."

Aunty Bell sank into a chair, her hands twisted in her apron, the tears starting in her eyes.

"Who says so?"

"Telegram — come in the night," he answered, almost breathless, throwing the yellow envelope into her lap. "Git me a clean shirt quick as God 'll let ye. I ain't got but ten minutes to catch that eight-ten train."

"But ye ain't a-goin' till ye see Caleb, be ye? He won't like it, maybe, if" —

"Don't ye stop there talkin', Aunty Bell. Do as I tell ye," he said, stripping off his suspenders and tugging at his blue flannel shirt. "I ain't a-goin' to stop for nobody nor nothin'. That little gal's fetched up hard jes' where I knowed she would, an' I won't have a minute's peace till I git my hands onto her. I ain't slep' a night since she left, an' you know it."

"How do ye know she'll come with ye?" asked Aunty Bell, as she gave him his shirt. Her hands were trembling.

"I ain't a-worritin'," he answered, thrusting his head and big chest into the stiff garment; fumbling, as he spoke, with his brown hands, for the buttons. "Gimme that collar."

"Well, I'm kind'er wonderin' if ye had n't better let Caleb know. I don't know what Caleb 'll say" —

"I ain't a-carin' what Caleb says. I'll stop that leak when I git to 't." He held his breath for a moment and clutched the porcelain button with his big fingers, trying to screw it into his collar, as if it had been a nut on a bolt. "Here, catch hold o' this button; it's so plaguy tight. No, — I don't want no toothbrush, nor nothin'. I would n't 'er come home at all, but I was so gormed up, an' she 's along with them Leroy folks Mr. Sanford knows. My — my" — he continued, forcing his great arms through the tight sleeves of his Sunday coat with a humping motion of his back, and starting toward the door. "Jes' to think o' Betty wanderin' 'bout them streets at night!"

"Why, ye ain't got no cravat on, Cap'n Joe!" called Aunty Bell, running after him, tie in hand, to the porch.

"Here, give it to me!" he cried, snatching it and cramming it into his pocket. "I'll fix it on the train." In another moment he was halfway down the plank walk, waving his hand, shouting back over his shoulder, "Send word to Cap'n Bob to load them other big stone an' git 'em to the Ledge to-day; the wind 's goin' to haul to the south'ard. I'll be back 'bout eight o'clock to-night."

Aunty Bell looked after his hurrying figure until the trees shut it from view; then, gasping with excitement, angry with herself for having asked so little, she reëntered the kitchen and again dropped into a chair.

Betty's flight had been a sore blow to the bustling little wife. She had been the last to believe that Betty had really deserted Caleb for Lacey, even after Captain Joe had told her how the mate of the Greenport boat had seen them board the New York train together.

As for the captain, he had gone about his work with his mind filled with varying emotions: sympathy for Caleb, sorrow and mortification over Betty's fall, and bitter, intense, dangerous hatred of Lacey. These were each in turn, as they assailed her, consumed by a never ending hunger to get the child home again, that she might begin the undoing of her fatal step. To him she was still the little girl he used to meet on the road, with her hair in a tangle about her head, her books under her arm. As he had never fully realized, even when she married Caleb, that anything had increased her responsibilities, or that she could be anything but the child she looked, — so he could not now escape the conviction that somehow or other "she 'd been hoodooed," as he expressed it, and that when she came to herself her very soul would cry out in bitter agony.

Every day since her flight he had been early and late at the telegraph office, and had directed Bert Simmons, the letter-carrier on the shore road, to hunt him up wherever he might be, — on the dock or aboard his boat, — should a letter come bearing his name. The telegram, therefore, was not a surprise. That Sanford should have found her was what he could not understand.

Aunty Bell, with the big secret weighing at her heart, busied herself about the house, so as to make the hours pass quickly. She was more conservative and less impulsive in many things than the captain; that is, she was apt to consider the opinions of her neighbors, and shape her course accordingly, unless stopped by one of her husband's outbursts and won over to his way of thinking. The captain knew no law but his own emotions, and his innate sense of right and wrong sustained by his indomitable will and courage. If the other folks did n't like it, the other folks had to get out of the way; he went straight on.

"Ain't nobody goin' to have nothin' to do with Betty, if she does git tired of Lacey an' wants to come home, poor child," Aunty Bell had said to Captain Joe only the night before, as they sat together at supper. "Them Nevins gals was sayin' yesterday they 'd pass her on the road and would n't speak to her, not if they see her starvin', and was a-goin' on awful about it; and Mis' Taft said" —

The captain raised his head quickly. "Jane Bell," — when the captain called Aunty Bell "Jane" the situation was serious, — "I ain't got nothin' to do with them Nevins gals, nor Mis' Taft, nor nobody else, and you ain't got nothin', neither. Ain't we hed this child runnin' in an' out here jes' like a kitten ever since we been here? Don't you know clean down in yer heart that there ain't no better gal ever lived 'n Betty? Ain't we all liable to go 'stray, and ain't we all of us so dirt mean that if we had our hatches off there ain't nobody who see our cargo would speak to us? Now don't let me hear no more about folks passin' her by. I ain't a-goin' to pass her by, and you ain't, neither, if them Nevins gals and old Mother Taft and the whole kit and caboodle of 'em walks on t'other side."

She remembered the very sound of these words, as she rested for a moment, rocking to and fro, in the kitchen, after the captain had gone, her fat little feet swinging clear of the floor. She could even hear the tone of his voice, and could see the flashing of his eye. The remembrance gave her courage. She wanted some one to come in, that she might put on the captain's armor and fight for the child herself.

She had not long to wait. Mrs. Taft was already coming up the walk, — for dinner, perhaps. Carleton was walking beside her. They had met at the gate.

"I heard the captain had to go to New York, Aunty Bell, and so I thought maybe you'd be alone," said Mrs. Taft, taking off her bonnet. "No news from the runaway, I suppose? Ain't it dreadful? She's the last girl in the world I would 'a' thought of doing a thing like that."

"We ain't none of us perfect, Mis' Taft. Take a chair, Mr. Carleton. If we was, we could most of us stay here; there would n't be no use o' heaven."

"But, Aunty Bell!" exclaimed the visitor, "you surely don't think— Why, it's awful for Betty to go and do what she did "—

"I ain't judgin' nobody, Mis' Taft. I ain't a-blamin' Betty, an' I ain't a-blamin' Caleb. I'm only thinkin' of all the sufferin' that poor child's got to go through now, an' what a mean world this is for her to have to live in."

"Serves the old man right for marrying a girl young enough to be his daughter," said Carleton, with a laugh, tilting back his chair, — his favorite attitude. "I made up my mind the first day I saw her that she was a little larky. She's been fooling West all summer, — anybody could see that." He had not forgiven the look in Caleb's eye that afternoon aboard the Screamer. "When's the captain coming home?"

Aunty Bell looked at the superintendent, her lips curling, as the hard, dry laugh rang in her ears. She had never fancied him, and she liked him less now than ever. Her first impulse was to give him a piece of her mind, — an indigestible morsel when served hot. Then she remembered that her husband was having some difficulty with him about the acceptance of the concrete disk, and so her temper, chilled by this more politic second thought, cooled down and stiffened into a frigid determination not to invite him to dinner if she ate nothing herself all day.

"Cap'n 'll be here in the mornin'," she answered curtly. "Got any message for him?"

"Yes. Tell him I was out to the Ledge yesterday with my transit, and the concrete is too low by six inches near the southeast derrick. It's got to come up to grade before I can certify. I thought I'd come in and tell him,— he wanted to know."

The door opened, and the tall form of Captain Bob Brandt, the Screamer's skipper, entered.

"Excuse me, Mis' Bell," he said, removing his hat and bowing good-humoredly to everybody. "I saw ye pass, Mr. Carleton, an' I wanted to tell ye that we're ready now to h'ist sail fur the Ledge. We got 'leven stone on. Caleb ain't workin' this week, an' one o' the other divers's a-goin' to set 'em. Guess it's all right; the worst is all done. Will you go out with us, or trust me to git 'em right?"

"Well, where are you going to put 'em?" asked Carleton in his voice of authority.

"Las' time Caleb was down, sir, he said he wanted four more stone near the boat-landin', in about twelve foot o' water, to finish that row; then we kin begin another layer nex' to 'em, if ye say so. S'pose you know Cap'n Joe ain't here?—gone to New York. Will you go with us?"

"No; you set 'em. I'll come out in the tug in the morning and drop a rod on 'em, and if they're not right you'll have to take 'em up again. That concrete's out of level, you know."

"What concrete?"

"Why, the big circular disk," snapped Carleton.

This was only another excuse of Carleton's for refusing to sign the certificate. The engineer had postponed his visit, and so this fresh obstruction was necessary to maintain his policy of delay.

"Not when I see it, sir, three days ago," said Captain Brandt in surprise. "It was dead low water, an' the tide jest touched the edges of the outer band all round even."

"Well, I guess I know," retorted the superintendent, flaring up. "I was out there yesterday with a level, an' walked all over it."

"Must'er got yer feet wet, then, sir," said the skipper, with a laugh, as he turned toward the door. "The tide's been from eight inches to a foot higher 'n usual for three days past; it's full-moon tides."

During the talk Aunty Bell and Mrs. Taft had slipped into the sitting-room, and the superintendent, finding himself alone, called to the skipper, and joined him on the garden walk.

As the afternoon hours wore on, and no other callers came in, — Mrs. Taft having gone, — Aunty Bell brought a big basket, filled with an assortment of yarn stockings of varied stains and repairs, out to a chair on the porch, and made believe to herself that she was putting them in order for the captain when he should need a dry pair. Now and then she would stop, her hand in the rough stocking, her needle poised, her mind going back to the days when she first moved to Keyport, and this curly-haired girl from the fishing-village a mile or more away had won her heart. Since the death of that baby girl of long ago, Betty, somehow, had filled day by day all the deep corners of the sore heart, still aching from this earlier sorrow. When the girl's mother died, a few months after Betty's marriage, Aunty Bell had thrown a shawl over her head, and, going to Caleb's cabin, had mounted the stairs to Betty's little room and shut the door. With infinite tenderness she had drawn the girl's head down on her own bosom, and had poured out to her all the mother's love she had in her own heart, and had told her of that daughter of her dreams. Betty had not forgotten it, and among all those she knew on the shore road she loved Aunty Bell the best. There were few days in the week — particularly in the summer, when Caleb was away — that she was not doing something for Aunty Bell, her bright face and merry, ringing laugh filling the house and the little woman's life, — an infectious, bubbling, girlish laugh that made it a delight to be with her.

But a fresh thought, like a draft from an open door, rushed into Aunty Bell's mind with a force that sent a shiver through her tender heart, and chilled every kind impulse. Suppose Caleb should turn his back on this girl wife of his. What then? Ought she to take her to her heart and brave it out with the neighbors? What sort of an example was it to other young women along the shore, Aunty Bell's world? Could they, too, run off with any young fellows they met, and then come home and be forgiven? It was all very well for the captain, — he never stopped to think about these things, — that was his way; but what was *her* duty in the matter? Would it not be better in the end for Betty if she were made to realize her wrong-doing, and to suffer for it?

These alternating memories and perplexities absorbed her as she sat on the porch, the stockings in her lap, her mind first on one course of action and then on another, until some tone of Betty's voice, or the movement of her hand, or the toss of her head came back, and with it the one intense, overwhelming desire to help and comfort the child she loved.

When it began to grow dark she lighted the lamp in the front room, and made herself a cup of tea in the kitchen. Every few minutes she glanced at the clock, her ears alert for the whistle of the incoming train. Losing confidence even in the clock, she again took her seat on the porch, her arms on the rail, her plump chin resting on her hands, straining her eyes to see far down the road.

When the signaling whistle of the train was heard, the long-drawn sound reverberating over the hills, she ran to the gate, and stood there, her apron thrown over her head. Soon a carriage passed, filled with summer visitors, their trunks piled in front, and drove on up the road. Then a man carrying a bag hurried by with two women, their arms full of bundles. After that the road was deserted. These appeared to be all the passengers coming her way. As the minutes dragged, and no sound of footsteps reached her ear, and no big burly figure with a slender girl beside it loomed against the dim light of the fading sky, her courage failed and her eyes began to grow moist. She saw it all now: Betty dared not come home and face Caleb and the others!

Suddenly she heard her name called from inside the house, and again from the kitchen door.

"Aunty Bell! Aunty Bell! where be ye?"

It was the captain's voice: he must have left the train at the drawbridge and crossed lots, coming in at the rear gate.

She hurried up the plank walk, and met him at the kitchen door. He was leaning against the jamb. It was too dark to see his face. A dreadful sense of some impending calamity overcame her.

"Where's Betty?" she faltered, scarcely able to speak.

The captain pointed inside.

The little woman pushed past him into the darkening room. For a moment she stood still, her eyes fixed on Betty's slender, drooping figure and bowed head, outlined against the panes of the low window.

"Betty!" she cried, running forward with outstretched arms.

The girl did not move.

"Betty — my child!" Aunty Bell cried again, taking the weeping woman in her arms.

Then, with smothered kisses and halting, broken speech, these two — the forgiving and the forgiven — sank to the floor.

Outside, on a bench by the door, sat the captain, rocking himself, bringing his hands down on his knees, and with every seesaw repeating in a low tone to himself, "She's home. She's home."

CHAPTER XII

CAPTAIN JOE'S CREED

WHEN Captain Joe flung open Caleb's cabin door, the same cry was on his lips: "She's home, Caleb, she's home! Run 'way an' lef' him, jes' 's I knowed she would, soon 's she got the spell off'n her."

Caleb looked up over the rim of his glasses into the captain's face. He was sitting at the table in his shirt-sleeves and rough overalls, the carpet slippers on his feet. He was eating his supper, — the supper that he had cooked himself.

"How d' ye know?" he asked. The voice did not sound like Caleb's; it was hoarse and weak.

"She come inter Mr. Sanford's place night 'fore last, scared almost to death, and he tuk her to them Leroy folks; they was stavin' good to her an' kep' 'er till mornin', an' telegraphed me. I got the eight-ten this mornin'. There warn't no time, Caleb," — in an apologetic tone, — "or I 'd sent for ye, jes' 's Aunty Bell wanted me to; but I knowed ye 'd understand. We jes' got back. I 'd brought 'er up, only she 's dead beat out, poor little gal."

It was a long answer of the captain's to so direct a question, and it was made with more or less misgiving. It was evident from his manner that he was a little nervous over the result. He did not take his eyes from the diver's face as he fired these shots at random, wondering where and how they would strike.

"Where is she now?" inquired Caleb quietly.

"Down on my kitchen floor with her head in Aunty Bell's lap. Git yer hat and come 'long." The captain leaned over the table as he spoke, and rested one hand on the back of Caleb's chair.

Caleb did not raise his eyes nor move. "I can't do her no good no more, Cap'n Joe. It was jes' like ye to try an' help her. Ye'd do it for anybody that was a-sufferin'; but I don't see *my* way clear. I done all I could for her 'fore she lef' me,—leastwise I thought I had." There was no change in the listless monotone of his voice.

"You allus done by her, Caleb." The captain's hand had slipped from the chair-back to Caleb's shoulder. "I know it, and she knows it now. She ain't ever goin' to forgive herself for the way she's treated ye,—tol' me so to-day comin' up. She's been hoodooed, I tell ye,—that's what's the matter; but she's come to now. Come along; I'll git yer hat. She ought'er go to sleep purty soon."

"Ye need n't look for my hat, Cap'n Joe.

I ain't a-goin'," said Caleb quietly, leaning back in his chair. The lamp shone full on his face and beard. Captain Joe could see the deep lines about the eyes, seaming the dry, shrunken skin. The diver had grown to be a very old man in a week.

"You say you ain't a-goin', Caleb?" In his heart he had not expected this.

"No, Cap'n Joe; I'm goin' to stay here an' git along th' best way I kin. I ain't blamin' Betty. I'm blamin' myself. I been a-thinkin' it all over. She done 'er best to love me and do by me, but I was too old for 'er. If it had n't been Billy, it would'er been somebody else, — somebody younger 'n me."

"She don't want nobody else but you, Caleb." The captain's voice rose quickly. He was crossing the room for a chair as he spoke. "She told me so to-day. She purty nigh cried herself sick comin' up. I was afeard folks would notice her."

"She's sorry now, cap'n, an' wants ter come back, 'cause she's skeered of it all, but she don't love me no more 'n she did when she lef' me. When Billy finds she's gone, he'll be arter her agin" —

"Not if I git my hands on him," interrupted the captain angrily, dragging the chair to Caleb's side.

"An' when she begins to hunger for him," continued Caleb, taking no notice of the outburst, "it 'll be all to do over agin. She won't be happy without him. I ain't got nothin' agin 'er, but I won't take 'er back. It 'll only make it wus for her in the end."

"Ye ain't a-goin' ter chuck that gal out in the road, be ye?" cried Captain Joe, seating himself beside the table, his head thrust forward in Caleb's face in his earnestness. "What's she but a chit of a child that don't know no better?" he burst out. "She ain't more 'n twenty now, and here's some on us more 'n twice 'er age and liable to do wus every day. Think of yerself when ye was her age. Do ye remember all the mean things ye done, and the lies ye told? S'pose you 'd been chucked out as ye want to do to Betty. It ain't decent for ye to talk so, Caleb, and I don't like ye fur it, neither. She's a good gal, and you know it," and the captain, in his restlessness, shifted the chair and planted it immediately in front of Caleb, where he could look him straight in the eye. Aunty Bell had told him just what Caleb would say, but he had not believed it possible.

"I ain't said she warn't, Cap'n Joe. I ain't blamin' her, nor never will. I'm blamin' myself. I ought'er stayed tendin' light-ship instead'er comin' ashore and spilin' 'er life. I was lonely, and the fust one was allus sickly, an' I thought maybe my time had come then; and it did while she was with me. I 'd ruther heared her a-singin', when I come in here at night, than any music I ever knowed." His voice broke for a moment. "I done by her all I could, but I begin to see lately she was lonelier here with me than I was 'board ship with nothin' half the time to talk to but my dog. I did n't think it was Billy she wanted, but I see it now."

Captain Joe rose from his chair and began pacing the room. His onslaughts broke against Caleb's indomitable will with as little effect as did the waves about his own feet the day he set the derricks.

His faith in Betty's coming to herself had never been shaken for an instant. If it had, it would all have been restored the morning she met him at Mrs. Leroy's, and, throwing her arms about him, clung to him like a frightened kitten. His love for the girl was so great that he had seen but one side of the question. Her ingratitude, her selfishness in ignoring the disgrace and misery she would bring this man who had been everything to her, had held no place in the captain's mind. To him the case was a plain one. She was young and foolish, and had committed a fault; she was sorry and repentant; she had run away from her sin; she had come back to the one she had wronged, and she wanted to be forgiven. That was his steadfast point of view, and this was his creed: "Neither do I condemn thee; go and sin no more." That Caleb did not view the question in the same way at first astonished, then irritated him. If she had broken the Master's command again, he would perhaps have let her go her way, — for what was innately bad he hated, — but not now, when she had awakened to a sense of her sin. He continued to pace up and down Caleb's kitchen, his hands behind his broad back, his horny, stubby fingers twisting nervously together. Caleb sat still in his chair, the lamplight streaming over his face. In all the discussion his voice had been one low monotone. It seemed but a phonographic echo of his once clear tones.

The captain resumed his seat with a half-baffled, weary air.

"Caleb," he said, — there was a softness now in the tones of his voice that made the diver raise his head, — "you and me hev knowed each other off 'n' on for nigh on to twenty years. We've had it thick and nasty, and we've had as clear weather as ever a man sailed in. You've tried to do square 'tween man and man, and so far's I know, ye have, and I don't believe ye're goin' to turn crooked now. From the time this child used to come down to the dock, when I fust come to work here, and talk to me 'tween school hours, and Aunty Bell would take her in to dinner, down to the time she got hoodooed by that smooth face and lyin' tongue, — damn him! I'll spile t'other side for him, some day, wus than the Screamer did,— from that time, I say, this 'ere little gal ain't been nothin' but a bird fillin' everything full of singin' from the time she got up till she went to bed agin. I ask ye now, man to man, if that ain't so?"

Caleb nodded his head.

"During all that time there ain't been a soul up and down this road, man, woman, nor child, that she would n't help if she could,— and there's a blame' sight of 'em she did help, as you an' I know: sick child'en, sittin' up with 'em nights; an' makin' bonnets for folks as could n't git 'em no other way, without payin' for 'em; and doin' all she could to make this place happier for her bein' in it. Since she's been yer wife, there ain't been a tidier nor nicer place along the shore road than yours, and there ain't been a happier little woman nor home nowheres. Is that so, or not?"

Again Caleb nodded his head.

"While all this is a-goin' on, here comes that little skunk, Bill Lacey, with a tongue like 'n ile-can, and every time she says she's lonely or tired — and she's had plenty of it, you bein' away — he up's with his can and squirts it into 'er ear about her bein' tied to an old man, and how if she'd married him he would n't 'a' lef' her a minute"—

Caleb looked up inquiringly, an ugly gleam in his eyes.

"Oh, I ketched him at it one day in my kitchen, and I tol' him then I'd break his head, and I wish to God I had, now! Purty soon comes the time with the Screamer, and his face gets stove in. What does Betty do? Leave them men to git 'long best way they could, — like some o' the folks round here that was just as well able to 'ford the time, — or did she stand by and ketch a line and make fast? I'll tell ye what she done, 'cause I was there, and you warn't. Fust one come ashore was Billy; he looked like he'd fallen off a topgall'nt mast and struck the deck with his face. Lonny Bowles come next; he warn't so bad mashed up. What did Betty do? Pick out the easiest one? No, she jes' anchored right 'longside that boy, and hung on, and never had 'er clo'es off for nigh on to forty-eight hours. If he's walkin' round now he owes it to her. Is that so, or not?"

"It's true, cap'n," said Caleb, his eyes fastened on the captain's face. The lids were heavy now; only his will held back the tears.

"For three weeks this went on, she a-settin' like a little rabbit with her paws up starin' at him, her eyes gettin' bigger all the time, an' he lyin', coiled up like a snake, lookin' up into her face until he'd hoodooed her and got her clean off her centre. Now there's one thing I'm a-goin' to ask ye, an' before I ask ye, an' before ye answer it, I'm a-goin' to ask ye an other: when the Three Sisters come ashore on Deadman Shoal las' winter in that sou'-easter, 'cause the light warn't lit, an' all o' them men was drownded, whose fault was it?"

"Why, you know, Cap'n Joe," Caleb interposed quickly, eager to defend a brother keeper, a pained and surprised expression overspreading his face. "Poor Charles Edwards had been out o' his head for a week."

"That's right, Caleb; that's what I heard, an' that's true, an' the dead men and the owners had n't nobody to blame, an' did n't. Now I'll ask ye the other question: When Betty, after livin' every day of her life as straight as a marlin spike, run away an' lef' ye a week ago, an' broke up yer home, who's to blame, — Betty, or the hoodoo that's put 'er out'er her mind ever since the Screamer blowed up?"

Caleb settled back in his chair and rested his chin on his hand, his big fluffy beard hiding his wrist and shirt-cuff. For a long time he did not answer. The captain sat, with his hands on his knees, looking searchingly into Caleb's face, watching every expression that crossed it.

"Cap'n Joe," said the diver in his calm, low voice, "I hearn ye talk, an' I know ye well 'nough to know that ye believe every word ye say, an' I don't know but it's all true. I ain't had much 'sperience o' women folks, only two

But I don't think ye git this right. It ain't for myself that I'm thinkin'. I kin git along alone, an' do my own cookin' an' washin' same as I allus used to. It's Betty I'm thinkin' of. She's tried me more 'n a year, an' done her best, an' give it up. She wouldn't 'a' been 'hoodooed,' as ye call it, by Bill Lacey if her own heart warn't ready for it 'fore he began. It's agin natur' for a gal as young 's Betty to be happy with a man 's old 's me. She can't do it, no matter how hard she tries. I didn't know it when I asked her, but I see it now."

"But she knows better now, Caleb; she ain't a-goin' to cut up no more capers." There was a yearning, an almost pitiful tone in the captain's voice. His face was close to Caleb's.

"Ye think so, an' maybe she won't; but there's one thing yer don't seem to see, Cap'n Joe: she can't git out'er love with me an' inter love with Billy an' back agin to me in a week."

These last words came slowly, as if they had been dragged up out of the very depths of his heart.

"She never was out'er love with ye, Caleb, nor in with Lacey. Don't I tell ye?" he cried impatiently, too absorbed in Betty's welfare to note the seriousness of Caleb's tone.

"Yes," said Caleb. His voice had fallen almost to a whisper. "I know ye think so, but th' bes' thing now for the little gal is to give 'er 'er freedom, an' let 'er go 'er way. She shan't suffer as long 's I 've got a dollar, but I won't have 'er come home. It 'll only break her heart then as well 's mine. Now — now — it 's only me — that is " — Caleb's head sank to the table until his face lay on his folded arms.

Captain Joe rose from his chair, bent down and laid his hand softly on the diver's shoulder. When he spoke his voice had the pleading tones of a girl.

"Caleb, don't keep nothin' back in yer heart; take Betty home. You need n't go down for her. I 'll go myself an' bring her here. It won't be ten minutes 'fore her arms 'll be round yer neck. Lemme go for her?"

The diver raised his head erect, looked Captain Joe calmly in the eye, and, without a trace of bitterness in his voice, said: "She 'll never set foot here as my wife agin, Cap'n Joe, as long 's she lives. I ain't got the courage to set still an' see her pine away day arter day, if she comes back, an' I won't. I love 'er too much for that. If she was my own child instead o' my wife, I 'd say the same thing. It 's Betty I 'm a-thinkin' of, not myself. It 'd be twict 's hard for 'er the next time she got tired an' wanted to go. It 's all over now, an' she 's free. Let it all stay so."

"Don't say that, Caleb." The shock of the refusal seemed to have stunned him. "Don't say that. Think o' that child, Caleb: she come back to ye, an' you shut your door agin 'er."

Caleb shook his head, with a meaning movement that showed the iron will of the man and the hopelessness of further discussion.

"Then she ain't good 'nough for ye, 's that it?"

The captain was fast losing his self-control. He knew in his heart that in these last words he was doing Caleb an injustice, but his anger got the better of him.

Caleb did not answer.

"That's it. Say it out. You don't believe in her." His voice now rang through the kitchen. One hand was straight up over his head; his lips quivered. "Ye think she's some low-down critter instead of a poor child that ain't done nobody no wrong intentional. I ask ye for th' las' time, Caleb. Be decent to yerself. Be a father to 'er, if ye can't be no more; an' if ye can't be that, — damn ye! — stan' up an' forgive her like a man."

Caleb made no sign. The cruel thrust had not reached his heart. He knew his friend, and he knew all sides of his big nature. The clear blue eyes still rested on the captain's face.

"You won't?" There was a tone almost of defiance in the captain's words.

The diver again shook his head.

"Then I'll tell ye one thing, Caleb, right here" (he was now bent forward, his forefinger in Caleb's face straight out like a spike): "ye're doin' the meanest thing I ever knowed a man to do in my whole life. I don't like ye fur it, an' I never will 's long 's I live. I would n't serve a dog so, let alone Betty. An' now I 'll tell ye another: if she ain't good 'nough to live with you, she 's good 'nough to live with Aunty Bell an' me, an' there 's where she 'll stay jes' 's long 's she wants to."

Without a word of good-night he picked up his hat and strode from the room, slamming the door behind him with a force that rattled every plate on the table.

Caleb half started from his chair as if to call him back. Then, with a deep indrawn sigh, he rose wearily from the chair, covered the smouldering fire with ashes, locked the doors, fastened the two shutters, and, taking up the lamp, went slowly upstairs to his empty bed.

The following Sunday Captain Joe shaved himself with the greatest care, — that is, he slashed his face as full of cuts as a Heidelberg student's after a duel; squeezed his big broad shoulders into his black coat, — the one inches too tight across the back, the cloth all in corrugated wrinkles; tugged at his stiff starched collar until his face was purple; hauled taut a sleazy cravat; and, in a determined quarter-deck voice rarely heard from him, ordered Aunty Bell to get on her best clothes, call Betty, and come with him.

"What in natur' 's got into ye, Cap'n Joe?"

"Church's got inter me, and you an' Betty's goin' along."

"Ye ain't never goin' to church, be ye?" No wonder Aunty Bell was thunderstruck. Neither of them had been inside of a church since they moved to Keyport. Sunday was the captain's day for getting rested, and Aunty Bell always helped him.

"I ain't, ain't I? That's all ye know, Jane Bell. You git Betty an' come along, jes' 's I tell ye. I'm a-runnin' this ship." There was that peculiar look in the captain's eye and tone in his voice that his wife knew too well. It was never safe to resist him in one of these moods.

Betty burst into tears when the little woman told her, and said she dared not go, and couldn't, until a second quick, not-to-be-questioned order resounded up the staircase:—

"Here, now, that church bell's purty nigh done ringin'. We got ter git aboard 'fore the gangplank's drawed in."

"Come along, child," said Aunty Bell. "'T ain't no use; he's got one o' his spells on. Which church be ye goin' to, anyway?" she called to him, as they came downstairs. "Methodist or Dutch?"

"Don't make no difference, — fust one we come to; an' Betty's goin' to set plumb in the middle 'tween you an' me, jes' so 's folks kin see. I ain't goin' to have no funny business, nor hand-whispers, nor head-shakin's about the little gal from nobody along this shore, from the preacher down, or somebody 'll git hurted."

All through the service — he had marched down the middle aisle and taken the front seat nearest the pulpit — he sat bolt upright, like a corporal on guard, his eyes on the minister, his ears alert. Now and then he would sweep his glance around, meeting the wondering looks of the congregation, who had lost interest in everything about them but the three figures in the front pew. Then, with a satisfied air, now that neither the speaker nor his hearers showed anything but respectful curiosity, and no spoken word from the pulpit bore the remotest connection with the subject uppermost in his mind, — no Magdalens nor Prodigal Sons, nor anything of like significance (there is no telling what would have happened had there been), — he settled himself again, and looked straight at the minister.

When the benediction had been pronounced he waited until the crowd got thickest around the door, — he knew why the congregation lagged behind; then he made his way into its midst, holding Betty by the arm as if she had been under arrest. Singling out old Captain Potts, a retired sea-captain, a great churchgoer and something of a censor over the morals of the community, he tapped him on the shoulder, and said in a voice loud enough to be heard by everybody : —

"This is our little gal, Betty West, Cap'n Potts. Caleb 's gin her up, and she 's come to live with us. When ye 're passin' our way with yer folks, it won't do ye no harm to stop in to see her"

CHAPTER XIII

A SHANTY DOOR

SANFORD had expected, when he led Betty from his door, that Mrs. Leroy would give her kindly shelter, but he had not been prepared for all that he heard the next day. Kate had not only received the girl into her house, but had placed her for the night in a bedroom adjoining her own; arranging the next morning a small table in her dressing-room where Betty could breakfast alone, free from the pryings of inquisitive servants. Mrs. Leroy told all these things to Sanford: describing the heart-broken weariness of the girl when she arrived; the little joyful cry she gave when big, burly Captain Joe, his eyes blinded by the hot midday glare outside, came groping his way into the darkened boudoir; and Betty's glad spring into his arms, where she lay while the captain held her with one hand, trying to talk to both Betty and herself at once, the tears rolling down his cheeks, his other great hand with the thole-pin fingers patting the girl's tired face. Mrs. Leroy told Sanford all these things and more, but she did not say how she herself had sat beside Betty on the divan that same morning, before Captain Joe arrived, winning little by little the girl's confidence, until the whole story came out. Neither did she tell him with what tact and gentleness she, the woman of the world, whose hours of loneliness had been more bitter and intense than any that Betty ever knew, had shown this inexperienced girl how much more noble it would have been to suffer and stand firm, doing and being the right, than to succumb as she had done. Nor yet did she tell Sanford how Betty's mind had cleared, as she talked on, and of the way in which the girl's brown hand had crept toward her own till it nestled among her jeweled fingers, while with tender words of worldly wisdom she had prepared her foster sister for what she still must face in penance for her sin; instructing her in the use of those weapons of self-control, purity of purpose, and patience, with which she must arm herself if she would win the struggle. Nor how, before the morning hours were gone, she had received the girl's promise to go back to her home, and, if her husband would not receive her, to fight on until she again won for herself the respect she had lost, and among those, too, who had once loved her. Least of all did she tell Sanford that when the talk was over and Betty was gone, she had thrown herself on her own bed in an agony of tears, wondering after all which one of the two had done the better for herself in the battle of life, — she or the girl.

Sanford knew nothing of this. As he sat in the train, on his way back to Keyport, his heart had gone out to the girl, for he had been greatly wrought up by the story Kate told him and by the pictures she had given of the interview. Yet, strange to say, he found himself bewildered by the fact that, even more than the story, he remembered the tones of Kate's voice and the very color of her eyes as she talked. He was constantly seeing, too, as he lingered over its details, a vision of Kate herself as she stood in the hall and bade him good-by, — her full white throat above the ruffles of her morning-gown. As he rode on, he found it difficult to turn his mind to other things, or to quiet his inner enthusiasm for her gentleness and charity.

And yet there were important affairs to which he owed immediate attention. Carleton's continued refusal to sign a certificate for the concrete disk, without which no payment would be made by the government, would, if persisted in, cause him serious embarrassment. The difficulty with Carleton had already reached an acute stage. Captain Joe had altogether failed in his efforts to make the superintendent sign the certificate, and Carleton had threatened to wire the Department and demand a board of survey if his orders were not complied with at once. The captain generally retired from the field and left the campaign to Sanford whenever, in the course of their work, it became necessary to fight the United States government — the sea was his enemy.

In this discussion, however, he had taken the pains to explain to Carleton patiently, and he thought intelligently, the falsity of the stand he took, showing him that his idea about the concrete base being too low was the result of a mere optical illusion, due to the action of the tide which backed the water up higher within the breakwater on the southeast side; that when the first course of masonry was laid, bringing the mass of concrete out of water, his — Carleton's — mistake would be instantly detected.

Captain Joe was as much out of patience as he ever permitted himself to be with Carleton, when he shook Sanford's hand on his arrival.

"Ain't no man on earth smart 'nough to make eleven inches a foot, let alone a critter like him!" he said, as he explained the latest development.

Once over the sloop's side, Sanford laid his bag on the deck and turned to the men.

"Who saw the concrete at dead low water during that low tide we had after the last northwest blow?" he inquired.

"I did, sir," answered Captain Brandt. "I told Mr. Carleton he was wrong. The water jes' tetched the outer iron band all round when I see it. It was dead calm an' dead low water."

"What do you say to that, Mr. Carleton?" asked Sanford, laughing.

"I'm not here to take no back talk from nobody," replied Carleton in a surly tone.

"Lonny," said Sanford, — he saw that further discussion with the superintendent was useless, — "go ashore and get my transit and target rod; you'll find them in my bedroom at the captain's; and please put them here in the skipper's bunk, so they won't get broken. I'll run a level on the concrete myself, Mr. Carleton, when we get to the Ledge."

"There ain't no use of your transit," retorted Carleton, with a sneer. "It's six inches too low, I tell you. You'll fix it as I want it, or I'll stop the work."

Sanford looked at him, but held his peace. It had not been his first experience with men of Carleton's class. He proposed, all the same, to know for himself who was right. He had seen Carleton use a transit, and had had a dim suspicion at the time that the superintendent was looking through the eyepiece while it was closed.

"Get ready for the Ledge, Captain Brandt, as soon as Lonny returns," said Sanford. "Where's Caleb, Captain Joe? We may want him."

The captain touched Sanford on the shoulder and moved down the deck with him, where he stood behind one of the big stones, out of hearing of the other men.

"He's all broke up, sir. He ain't been to work since the little gal left. I want to thank ye, Mr. Sanford, for what ye did for 'er; and that friend o' yourn couldn't 'a' been no better to her if she'd been her sister."

"Oh, that's all right, captain," said Sanford, laying a hand on his shoulder. "Betty is at your house, I hear. How does she bear it?"

"Gritty as she kin be, but she ain't braced up much; Aunty Bell's got 'er arms round 'er most of the time. I wish you'd send for Caleb; nothin' else 'll bring him out. He won't come for me. I'll go for him myself, if ye say so."

"Go get him. I may want him to hold a rod in four or five feet of water. He won't need his helmet, but he'll need his dress. Do you hear anything about Lacey?"

"He ain't been round where any of us could see him — and git hold of him," answered Captain Joe, knitting his brows. "I jes' wish he'd come once. I heared he was over to Stonin'ton, workin' on the railroad."

The captain jumped into the yawl and sculled away toward the diver's cabin. He had not felt satisfied with himself since the night when Caleb had refused to take Betty back. He had said then, in the heat of the moment, some things which had hurt him as much as they had hurt Caleb. He would have told him so before, but he had been constantly at the Ledge receiving the big cut stones for the masonry, nine of which were then piled up on the Screamer's deck. After that there had arisen the difficulty with Carleton. This now was his opportunity.

The men on the sloop, somehow, knew Caleb was coming, and there was more or less curiosity to see him. Nickles, standing inside the galley and within earshot, had probably overheard Sanford's request.

All the men liked the old diver. His courage, skill, and many heroic acts above and under water had earned their respect, while his universal kindness and cheeriness had won their confidence. The calamity that had overtaken him had been discussed and re-discussed; and while many hopes were indulged in regarding the future condition of Lacey's soul and the present state of his eyes, profane hopes that would have interfered seriously with the eternal happiness of the first and the seeing qualities of the second, and while numerous criticisms were as freely passed upon Betty, nothing but kindness and sympathy was felt for Caleb.

When Caleb came up over the sloop's rail, followed by Captain Joe, it was easy to see that all was right between him and the captain. One hearty handshake inside the cabin's kitchen, and a frank outspoken " I'm sorry, Caleb; don't lay it up agin me," had done that. When Caleb spoke to the men, in his usual gentle manner, each one of them said or did some little thing, as chance offered an unobtrusive opportunity, that conveyed to the diver a heartfelt sorrow for his troubles, — every one but Carleton, who purposely, perhaps, had gone down into the cabin, his temper still ruffled over his encounter with Captain Joe and Sanford.

And so Caleb once more took his place on the working force.

As the Screamer rounded to and made fast in the eddy, the Ledge gang were engaged in using the system of derricks, which since the final anchoring had never needed an hour's additional work. They were moving back from the landing-wharf the big cut stones required to lay the first course of masonry, the work to begin as soon as the controversy over the proper level of the concrete was settled.

With the making fast of the Screamer to the floating buoys in the eddy, the life-boat from the Ledge pulled alongside, and landed Sanford, Carleton, Captain Joe, Caleb, and the skipper, — Lonny Bowles carrying the transit and rod as carefully as if they had been two long icicles. When the party reached the Ledge the concrete was found to be awash with three feet of water; nothing of the mass itself could be seen by the naked eye. It was therefore apparent that if the dispute was to be settled it could be done only by a series of exact measurements. Carleton showed every evidence of satisfaction. He had begun to suspect he might be wrong, but his obstinacy sustained him. Now that the disk was covered with water there was still reason for dispute.

Caleb squeezed himself into his diving-dress, and began operations, Captain Joe fastening the water-tight cuffs over his wrists, leaving his hands free. The diver then picked up the rod with its adjustable target and plunged across the shallow basin, the water coming up to his hips. Sanford meanwhile arranged the tripod on the platform, leveled his instrument, directing Caleb where to hold the rod, and began his survey. Captain Joe stood one side recording his findings with a big blue lead pencil on a short strip of plank.

The first entries showed that the two segments of the circle — the opposite segments, southeast and northwest — varied barely three tenths of an inch in height. This, of course, was immaterial over so large a surface. The result proved conclusively that Carleton's claim that one section of the concrete was six inches too low was absurd.

"I'm afraid I shall have to decide against you this time, Mr. Carleton," said Sanford pleasantly. "Run your eye through this transit; you can see yourself what it shows."

A SHANTY DOOR

"Right or wrong," broke out Carleton, now thoroughly angry, both over his defeat and at the half-concealed, jeering remarks of the men, "it's got to go up six inches, or not a cut stone will be laid. That's what I'm here for, and what I say *goes*."

"But please take the transit and see for yourself, Mr. Carleton," urged Sanford.

"I don't know nothin' about *your* transit, nor who fixed it to suit you," snarled Carleton.

Sanford bit his lip, and made no answer. There were more important things to be done in the building of a light than the resenting of such insults or quarreling with a superintendent. The skipper, however, to whom the superintendent was a first experience, and who took his answer as in some way a reflection on his own veracity, walked quickly toward him with his fist tightly clinched. His big frame towered over Carleton's.

"Thank you, Captain Brandt," said Sanford, noticing the skipper's expression and intent. "But Mr. Carleton isn't in earnest. *His* transit is not here, and we cannot tell who fixed that."

The men laughed, and the skipper stopped and stood aside, awaiting any further developments that might require his aid.

"In view of these measurements," asked Sanford, as he held before Carleton's eyes the piece of plank bearing Captain Joe's record, "do you still order the six inches of concrete put in?"

"Certainly I do," said Carleton. His ugly temper was gradually being hidden under an air of authority. Sanford's tact had regained him a debating position.

"And you take the responsibility of the change?"

"I do," replied Carleton in a blustering voice.

"Then please put that order in writing," said Sanford quietly, "and I will see it done as soon as the tide lowers."

Carleton's manner changed; he saw the pit that lay before him. If he were wrong, the written order would fix his responsibility; without that telltale record he could deny afterward having given the order, if good policy so demanded.

"Well, that ain't necessary; you go ahead," said Carleton, with less vehemence.

"I think it is, Mr. Carleton. You ask me to alter a bench-mark level which I know to be right, and which every man about us knows to be right. You refuse a written certificate if I do not carry out your orders, and yet you expect me to commit this engineering crime because of your personal opinion,— an opinion which you now refuse to back up by your signature."

"I ain't given you a single written order

this season: why should I now?" in an evasive tone.

"Because up to this time you have asked for nothing unreasonable. Then you refuse?"

"I do, and I'm not to be bulldozed, neither."

"Caleb," said Sanford, with the air of a man who had made up his mind, raising his voice to the diver, still standing in the water, "put that rod on the edge of the iron band."

Caleb felt around under the water with his foot, found the band, and placed on it the end of the rod. Sanford carefully adjusted the instrument.

"What does it measure?"

"Thirteen feet six inches, sir!" shouted Caleb.

"Lonny Bowles," continued Sanford, "take three or four of the men and go along the breakwater and see if Caleb is right."

The men scrambled over the rocks, Lonny plunging into the water beside Caleb, so as to get closer to the rod.

"Thirteen feet six inches!" came back the voices of Lonny and the others, speaking successively.

"Now, Captain Joe, look through this eyepiece and see if you find the red quartered target in the centre of the spider-web lines. You, too, skipper."

The men put their eyes to the glass, each announcing that he saw the red of the disk.

"Now, Caleb, make your way across to the northwest derrick, and hold the rod on the band there."

The old diver waded across the concrete, and held the rod and target over his head. The men followed him around the breakwater, — all except Bowles, who, being as wet as he could be, plunged in waist-deep.

Sanford turned the transit without disturbing the tripod, and adjusted it until the lens covered the target.

"Raise it a little, Caleb!" shouted Sanford, — "so! What is she now?"

"Thirteen feet six inches and — a — half!"

"Right! How is it, men?"

"Thirteen six and a half!" came back the replies, after each man had assured himself.

"Now bring me a clean, dry plank, Captain Joe," said Sanford. "That's too small," as the captain held out the short piece containing the record. Clean planks were scarce on the cement-stained work; dry ones were never found.

Everybody went in search of a suitable plank. Carleton looked on at this pantomime with a curl on his lips, and now and then a little shiver of uncertain fear creeping over him. Sanford's quiet, determined manner puzzled him.

"What's all this circus about?" he broke out impatiently.

"One minute, Mr. Carleton. I want to make a record which will be big enough for the men to sign; one that won't get astray, lost, or stolen."

"What's the matter with this?" asked Captain Joe, opening the wooden door of the new part of the shanty. "Ye can't lose this 'less ye take away the house."

"That's the very thing!" exclaimed Sanford. "Swing her wide open, Captain Joe. Please give me that big blue pencil."

When the door flew back it was as white and clean as a freshly scrubbed pine table.

Sanford wrote as follows:—

August 29, SHARK LEDGE LIGHT.

We, the undersigned, certify that the concrete disk is perfectly level except opposite the northwest derrick, where it is three tenths of an inch too high. We further certify that Superintendent Carleton orders the concrete raised six inches on the southeast segment, and refuses to permit any cut stone to be set until this is done.

HENRY SANFORD, Contractor.

"Come, Captain Joe," said Sanford, "put your signature under mine."

The captain held the pencil in his bent fingers as if it had been a chisel, and inscribed his full name, "Joseph Bell," under that of

Sanford. Then Caleb and the others followed, the diver fumbling inside his dress for his glasses, the search proving fruitless until Captain Joe ran his arm down between the rubber collar of the diving-dress and Caleb's red shirt and drew them up from inside his undershirt.

"Now, Captain Joe," said Sanford, "you can send a gang in the morning at low water and raise that concrete. It will throw the upper masonry out of level, but it won't make much difference in a circle of this size."

The men gave a cheer, the humor of the situation taking possession of every one. Even Caleb forgot his sorrow for a moment. Carleton laughed a little halting laugh himself, but there was nothing of spontaneity in it. Nickles, the cook, who, now that the cut stone was about to be laid, was permanently transferred from the Screamer to the shanty, and under whose especial care this door was placed by reason of its position, — it opened into the kitchen, — planted his fat, oily body before the curious record, read it slowly word for word, and delivered himself of this opinion : "That 'ere door 's th' biggest receipt for stores I ever see come into a kitchen."

"Big or little," said Captain Joe, who could not see the drift of most of Nickles's jokes, "you spatter it with yer grease or spile it any, and ye go ashore."

CHAPTER XIV

TWO ENVELOPES

BETTY's flight had been of such short duration, and her return home accomplished under such peculiar circumstances, that the stories in regard to her elopement had multiplied with the hours. One feature of her escapade excited universal comment, — her spending the night at Mrs. Leroy's. The only explanation that could be given of this extraordinary experience was that so high a personage as Mrs. Leroy must have necessarily been greatly imposed upon by Betty, or she could never have disgraced herself and her home by giving shelter to such a woman.

Mrs. Leroy's hospitality to Betty inspired another theory, — one that, not being contradicted at the moment of its origin by Aunty Bell, had seemed plausible. Miss Peebles, the schoolmistress, who never believed ill of anybody, lent all her aid to its circulation. The conversation out of which the theory grew took place in Aunty Bell's kitchen. Betty was upstairs in her room, and the talk went on in lowered tones, lest she should overhear.

"I never shall believe that a woman holding Mrs. Leroy's position would take Betty West into her house if she knew what kind of a woman she was," remarked the elder Miss Nevins.

"And that makes me think there's some mistake about this whole thing," said Miss Peebles. "Who saw her with Lacey, anyhow? Nobody but the butcher, and he don't know half the time what he's talking about, he rattles on so. Maybe she never went with Lacey at all."

"What did she go 'way for, then?" asked the younger Nevins girl, who was on her way to the store, and had stopped in, hoping she might, by chance, get a look at Betty. "I guess Lacey's money was all gone — that's why she imposed on Mrs. Leroy."

"I don't believe it," said Miss Peebles. "Betty may have been foolish, but she never told a lie in her life."

"Well, it may be," admitted the younger sister in a softened tone. "I hope so, anyhow."

Aunty Bell kept still. Betty was having trouble enough; if the neighbors thought her innocent, and would give her the benefit of the doubt, better leave it so. There were one or two threads of worldly wisdom and canny policy twisted about the little woman's heart which now and then showed their ends.

Captain Joe was in the sitting-room, reading. He had come in from the Ledge, wet, as usual, had put on some dry clothes, and while waiting for supper had picked up the "Noank Times." Aunty Bell and the others saw him come in, but thought he had changed his clothes and had gone to the dock.

He had overheard every word of the discussion. There were no raveled threads in the captain's make-up. He threw down his paper, pushed his way into the group, and said: —

"There's one thing I don't want no mistake over, and I won't have it. Betty did n't tell no lies to Mrs. Leroy nor to nobody else, an' I ain't a-goin' to have nobody lie for 'er. Mrs. Leroy knows all about it. She took care of her 'cause she's got a heart inside of her. Betty went off with Bill Lacey 'cause he'd hoodooed 'er, an' when she come to herself she come home agin: that's all ther' is to that. She's sorry for what she's done, an' ther' ain't nobody outside o' heaven can do more. She's goin' to stay here 'cause me and Aunty Bell love her now more 'n we ever did before. But she's goin' to start life agin fair an' square, with no lies of her own an' no lies told about 'er by nobody else." The captain looked at Aunty Bell. "Them that don't like it can lump it. Them as don't like Betty after this can stay away from me," and he turned about on his heel and went down to the dock.

Two currents had thus been started in Betty's favor: one the outspoken indorsement of Captain Joe; and the other the protection of Mrs. Leroy, "the rich lady who lived at Medford, in that big country-seat where the railroad crossed, and who had the yacht and horses, and who must be a good woman, or she would n't have come to nurse the men, or sent them delicacies, and who came herself to put up the mosquito-nets over their cots."

As the August days slipped by and the early autumn came, the gossip gradually died. Caleb continued to live alone, picking up once more the manner of life he had practiced for years aboard the light-ship: having a day every two weeks for his washing, — always Sunday, when the neighbors would see him while on their way to church, — hanging out his red and white collection on the line stretched in the garden. He cooked his meals and cleaned the house himself. Nobody but Captain Joe and Aunty Bell crossed his threshold, except the butcher who brought him his weekly supplies. He had been but seldom to the village in the daytime, — somehow he did not like to pass Captain Joe's when any one could see him, — and had confined his outings to going from the cabin to the Ledge and back again as his duties required, locking the rear door and hanging the key on a nail beside it until his return.

He had seen Betty only once, and that was

when he had passed her on the road. He came upon her suddenly, and he thought she started back as if to avoid him, but he kept his eyes turned away and passed on. When he reached the hill and looked back he could see her sitting by the side of the road, a few rods from where they met, her head resting on her hand.

Only one man had dared to speak to him in an unsympathetic way about Betty's desertion, and that was his old friend Tony Marvin, the keeper of Keyport Light. They had been together a year on Bannock Rip during the time the Department had doubled up the keepers. He had not heard of Caleb's trouble until several weeks after Betty's flight; lighthouse-keepers staying pretty close indoors.

"I hearn, Caleb, that the new wife left ye for that young rigger what got his face smashed. 'Most too young, warn't she, to be stiddy?"

"No, I ain't never thought so," replied Caleb quietly. "Were n't no better gal 'n Betty; she done all she knowed how. You 'd 'a' said so if ye knowed her like I did. But 't was agin natur', I bein' so much older. But I 'd rather had her go than suffer on."

"Served ye durn mean, anyhow," said the keeper. "Did she take anything with 'er?"

"Nothin' but the clo'es she stood in. But she did n't serve me mean, Tony. I don't want ye to think so, an' I don't want ye to say so, nor let nobody say so, neither; an' ye won't if you 're a friend o' mine, which you allers was."

"I hearn there was some talk o' yer takin' her back," the keeper went on in a gentler tone, surprised at Caleb's blindness, and anxious to restore his good feeling. "Is that so?"

"No, that ain't so," Caleb answered firmly, ending the conversation on that topic and leading it into other channels.

This interview of the light-keeper's was soon public property. Some of those who heard of it set Caleb down as half-witted over his loss, and others wondered how long it would be before he would send for Betty and patch it all up again, and still others questioned why he did n't go over to Stonington and smash the other side of Lacey's face; they heard that Billy had been seen around there.

As for Betty, she had found work with a milliner on the edge of the village, within a mile of Captain Joe's cottage, where her taste in trimming bonnets secured her ready employment, and where her past was not discussed. That she was then living with Captain Joe and his wife was enough to gain her admission.

There had been days, however, after her return, when she would have given way under the strain, had it not been for her remembered promise to Mrs. Leroy, — the only woman, except Aunty Bell, who had befriended her, — and for the strong supporting arm of Captain

Joe, who never lost an opportunity to show his confidence in her.

And yet in spite of these promises and supports she could have plunged into the water many a time at the end of the dock and ended it all. She would sit for hours in her little room next Aunty Bell's, on Saturday afternoons, when she came earlier from work, and watch for the Screamer or one of the tugs to round in, bringing Caleb and the men. She could not see her own cottage from the window where she sat, but she could see her husband come down the sloop's side and board the little boat that brought him to his landing. She would often think that she could catch his good-night as he pushed off. On Monday mornings, too, when she knew he was going out, she was up at daylight, watching for a meagre glimpse of him when the skiff shot out from behind the dock and took him aboard to go to his work on the Ledge.

Little by little the captain's devotion to Betty's interests, and the outspoken way in which he praised her efforts to maintain herself, began to have their effect. People who had passed her by without a word, as they met her on the road, volunteered a timid good-morning, which was answered by a slight nod of the head by Betty. Even one of the Nevins girls — the younger one — had joined her and walked as far as the milliner's, with a last word on the doorstep, which had detained them both for at least two minutes in full sight of the other girls who were passing the shop.

Betty met all advances kindly, but with a certain reserve of manner. She appreciated the good motive, but in her own eyes it did not palliate her fault, — that horrible crime of ingratitude, selfishness, and waywardness, the memory of which hung over her night and day like a pall.

Most of her former acquaintances respected her reserve, — all except Carleton. Whenever he met her under Captain Joe's roof he greeted her with a nod, but on the road he had more than once tried to stop and talk to her. At first the attempt had been made with a lifting of the hat and a word about the weather, but the last time he had stopped in front of her and tried to take her hand.

"What's the matter with you?" he said in a coaxing tone. "I ain't going to hurt you."

Betty darted by him, and reached the shop all out of breath. She said nothing to any one about her encounter, not being afraid of him in the daytime, and not wanting her affairs talked of any more.

If Caleb knew how Betty lived, he never mentioned it to Captain Joe or Aunty Bell. He would sometimes ask after her health and whether she was working too hard, but never more than that.

One Saturday night — it was the week Betty had hurt her foot and could not go to the shop — Caleb came down to Captain Joe's and called him outside the kitchen door. It was pay-day with the men, and Caleb had in his hand the little envelope, still unopened, containing his month's pay. The lonely life he led had begun to tell upon the diver. The deathly pallor that had marked his face the first few days after his wife's departure was gone, and the skin was no longer shrunken, but the sunken cheeks remained, and the restless, eager look in the eyes that told of his mental strain.

Caleb was in his tarpaulins; it was raining at the time.

"Come in, Caleb, come in!" cried Captain Joe in a cheery voice, laying his hand on the diver's shoulder. "Take off yer ileskins." The captain never despaired of bringing husband and wife together, somehow.

Betty was sitting inside the kitchen, reading by the kerosene lamp, out of sound of the voices.

"No, I ain't washed up nor had supper yit, thank ye. I heared from Aunty Bell that Betty was laid up this week, an' so I come down." Here Caleb stopped, and began slitting the pay-envelope with a great thumb-nail shaped like a half-worn shoe-horn. "I come down, thinkin' maybe you'd kind'er put this where she could git it," slowly unrolling two of the four bills and handing them to the captain. "I don't like her to be beholden to ye for board nor nothin'."

"Ye can't give me a cent, Caleb. I knowed her 'fore you did," said the captain, protesting with his hand upraised, a slightly indignant tone in his voice. Then a thought crept into his mind. "Come in and give it to her yerself, Caleb," putting his arm through the diver's.

"No," said Caleb slowly, "I ain't come here for that, and I don't want ye to make no mistake, cap'n. I come here 'cause I been a-thinkin' it over, and somehow it seems to me that half o' this is hern. I don't want ye to tell 'er that I *give* it to her, 'cause it ain't so. I jes' want ye to lay it som'eres she'll find it; and when she asks about it, say it's hern."

Captain Joe crumpled the bills in his hand.

"Caleb," he said, "I ain't goin' to say nothin' more to ye. I've said all I could, and las' time I said too much; but what seems to me to be the cussedest foolishness out is for ye to go back an' git yer supper by yerself, when the best little gal you or I know is a-settin' within ten feet o' ye with her heart breakin' to git to ye."

"I'm sorry she's sufferin', Cap'n Joe. I don't like to see nobody suffer, leastways

Betty, but ye don't know it all. Jes' leave them bills as I asked ye. Tell Aunty Bell I got the pie she sent me when I come home, — I'll eat it to-morrow. I s'pose ye ain't got no new orders 'bout that last row of enrockment? I set the bottom stone to-day, an' I ought'er get the last of 'em finished nex' week. The tide cut turrible to-day, an' my air comin' so slow through the pump threw me 'mong the rocks an' seaweed, an' I got a scrape on my hand," showing a deep cut on its back; "but it's done hurtin' now. Good-night."

On his way home, just before he reached his cabin, Caleb came upon Bert Simmons, the shore road letter-carrier, standing in the road, under one of the village street lamps, overhauling his package of letters.

"About these letters that's comin' for yer wife, Caleb? Shall I leave 'em with you or take 'em down to Cap'n Joe Bell's? I give the others to her. Here's one now."

Caleb took the letter mechanically, looked it over slowly, noted its Stonington postmark, and, handing it back, answered calmly, "Better leave 'em down to Cap'n Joe's, Bert."

CHAPTER XV

A NARROW PATH

WHEN Sanford, after dining, rang her bell, Mrs. Leroy was seated on the veranda that overlooked the garden, — a wide and inviting veranda, always carpeted in summer with mats and rugs, and made comfortable with cane chairs and straw divans that were softened into luxurious delights by silk cushions. During the day the sunshine filtered its way between the thickly matted vines, lying in patterns on the floor, or was held in check by thin Venetian blinds. At night the light of a huge eight-sided lantern festooned with tassels shed its glow through screens of colored gauze.

Mrs. Leroy was dressed in a simple gown of white crêpe, which clung and wrinkled about her slight figure, leaving her neck and arms bare. On a low table beside her rested a silver tray with a slender-shaped coffee-pot and tiny egg-shell cups and saucers.

She looked up at him, smiling, as he pushed aside the curtains. "Two lumps, Henry?" she called, holding the sugar-tongs in her hand. Then, as the light of the lantern fell upon his face, she exclaimed, "Why, what's the matter? You are worried: is there fresh trouble at the Ledge?" and she rose from her chair.

"No; only Carleton," he replied, looking down at her. "He holds on to that certificate, and I can get no money until he gives it up; yet I have raised the concrete six inches to please him. I wired Captain Joe yesterday to see him at once and to get his answer, — yes or no. What do you suppose he replied? 'Tell him he don't own the earth. I'll sign it when I get to it.' Not another word, nor would he give any reason for not signing it."

"Why don't you appeal to the Board? General Barton would not see you suffer an unjust delay. I'll write him myself," she said, sitting bolt upright on the divan.

Sanford smiled. Her rising anger soothed him as flattery might have done at another time. He felt in it a proof of how close to her heart she really held his interests and his happiness.

"That would only prolong the agony, and might lose us the season's work. The Board is always fair and honest, only it takes so long for it to move." As he spoke he piled the cushions high behind her head, and drew a low chair opposite to her. "It's torture to a contractor who is behind time," he continued, flecking the ashes of his cigar into his saucer. "It means getting all tangled up in the red tape of a government bureau. I must give up my holiday and find Carleton; there is nothing else to be done now. I leave on the early train to-morrow. But what a rest this is!" he exclaimed, breaking into the strained impetuosity of his own tones with a long-drawn sigh of relief, as he looked about the dimly lighted veranda. "Nothing like it anywhere."

As he spoke his eyes wandered over her dainty figure, half reclining before him, — the delicately modeled waist, the shapely wrists, and the tiny slippers peeping beneath the edge of her dress that fell in folds to the floor. "Another new gown, I see?"

"Never mind about my gown. I want to hear more about this man Carleton," she said. Her face was alight with the pleasure of his tribute, but she spoke as though she had hardly heard it. "What have you done to him to make him hate you?"

"Nothing but try to keep him from ruining the work."

"And you told him he was ruining it?"

"Certainly; there was nothing else to do. He's got the concrete now six inches out of level; you can see it plainly at low water."

"No wonder he takes his revenge," she said, cutting straight into the heart of the matter with that marvelous power peculiar to some women. "What else has gone wrong?" She meant him to tell her everything, knowing that to let him completely unburden his mind would give him the only real rest that he needed. She liked, too, to feel her influence over him. That he always consulted her in such matters was to Kate one of the keenest pleasures that his friendship brought.

"Everything, I sometimes think. We are very much behind. That concrete base should have been finished two weeks ago. The equinoctial gale is nearly due. If we can't get the first two courses of masonry laid by the middle of November, I may have to wait until spring for another payment, and that about means bankruptcy."

"What does Captain Joe think?"

"He says we shall pull through if we have no more setbacks. Dear old Captain Joe! nothing upsets him. We certainly have had our share of them this season: first it was the explosion, and now it is Carleton's spite."

"Suppose you *do* lose time, Henry, and *do* have to wait until spring to go on with the work. It will not be for the first time." There was a sympathetic yet hopeful tone in her voice. "When you sunk the coffer-dam at Kingston, three years ago, and it lay all winter in the ice, didn't you worry yourself half sick? And yet it all came out right. Oh, you needn't raise your eyebrows; I saw it myself. You know you are better equipped now, both in experience and in means, than you were then. Make some allowance for your own temperament, and please don't forget the nights you have lain awake worrying over nothing. It will all come out right." She leaned toward him and laid her hand on his, as an elder sister might have done, and in a gayer tone added, "I'm going to Medford soon, myself, and I'll invite this dreadful Mr. Carleton to come over to luncheon, and you'll get your certificate next day. What does he look like?"

Sanford broke into a laugh. "You wouldn't touch him with a pair of tongs, and I wouldn't let you, — even with them."

"Then I'll do it, anyway, just to show you how clever I am," she retorted, with a pretty, bridling toss of her head. She had taken her hand away. Sanford still held his own extended.

Kate's tact was having its effect. Under the magic of her sympathy his cares had folded their tents. Carleton was fast becoming a dim speck on the horizon, and his successive troubles were but a string of camels edging the blue distance of his thoughts.

It was always like this. She never failed to comfort and inspire him. Whenever his anxieties became unbearable it was to Kate that he turned, as he had done to-night. The very touch of her soft hand, so white and delicate, laid upon his arm, and the exquisite play of melody in her voice, soothed and strengthened him. Things were never half so bad as they seemed, when he could see her look at him mischievously from under her lowered eyelids as she said, "Mercy, Henry! is that all? I thought the whole lighthouse had been washed away." And he never missed the inspiration of the change that followed, — the sudden quiet of her face, the very tensity of her figure, as she added in earnest tones, instinct with courage and sympathy, some word of hopeful interest that she of all women best knew how to give.

With the anxieties dispelled which had brought him hurrying to-night to Gramercy Park, they both relapsed into silence, — a silence such as was common to their friendship, one which was born neither of ennui nor of discontent, the boredom of friends nor the poverty of meagre minds, but that restful silence which comes only to two minds and hearts in entire accord, without the necessity of a single spoken word to lead their thoughts; a close, noiseless fitting together of two temperaments, with all the rough surfaces of their natures worn smooth by long association each with the other. In such accord is found the strongest proof of true and perfect friendship. It is only when this estate no longer satisfies, and one or both crave the human touch, that the danger-line is crossed. When stealthy fingers set the currents of both hearts free, and the touch becomes electric, discredited friendship escapes by the window, and triumphant love enters by the door.

The lantern shed its rays over Kate's white draperies, warming them with a pink glow. The smoke of Sanford's cigar curled upward in the still air and drifted out into the garden, or was lost in the vines of the jessamine trailing about the porch. Now and then the stillness was broken by some irrelevant remark suggested by the perfume of the flowers, the quiet of the night, the memory of Jack's and Helen's happiness; but silence always fell again, except for an occasional light tattoo of Kate's dainty slipper on the floor. A restful lassitude, the reaction from the constant hourly strain of his work, came over Sanford; the world of perplexity seemed shut away, and he was happier than he had been in weeks. Suddenly and without preliminary question, Mrs. Leroy asked sharply, with a strange, quivering break in her voice, "What about that poor girl Betty? Has she patched it up yet with Caleb? She told me, the night she stayed with me, that she loved him dearly. Poor girl! she has nothing but misery ahead of her if she does n't." She spoke with a certain tone in her voice that showed but too plainly the new mood that had taken possession of her.

"Pity she did n't find it out before she left him!" exclaimed Sanford.

"Pity he did n't do something to show his appreciation of her, you mean!" she interrupted, with a quick toss of her head.

"You are all wrong, Kate. Caleb is the gentlest and kindest of men. You don't know that old diver, or you wouldn't judge him harshly."

"Oh, he didn't beat her, I suppose. He only left her to get along by herself. I wish such men would take it out in beating. Some women could stand that better. It's the cold indifference that kills." She had risen from her seat, and was pacing the floor of the veranda.

"Well, that was not his fault, Kate. While the working season lasts he must be on the Ledge. He couldn't come in every night."

"That's what they all say! If it's not one excuse, it's another. I'm tired to death of hearing about men who would rather make money than make homes. Now that he has driven her out of her wits by his brutality, he closes his door against her, even when she crawls back on her knees. But don't *you* despise her." She stood before him, looking down into his face for a moment. "Be just as sweet and gentle to her as you can. If she ever goes wrong again, it will be the world's fault or her husband's, — not her own. Tell her from me that I trust her and believe in her, and that I send her my love."

Sanford listened to her with ill-concealed admiration. It was when she was defending or helping some one that she appealed to him most. At those times he recognized that her own wrongs had not imbittered her, but had only made her the more considerate.

"There's never a day you don't teach me something," he answered quietly, his eyes fixed on her moving figure. "Perhaps I have been a little hard on Betty, but it's because I've seen how Caleb suffers."

She stopped again in her walk and leaned over the rail of the veranda, her chin on her hand. Sanford watched her, following the bend of her exquisite head and the marvelous slope of her shoulders. He saw that something unusual had stirred her, but he could not decide whether it was caused by the thought of Betty's misery or by some fresh sorrow of her own. He threw away his cigar, rose from his chair, and joined her at the railing. He could be unhappy himself and stand up under it, but he could not bear to see a shade cross Kate's face.

"You are not happy to-night," he said.

She did not answer.

Sanford waited, looking down over the garden. He could see the shadowy outlines of the narrow walks and the white faces of the roses drooping over the gravel. When he spoke again there were hesitating, halting tones in his voice, as if he were half afraid to follow the course he had dared to venture on.

"Is Morgan coming home, Kate?"

"I don't know," she replied dreamily, after a pause.

"Didn't he say in his last letter?"

"Oh yes; answered as he always does,—when he gets through."

"Where is he now?"

"Paris, I believe."

She had not moved nor lifted her chin from her hand.

Minutes went by without her speaking again. A strange hush fell about them. Sanford could hear the click of the old clock in the hall, and the monotonous song of the crickets in the grass below.

A sense of great remoteness from her came over him. It was as though she had gone into a room alone with her griefs and her sobs, and had locked the door behind her. He had not meant to wound her by his questions, only to discover whether some new phase of the old grief were hurting her. If it were anything else but the sorrow he never touched, he stood ready to give her all his strength.

He looked at her intently. She had never appeared to him so beautiful, so pathetic: there was a hopeless weariness in her pose that vibrated through him as nothing had done in months. The change in her mood had come suddenly, as all changes did in her, but to-night he seemed unable to meet them. A great rush of feeling surged over him. He stepped closer, lifting his hand to lay on her head. Then, with an abrupt gesture, he turned and began pacing the veranda, his head bowed, his hands clasped behind his back. Strange, unutterable thoughts whirled through his brain; unbidden, unspeakable words crowded in his throat. He made one great effort at self-control, stopped once more, this time laying his hand upon her shoulder. He felt in his heart that it was the same old sorrow which now racked her, but an uncontrollable impulse swept him on. All the restraint of years seemed slipping from him.

"Kate, what is it? You break my heart. Is there something else to worry you, — something you have n't told me?"

She shivered slightly as she felt the hand tighten on her shoulder. Then a sudden, tingling thrill ran through her.

"I have never any right to be unhappy when I have you, Henry. You are all the world to me, — all I have."

It was not the answer he had expected. For an instant the blood left his face, his heart stood still.

Kate raised her head, and their eyes met.

There are narrow paths in life where one fatal step sends a man headlong. There are eyes in women's heads as deep as the abyss below. Hers were wide open, with the fearless confidence of an affection she was big enough to give. He saw down into their depths, and read there — as they flashed toward him in intermittent waves over the barrier of the reserve she sometimes held — love, truth, and courage. To disturb these, even by the sympathy she longed to receive and he to give, might, he knew, endanger the ideal of that loyalty to another in her which he venerated most. To go behind it and break down the wall of that self-control of hers which held in check the unknown, untouched springs of her heart might loosen a flood that would wreck the only bark which could keep them both afloat on the troubled waters of life, — their friendship.

Sanford bent his head, raised her hand to his lips, kissed it reverently, and without a word walked slowly toward his chair.

As he regained his seat the butler pushed aside the light curtains of the veranda, and in his regulation monotone announced, "Miss Shirley, Major Slocomb, and Mr. Hardy."

"My dear madam," broke out the major in his breeziest manner, before Mrs. Leroy could turn to greet him, "what would life be in this bake-oven of a city but for the joy of yo'r presence? And Henry! You here, too? Do you know that that rascal Jack has kept me waiting for two hours while he took Helen for a five minutes' walk round the square, or I would have been here long ago. Where are you, you young dog?" he called to Jack, who had lingered in the darkened hall with Helen.

"What's the matter now, major?" inquired Jack, shaking hands with Mrs. Leroy, and turning again toward the Pocomokian. "I asked your permission. What would you have me do? Let Helen see nothing of New York, because you"—

"Do hush up, cousin Tom," said Helen, pursing her lips at the major. "We stayed out because we wanted to, did n't we, Jack? Don't you think he is a perfect ogre, Mrs. Leroy?"

"He forgets his own younger days, my dear Miss Shirley," she answered. "He shan't scold you. Henry, make the major join you in a cigar, while I give Miss Helen a cup of coffee."

"They are both forgiven, my dear madam, when so lovely an advocate pleads their cause," said the Pocomokian grandiloquently, bowing low, his hand on his chest. "Thank you; I will join you," and leaned over Sanford as he spoke, and lighted a cigar in the blue flame of the tiny silver lamp.

It was delightful to note how the coming alliance of the Hardy and Slocomb families had developed the paternal, not to say patriarchal attitude of the major toward his once boon companion. He already regarded Jack as his own son,—somebody to lean upon in his declining years, a prop and a staff for his old age. He had even sketched out in his mind a certain stately mansion on the avenue, to say nothing of a series of country-seats,—one on Crab

Island in the Chesapeake, — all with porticoes and an especial suite of rooms on the ground floor; and he could hear Jack say, as he pointed them out to his visitors, "These are for my dear old friend Major Slocomb of Pocomoke, — member of my wife's family." He could see his old enemy, Jefferson, Jack's servant, cowed into respectful obedience by the new turn in his master's affairs, in which the Pocomokian had lent so helpful a hand.

"She is the child of my old age, so to speak, suh, and I, of co'se, gave my consent after great hesitation," he would frequently say, fully persuading himself that Helen had really sought his approbation, and never for one moment dreaming that, grateful as she was to him for his chaperonage of her while in New York, he was the last person in the world she would have consulted in any matter so vital to her happiness.

Jack accepted the change in the major's manner with the same good humor that seasoned everything that came to him in life. He had known the Pocomokian for too many years to misunderstand him now, and this new departure, with its patronizing airs and fatherly oversight, only amused him.

Mrs. Leroy had drawn the young girl toward the divan, and was already discussing her plans for the summer.

"Of course you are both to come to me this

fall, when the beautiful Indian summer weather sets in. The Pines is never so lovely as then. You shall sail to your heart's content, for the yacht is in order; and we will then see what this great engineer has been doing all summer," she added, glancing timidly from under her dark eyelashes at Sanford. "Mr. Leroy's last instructions were to keep the yacht in commission until he came home. I am determined you shall have one more good time, Miss Helen, before this young man ties you hand and foot. You will come, major?"

"I cannot promise, madam. It will depend entirely on my arrangin' some very important matters of business. I hope to be able to come for perhaps a day or so."

Jack looked at Sanford and smiled. Evidently Mrs. Leroy did not know the length of the major's "day or so." Nor that it was apt to depend upon the date of the next invitation. He was still staying with Jack, and had been there since the spring.

Buckles, the butler, had been bending over the major as that gentleman delivered himself of this announcement of his hopes. When he had filled to the brim the tiny liqueur glass, the major — perhaps in a moment of forgetfulness — said, "Thank you, suh," at which Buckles's face hardened. Such slips were not infrequent. The major was, in fact, always a little uncomfortable in Buckles's presence. Jack, who had often noticed his attitude, thought that these conciliatory remarks were intended as palliatives to the noiseless English flunky with the immovable face and impenetrable manner. The Pocomokian never extended such deference to Sam, Sanford's own servant, or even to Jefferson. "Here, Sam, you black scoundrel, bring me my hat," he would say whenever he was leaving Sanford's apartments, at which Sam's face would relax quite as much as Buckles's had hardened. But then the major knew Sam's kind, and Sam knew the major, and, strange to say, believed in him.

When Buckles had retired, Sanford started the Pocomokian on a discussion in which all the talking would fall to the latter's share. Mrs. Leroy turned to Helen and Jack again. There was no trace, in her voice nor on her features, of the emotion that had so stirred her. All that side of her nature had been shut away the moment her guests appeared.

"Don't mind a word Jack says to you, my dear, about hurrying up the wedding-day," she laughed, in a half-earnest and altogether charming way, — not cynical, but with a certain undercurrent of genuine anxiety in her voice, all the more keenly felt by Sanford, who waited on every word that fell from her lips. "Put it off as long as possible. So many troubles and disappointments come afterwards, and it is so hard to keep everything as it should be. There is no happier time in life than that just before marriage. Oh, you need n't scowl at me, you young Bluebeard; I know all about it, and you don't know one little bit."

Helen looked at Jack in some wonder. She was at a loss to know how much of the talk was pure badinage, and how much, perhaps, the result of some bitter worldly experience. The young girl shuddered, yet without knowing what inspired the remark or what lay behind it. But she laughed quite heartily, as she said, "It is all true, no doubt; only I intend to begin by being something of a tyrant myself, don't I, Jack?"

Before Jack could reply, Smearly, who had hurried by Buckles, entered unannounced, and with a general smile of recognition, and two fingers to the major, settled himself noiselessly in an easy-chair, and reached over the silver tray for a cup. It was a house where such freedom was not commented on, and Smearly was one of those big Newfoundland-dog kind of visitors who avail themselves of all privileges.

"What is the subject under discussion?" the painter asked, as he dropped a lump of sugar into his cup and turned to his hostess.

"I have just been telling Miss Shirley how happy she will make us when she comes to The Pines this autumn."

"And you have consented, of course?" he inquired carelessly, lifting his bushy eyebrows.

"Oh yes," answered Helen, a faint shadow settling for a moment on her face. "It's so kind of Mrs. Leroy to want me. You are coming, too, are you not, Mr. Sanford?" and she moved toward Henry's end of the divan, where Jack followed her. She had never liked Smearly. She did not know why, but he always affected her strangely. "He looks like a bear," she once told Jack, "with his thick neck and his restless movements."

"Certainly, Miss Helen, I am going, too," replied Sanford. "I tolerate my work all summer in expectation of these few weeks in the autumn."

The young girl raised her eyes quickly. Somehow it did not sound to her like Sanford's voice. There was an unaccustomed sense of strain in it. She moved a little nearer to him, however, impelled by some subtle sympathy for the man who was not only Jack's friend, but one she trusted as well.

"Lovely to be so young and hopeful, isn't it?" said Mrs. Leroy to Smearly, with a movement of her head toward Helen. "Look at those two. Nothing but rainbows for her and Jack."

"Rainbows come after the storm, my dear lady, not before," rejoined Smearly. "If they have any prismatics in theirs, they will appear in a year or two from now." He had lowered his voice so that Helen should not hear.

"You never believe in anything. You hate women," said Mrs. Leroy impatiently in an undertone.

"True, but with some exceptions; you, for instance," with a mock bow. "But why fool ourselves, my dear lady? The first year is one of sugar-plums, flowers, and canary-birds. We can't keep our hands off them; we love them so we want to eat them up."

"Just like any other wild beast," interrupted Mrs. Leroy, with a gurgling laugh, her head bent coquettishly on one side.

"The second year both are pulling in opposite directions." (He affected not to have heard her thrust.) "Then comes a snap of the matrimonial cord, and over they go. Of course neither of these two turtle-doves has the slightest idea of anything of the kind. They expect to go on and on and on, like the dear little babes in the wood; but they won't, all the same. Some day an old crow of an attorney will come and cover them over with dried briefs, and that will be the last of it."

Sanford took no part in the general talk. He was listless, absorbed. He felt an irresistible desire to be alone, and stayed on only because Helen's many little confidences, told to him in her girlish way, as she sat beside him on the divan, required but an acquiescing nod now and then, or a random reply, which he could give without betraying himself.

He was first of all the guests to rise. In response to Mrs. Leroy's anxious glance, as he bade her good-night between the veranda curtains, he explained, in tones loud enough to be heard by everybody, that it was necessary to make an early start in the morning for the Ledge, and that he had some important letters to write that night.

"Don't forget to telegraph me if you get the certificate," was all she said.

Helen and Jack followed Sanford. They too wanted to be alone; that is, together,— in their case the same thing.

Once outside and under the trees of the park, Helen stopped in a secluded spot, their shadows under the electric light flecking the pavement, took the lapels of Jack's coat in her hands, and said, "Jack, dear, I wasn't happy there to-night. She never could have loved anybody."

"Who, darling?"

"Why, Mrs. Leroy. Did you hear what she said?"

"Yes, but it was only Kate. That's her way, Helen. She never means half she says."

"Yes, but the *way* she said it, Jack. She doesn't know what love means. Loving is not being angry all the time. Loving is helping,— helping everywhere and in everything. Whatever either needs the other gives. I can't say it just as I want to, but you know what I mean.

And that Mr. Smearly; he did n't think I heard, but I did."

"Dear heart," said Jack, smoothing her cheek with his hand, "don't believe everything you hear. You are not accustomed to the ways of these people. Down in your own home in Maryland people mean what they say; here they don't. Smearly is all right. He was 'talking through his hat,' as the boys say at the club, — that's all. You'd think, to hear him go on, that he was a sour, crabbed old curmudgeon, now, would n't you? Well, you never were more mistaken in your life. Every penny he can save he gives to an old sister of his, who has n't seen a well day for years. That's only his talk."

"But why does he speak that way, then? When people love as they ought to love, every time a disappointment in the other comes, it is just one more opportunity to help, — not a cause for ridicule. I love you that way, Jack; don't you love me so?" and she looked up into his eyes.

"I love you a million ways, you sweet girl," and, with a rapid glance about him to see that no one was near, he slipped his arm about her and held her close to his breast.

He felt himself lifted out of the atmosphere of romance in which he had lived for months. This gentle, shrinking Southern child whom he had loved and petted and smothered with roses, this tender, clinging girl who trusted him so implicitly, was no longer his sweetheart, but his helpmate. She had all at once become a woman, — strong, courageous, clear-minded, helpful, ready to lead him if need be.

A new feeling rose in his heart and spread itself through every fibre of his being, — a feeling without which love is a plaything. It was reverence.

When Sanford reached his apartments Sam was waiting for him, as usual. The candles were lighted instead of the lamp. The windows of the balcony were wide open.

"You need not wait, Sam; I'll close the blinds," he said, as he stepped out and sank into a chair.

Long after Sam had gone he sat there without moving, his head bent, his forehead resting on his hand. He was trying to pick up the threads of his life again, to find the old pattern which had once guided him in his course, and to clear it from the tangle of lines that had suddenly twisted and confused him.

For a long time he saw nothing but Kate's eyes as they had met his own, with the possibilities which he had read in their depths. He tried to drive the picture from him; then baffled by its persistence he resolutely faced it; held it as it were in his hands, and, looking long and unflinchingly at it, summoned all his courage.

He had read Kate's heart in her face. He knew that he had revealed his own. But he meant that the future should be unaffected by the revelations made. The world must never share her confidence nor his, as it would surely do at their first false step. It should not have the right to turn and look, and to wonder at the woman whom he was proud to love. That open fearlessness which all who knew her gloried in should still be hers. He realized the value of it to her, and what its loss would entail should a spoken word of his rob her of it, or any momentary weakness of theirs deprive her of the strength and comfort which his open companionship could give.

No! God willing, he would stand firm, and so should she.

An hour later he was still there, his unlighted cigar between his lips, his head on his hands.

CHAPTER XVI

UNDER THE WILLOWS

THE mile or more of shore skirting the curve of Keyport harbor from Keyport Village to Captain Joe's cottage was lighted by only four street lamps. Three of these were hung on widely scattered telegraph-poles; the fourth was nailed fast to one end of old Captain Potts's fish-house.

When the nights were moonless, these faithful sentinels, with eyes alert, scanned the winding road, or so much of it as their lances could protect, watching over deep culverts, and in one place guarded a treacherous bridge without a rail.

When the nights were cloudy and the lantern-panes were dimmed by the driving sleet, these beacons confined their efforts to pointing out for the stumbling wayfarer the deep puddles or the higher rows of soggy seaweed washed up by the last high tide into the highway itself. Only on thick nights, when the fog-drift stole in from the still sea, and even Keyport Light burned dim, did their scouting rays retreat discomfited, illumining nothing but the poles on which the lanterns hung.

Yet in spite of this vigilance there were still long stretches of road between, which even on clear nights were dark as graveyards and as lonesome. Except for the ruddy gleam slanted across the path from some cabin window, or the glare of a belated villager's swinging lantern flecking the pale, staring fences with seesawing lights and shadows, not a light was visible.

Betty knew every foot of this road. She had trundled her hoop on it, her hair flying in the wind, when she first came to Keyport to school. She had trodden it many a time with Caleb; had idled along its curves with Lacey before the day when her life came to an end, and had plodded over it many a weary hour since, as she went to her work in the village or returned to Captain Joe's. Every stone and tree and turn were familiar to her, and she could have found her way in the pitch-dark to the captain's or to Caleb's, just as she had done again and again in the days before the street lights were set, or when Caleb would be standing on the porch, if she were late, shading his eyes and peering down the road, the kitchen lamp in his hand. "I was gittin' worried, little woman; what kep' ye?" he would say. She had never been afraid in those days, no matter what the hour. Everybody knew her. "Oh, that's you, Mis' West, is it? I kind o' mistrusted it was," would come from some shadowy figure across the road.

UNDER THE WILLOWS

All this was changed for her now. There were places along the highway that made her draw her shawl closer, often half hiding her face. She would shudder as she turned the corner by the church, the one where the captain and Aunty Bell had taken her the first Sunday after her coming back. The big, gloomy oil warehouse where she had nursed Lacey seemed to her haunted and uncanny, and at night more gloomy than ever without a ray of light in any one of its broken, staring windows. Even the fishing-smacks, anchored out of harm's way for the night, looked gruesome and mysterious, with single lights aloft, and black hulls and masts reflected in the water. It was never until she reached the willows that her agitation disappeared. These grew just opposite Captain Potts's fish-house. There were three of them, and their branches interlocked and spread across the road, the spaces between the trunks being black at night, despite the one street lamp nailed to the fish-house across the way. When Betty gained these trees her breath always came freer. She could then see along the whole road, away past Captain Joe's, and up the hill. She could see, too, Caleb's cabin from this spot, and the lamp burning in the kitchen window. She knew who was sitting beside it. From these willows, also, she could run for Captain Joe's swinging gate with its big ball and chain, getting safely inside before Caleb could pass and see her, if by any chance he should be on the road and coming to the village. Once she had met him this side of their dark shadows. It was on a Saturday, and he was walking into the village, his basket on his arm. He was going for his Sunday supplies, no doubt. The Ledge gang must have come in sooner than usual, for it was early twilight. She had seen him coming a long way off, and had looked about for some means of escape. There was no mistaking his figure. She would know him as far as she could see him, — that strong, broad figure, with the awkward, stiff walk peculiar to so many seafaring men, particularly lightship-keepers like Caleb, who have walked but little. She knew, too, the outline of the big, fluffy beard that the wind caught and blew over his ruddy face. No one could be like her Caleb but himself.

These chance meetings she dreaded with a fear she could not overcome. On this last occasion, finding no concealing shelter, she had kept on, her eyes on the ground. When Caleb had passed, his blue eyes staring straight ahead, his face drawn and white, the lips pressed close, she turned and looked after him, and he turned, too, and looked after her, — these two, man and wife, within reach of each other's arms and lips, yet with only the longing hunger of a dead happiness in their eyes. She could have run toward him, and knelt down in the road, and begged him to forgive her and take her home again, had not Captain Joe's words restrained her: "Caleb says he ain't got nothin' agin ye, child, but he won't take ye back s' long 's he lives."

Because, then, of the dread of these chance meetings, and because of the shy looks of many of the villagers, who, despite Captain Joe's daily fight, still passed her with but a slight nod of recognition, she was less unhappy when she walked the road at night than in the daylight. The chance of being recognized was less. Caleb might pass her in the dark and not see her, and then, too, there were fewer people passing after dark.

On the Saturday night succeeding that on which they had met and looked at each other, she determined to wait until it was quite dark. He would have come in then, and she could slip out from the shop where she worked and gain the shore road before he had finished making his purchases in the village.

Her heart had been very heavy all day. The night before she had left her own bed and tapped at Aunty Bell's door, and had crept under the coverlid beside the little woman, the captain being at the Ledge, and had had one of her hearty cries, sobbing on the elder woman's neck, her arms about her, her cheek to hers. She had gone over with her for the hundredth time all the misery of her position, wondering what would become of her; and how hard it was for Caleb to do all his work alone, — washing his clothes and cooking his meals just as he had done on board the lightship; pouring out her heart until she fell asleep from sheer exhaustion. All of her thoughts were centred in him and his troubles. She longed to go back to Caleb to take care of him. It was no longer to be taken care of, but to care for him.

As she hurried through the streets, after leaving the shop, and gained the corner leading to the shore road, she glanced up and down, fearing to see the sturdy figure with the basket. But there was no one in sight whom she knew. At this discovery she slackened her steps and looked around more quietly. When she reached the bend in the road, a flash of light from an open door in a cabin near by gave her a momentary glimpse of a housewife bending over a stove and a man putting a dinner-pail on the kitchen table. Then all was dark again. It was but a momentary glimpse of a happiness the possibility of which in her own life she had wrecked, but it sent the blood tingling to her face. She stopped, steadying herself by the stone wall, then she walked on.

When she passed into the black shadows of the overhanging willows, a man stepped from behind a tree-trunk.

"Are n't you rather late this evening?" he asked.

Betty stood still, the light of the street lamp full on her face. The abruptness of the sound startled her.

"Oh, you needn't be afraid; I'm not going to hurt you."

The girl peered into the gloom. She thought the voice was familiar, though she was not sure. She could distinguish only a shadowy face.

"What makes you so skittish, anyhow?" the man asked again, — in a lower tone this time. "You didn't use to be so. I thought maybe you might like to drive over to Medford and see the show to-night."

Betty made no answer, but she took a step nearer to him, trying to identify him. She was not afraid; only curious. Then all at once it occurred to her that it could be for no good purpose he had stopped her. None of the men had spoken to her in the street, even in the daytime, since her return home.

"Please let me pass," she said quietly and firmly.

"Oh, you needn't be in a hurry. We've got all night. Come along, now, won't you? You used to like me once, before you shook the old man."

Betty knew him now!

The terror of her position overcame her; a deathly faintness seized her.

She saw it all; she knew why this man dared. She realized the loneliness and desolation of her position, poor child that she was. Every cabin near her filled with warmth and cheer and comfort, and she friendless and alone! Not a woman near but had the strong arm of husband or brother to help and defend her. The very boats in the harbor, with their beacon-lights aloft, protected and safe. Only she in danger; only she unguarded, waylaid, open to insult, even by a man like this.

She stood shivering, looking into his cowardly face. Then rousing herself to her peril, she sprang toward the road. In an instant the man had seized her wrist. She felt his hot breath on her face.

"Oh, come now, none of that! Say, why ain't I as good as Bill Lacey? Give me a kiss."

"Let me go! *Let me go!* How dare you!" she cried, struggling in his grasp. When she found his strength gaining on her, she screamed.

Hardly had she made her outcry, when from behind the fish-house a man with a flowing beard darted into the shadows, flung himself on Betty's assailant, and dragged him out under the glare of the street lamp. The girl fled up the road without looking behind.

"That's what ye're up to, is it, Mr. Carleton?" said the man, holding the other with the grip of a steel vise. "I 'spected as much when I see ye passin' my place. Damn ye! If it warn't that it would be worse for her, I'd kill ye!"

Every muscle in the speaker's body was tense with anger. Carleton's head was bent back, his face livid from the pressure of his assailant's fingers twisted about his throat.

The man slowly relaxed his hold. "Ain't she got trouble 'nough without havin' a skunk like you a-runnin' foul o' her?"

Carleton made a quick gesture as if to spring aside and run. The diver saw the movement and stepped in front of him.

"Ain't ye ashamed o' yerself? Ain't it mean o' ye to make up to a gal like Betty?" His voice was low and measured.

"What's it your business, anyhow?" Carleton gasped between his breaths, shaking himself like a tousled dog. "What are you putting on frills about her for, anyhow? She's nothing to you, if she is your wife. I guess I know what I'm doing."

Caleb's fingers grew hard and rigid as claws.

"So do I know what ye're a-doin'. Ye'd drag that child down an' stomp on her, if ye could. Ye'd make a *thing* of her," — the words came with a hiss, — "you — you — callin' yerself a man!"

"Why don't you take care of her, then?" snarled Carleton, with an assumed air of composure, as he adjusted his collar and cuffs.

"That's what I'm here for; that's why I

follered ye; there ain't a night since it begun to git dark I ain't watched her home. She's not yourn; she's mine. Look at me,"—Caleb stepped closer and raised his clinched fist. "If ever ye speak to her agin, so help me God, I *will* kill ye!"

With one swing of his arm he threw the superintendent out of his way, and strode up the street.

Carleton staggered from the blow, and would have fallen but for the wall of the fish-house. For a moment he stood in the road looking after Caleb's retreating figure. Then, with a forced bravado in his voice, he called out in the darkness, "If you think so damn much of her, why don't you take her home?" and slunk away toward the village.

The old man did not turn. If he heard, he made no sign. He walked on, with his head down, his eyes on the road. As he passed Captain Joe's he loitered at the gate until he saw the light flash up in Betty's bedroom; then he kept on to his own cabin.

CHAPTER XVII

THE SONG OF THE FIRE

THE fire was nearly out when Caleb entered his kitchen door and drew a chair to the stove. Carleton's taunting words, "Why don't you take her home?" rang in his ears. Their sting hurt him. Everything else seemed to fall away from his mind. He knew why he did not take her home, he said to himself; every one else knew why, — every one up and down Keyport knew what Betty had done to ruin him. If she was friendless, tramping the road, within sight of her own house, whose fault was it? Not his. He had never done anything but love her and take care of her.

He reached for a pair of tongs, stirred the coals, and threw on a single piece of driftwood. The fire blazed up brightly at once, its light flickering on the diver's ruddy face, and as quickly died out.

"Why don't I take care of 'er, eh? Why did n't she take care of herself?" he cried aloud, gazing into the smouldering embers. "She sees what it is now trampin' the road nights, runnin' up agin such curs as him. He's a nice un, he is. I wish I'd choked the life out'er him; such fellers ain't no right to live," looking about him as if he expected to find Carleton behind the door, and as quickly recovering himself. "I wonder if he hurt 'er," — his voice had softened. "She screamed turrible. I ought, maybe, to 'a' ketched up to her. Poor little gal, she ain't used to this." He was silent awhile, his head bent, his shoulders updrawn, his big frame stretched out in the chair.

"She ain't nothin' but a child, anyhow," he broke out again, — "Cap'n Joe says so. He says I don't think o' this; maybe he's right. He says I'm bigger an' twice as old's she be, an' ought'er know more; that it ain't me she's hurted, — it's herself; that I married her to take care of 'er; and that the fust time she got in a hole I go back on 'er, 'cause she's dragged me in arter 'er. Well, ain't I a-takin' care of 'er? Ain't I split squar' in two every cent I've earned since she run away with that" —

Caleb paused abruptly. Even to himself he never mentioned Lacey's name. Bending forward he poked the fire vigorously, raking the coals around the single stick of driftwood. "It's all very well for th' cap'n to talk; he ain't gone through what I have."

Pushing back his chair he paced the small room, talking to himself as he walked, pausing to address his sentences to the several articles of furniture, — the chairs, the big table, the kitchen sink, whatever came in his way. It was an old trick of his when alone. "I ain't a-goin' to have 'er come home so late no more," he continued. His voice had sunk to a gentle whisper. "I'm goin' to tell them folks she works for that they've got to let 'er out afore dark, or she shan't stay." He was looking now at an old rocker as if it were the shopkeeper himself. "She'll be so scared arter this she won't have a minute's peace. She needn't worrit herself, though, 'bout that skunk. She's shut o' *him*. But there'll be more of 'em. They all think that now I've throwed 'er off they kin do as they've a mind to." He stopped again and gazed down at the floor, seemingly absorbed in a hole in one of the planks. "Cap'n Joe sez I ain't got no business to throw 'er off. He wouldn't treat a dog so, — that's what ye said, cap'n; I ain't never goin' to forgit it. *I* ain't throwed *her* off. She throwed *me* off, — lef' me here without a word; an' ye know it, cap'n. Ye want me to take 'er back, do ye?" He spoke with as much earnestness as though the captain stood before him. "S'pose I do, an' she finds out arter all that her comin' home was 'cause she was skeared of it all, and that she still loved" —

He stopped, reseated himself, and picking up another stick threw it on the fire, snuggling the two together. The sticks, cheered by each other's warmth, burst into a crackling flame.

"Poor little Betty!" he began again aloud. "I'm sorry for ye. Everybody's agin ye, child, 'cept Cap'n Joe's folks. I know it hurts ye turrible to have folks look away from ye. Ye always loved to have folks love ye. I ain't got nothin' agin ye, child, indeed I ain't. It was my fault, not yourn. I told Cap'n Joe so; ask him, — he'll tell ye." He turned toward the empty chair beside him, as if he saw her sad face there. "I know it's hard, child," shaking his head. "Ain't nobody feels it more 'n me, — ain't nobody feels it more 'n me. I guess I must take care o' ye; I guess there ain't nobody else but me kin do it."

The logs blazed cheerily; the whole room was alight. "I wish ye loved me like ye did onct, little woman, — I wouldn't want no better happiness; jest me an' you, like it useter was. I wonder if ye do? No, I know ye don't." The last words came with a positive tone.

For a long time he remained still, gazing at the blazing logs locked together, the flames dancing about them. Then he got up and roamed mechanically around the room, his thoughts away with Betty and her helpless condition, and her rightful dependence on him. In the same dreary way he opened the cupboard, took out a piece of cold meat and some slices of stale bread, laying them on the table, poured some tea into a cup and put it on the stove; it was easier making the tea that way than in a pot. He drew the table toward the fire, so that his supper would be within reach, stirring the brewing tea meanwhile with a fork he had in his hand, and began his frugal meal. Since Betty left he had never set the table. It seemed less lonely to eat this way.

Just as he had finished there came a knock at the front door. Caleb started, and put down his cup. Who could come at this hour? Craning his head toward the small open hall, he saw through the glass in the door the outlines of a woman's figure approaching him through the hall. His face flushed, and his heart seemed to jump in his throat.

"It's me, Caleb," said the woman. "It's Aunty Bell. The door was open, so I did n't wait. Cap'n sent me up all in a hurry. He's jes' come in from the Ledge, and hollered to me from the tug to send up and get ye. The pump's broke on the big h'ister. A new one's got to be cast to-night and bored out to-morrer, if it *is* Sunday. Cap'n says everything's stopped at the Ledge, and they can't do another stroke till this pump's fixed. Were n't nobody home but Betty, and so I come myself. Come right along; he wants ye at the machine shop jes' 's quick as ye kin git there."

Caleb kept his seat and made no reply. Something about the shock of discovering who the woman was had stunned him. He did not try to explain it to himself; he was conscious only of a vague yet stinging sense of disappointment. Automatically, like a trained soldier obeying a command, he bent forward in his chair, drew his thick shoes from under the stove, slipped his feet into them, and silently followed Aunty Bell out of the house and down the road. When they reached Captain Joe's gate he looked up at Betty's window. There was no light.

"Has Betty gone to bed?" he asked quietly.

"Yes, more 'n an hour ago. She come home late, all tuckered out. I see 'er jes' before I come out. She said she warn't sick, but she would n't eat nothin'."

Caleb paused, looked at her as if he were about to speak again, hesitated, then, without a word, walked away.

"Stubborn as a mule," said Aunty Bell, looking after him. "I ain't got no patience with such men."

CHAPTER XVIII

THE EQUINOCTIAL GALE

WHEN Sanford arrived at Keyport, a raw, southeast gale swept through the deserted streets. About the wharves of the village itself idle stevedores lounged under dripping roofs, watching the cloud-rack and speculating on the chances of going to work. Out in the harbor the fishing-boats rocked uneasily, their long, red pennants flattened against the sky. Now and then a frightened sloop came hurrying in with close-reefed jib, sousing her bow under at every plunge.

Away off in the open a dull gray mist, churned up by the tumbling waves, dimmed the horizon, blurring here and there a belated coaster laboring heavily under bare poles, while from Crotch Island way came the roar of the pounding surf dashed headlong on the beach. The long-expected equinoctial storm was at its height.

So fierce and so searching were the wind and rain that Sanford was thoroughly drenched when he reached Captain Joe's cottage.

"For the land's sake, Mr. Sanford, come right

in! Why, ye 're jest 's soakin' as though ye 'd fell off the dock. Cap'n said ye was a-comin', but I hoped ye would n't. I ain't never see it blow so terrible, I don't know when. Gimme that overcoat," slipping it from his shoulders and arms. "Be yer feet wet?"

"Pretty wet, Mrs. Bell. I 'll go up to my room and get some dry socks" —

"Ye ain't a-goin' to move one step. Set right down an' get them shoes off. I 'll go for the socks myself. I overhauled 'em last week with the cap'n's, and sot a new toe in one o' them. I won't be a minute!" she cried, hurrying out of the room, and returning with heavy woolen socks and a white worsted sweater.

"Guess ye 'll want these, too, sir," she said, picking up a pair of slippers.

"Where is Captain Joe?" asked Sanford, as he pulled off his wet shoes and stockings and moved closer to the fire. It was an every-day scene in Aunty Bell's kitchen, where one half of her visitors were wet half the time, and the other half wet all the time.

"I don't jes' know. He ain't been home sence Saturday night but jes' long 'nough to change his clothes an' git a bite to eat. Come in from the Ledge Saturday night on the tug two hours after the Screamer brought in the men, an' hollered to me to go git Caleb ah' come down to the machine shop. You heared they broke the pump on the h'istin'-engine, did n't ye? They both been a-workin' on it pretty much ever sence."

"Not the big hoister?" Sanford exclaimed, with a start, turning pale.

"Well, that's what the cap'n said, sir. He an' Caleb worked all Saturday night an' Sunday, an' got a new castin' made, an' bored it out yesterday. I told him he would n't have no luck, workin' on Sunday, but he did n't pay no more 'tention to me than th' wind a-blowin'. It was to be done this mornin'. He was up at five, an' I ain't seen him sence. Said he was goin' to git to the Ledge in Cap'n Potts' cat-boat, if it mod'rated."

"He won't go," said Sanford, with a sigh of relief now that he knew the break had been repaired without delay. "No cat-boat can live outside to-day."

"Well, all I know is, I heared him tell Lonny Bowles to ask Cap'n Potts for it 'fore they went out," she replied, as she hung Sanford's socks on a string especially reserved for such emergencies. "Said they had two big cut stone to set, an' they could n't get a pound o' steam on the Ledge till he brought the pump back."

Sanford instinctively looked out of the window. The rain beat against the panes. The boom of the surf sounded like distant cannon.

"Ye can't do nothin' with him when he gits one o' his spells on, noways," continued Aunty Bell, as she raked out the coals. "Jes' wait till I grind some fresh coffee, — won't take a minute. Then I'll git breakfast for ye."

Sanford stepped into the sitting-room, closed the door, took off his coat and waistcoat, loosened his collar, pulled on the sweater, and came back into the kitchen, looking like a substitute in a game of football. He always kept a stock of such dry luxuries in his little room upstairs, Aunty Bell looking after them as she did after the captain's, and these rapid changes of dress were not unusual.

"How does Betty get on?" asked Sanford, drawing up a chair to the table. The bustling little woman was bringing relays of bread, butter, and other comforts, flitting between the pantry and the stove.

"Pretty peaked, sir; ye would n't know her, poor little girl; it 'd break yer heart to see her," she answered, as she placed a freshly baked pie on the table. "She's upstairs now. Cap'n would n't let her git up an' go to work this mornin', it blowed so. That's her now a-comin' downstairs."

Sanford rose and held out his hand. He had not seen Betty since the memorable night when she had stood in his hallway, and he had taken her to Mrs. Leroy's. He had been but seldom at the captain's of late, going straight to the Ledge from the train, and had always missed her.

Betty started back, and her color came and

went when she saw who it was. She did n't know anybody was downstairs, she said half apologetically, addressing her words to Aunty Bell, her eyes averted from Sanford's face.

"Why, Betty, I'm glad to see you!" exclaimed Sanford in a cheery tone, his mind going back to Mrs. Leroy's admonition.

Betty raised her eyes with a timid, furtive glance, her face flushed scarlet, but, reading Sanford's entire sincerity in his face, she laid her hand in his, saying it was a bad day, and that she hoped he was not wet. Then she turned to help Mrs. Bell with the table.

Sanford watched her slight figure and careworn face as she moved about the room — hardly a trace in them of the Betty of old. When Aunty Bell had gone down into the cellar, he called Betty to him and said in a low voice, "I have a message for you."

She turned quickly, as if anticipating some unwelcome revelation.

"Mrs. Leroy told me to give you her love."

Betty's eyes filled. "Is that what she said, Mr. Sanford?"

"Every word, Betty, and she means it all."

The girl stood fingering the handles of the knives she had just laid upon the cloth. After a pause, Sanford's eyes still upon her face, she answered slowly, with a pathos that went straight home to his heart: —

"Tell her, please, sir, that I thank her so

much, and that I never forget her. I am trying so hard — so hard — I promised her I would. You don't know, Mr. Sanford, — nobody won't never know how good she was to me. If I'd been her sister she could n't 'a' done no more."

It was but a slight glimpse of the girl's real nature, but it settled for Sanford all the misgivings he had had. It sent a quiver through him, too, as his mind reverted to Kate's own account of the interview. He was about to tell her of Mrs. Leroy's expected arrival at Medford, and urge her to go over some Sunday, when Aunty Bell bustled in with a covered dish.

"Come, child," she said, "sit right down alongside o' Mr. Sanford an' git your breakfas'. You ain't eat a morsel yet."

There were no seats of honor and no second table in this house, except for those who came late.

Here a sharp, quick knock sounded on the outer door, and in stalked Captain Bob Brandt, six feet or more of wet oilskins, the rain dripping from his sou'wester, his rosy, good-natured face peering out from under the puckered brim.

"Cap'n Joe sent me down to the station for ye, sir, in case ye come, but I missed ye, somehow. Mr. Carleton was on the platform, an' said he see ye git off. Guess ye must 'a' come cross lots."

"Did Mr. Carleton mention anything about

receiving a telegram from me, saying I wanted to see him?" inquired Sanford, as he shook the skipper's hand.

"Yes, sir; said he knew yer was comin', but that he was goin' over to Medford till the storm was over."

Sanford's brow knit. Carleton had evidently avoided him.

"Did he leave any message or letter with Captain Joe?" Sanford asked, after a pause. He still hoped that the coveted certificate had finally been signed.

"Guess not, sir. Don't think he see 'im. I suppose ye know Cap'n Joe's gone to the Ledge with the new pump?"

"Not in this storm?" cried Sanford, a look of alarm overspreading his face.

"Yes, sir, half an hour ago, in Cap'n Potts' Dolly. I watched 'em till they run under the P'int, then I come for you; guess that's what got me late. She was under double reefs then, an' a-smashin' things for all she was worth. I tell ye, 't ain't no good place out there for nobody, not even Cap'n Joe." As he spoke he took off his hat and thrashed the water from it against the jamb of the door. "No, thank ye, ma'am," with a wave of his hand in answer to Mrs. Bell's gesture to sit down opposite Betty. "I had breakfast 'board the Screamer."

"Who's with him?" exclaimed Sanford, now really uneasy. Captain Joe's personal safety was worth more to him than the completion of a dozen lighthouses.

"Caleb and Lonny Bowles. They 'd go anywheres cap'n told 'em. He was holdin' tiller when I see him last; Caleb layin' back on the sheet and Lonny bailin'. Cap'n said he would n't 'a' risked it, only we was behind an' he did n't want ye worried. I 'm kind'er sorry they started; it ain't no picnic out there, I tell ye."

Betty gave an anxious look at Aunty Bell.

"Is it a very bad storm, Cap'n Brandt?" she asked, almost in a whisper.

"Wust I ever see, Mis' West, since I worked round here," nodding kindly to Betty as he spoke, his face lighting up. He had always believed in her because the captain had taken her home. "Everything comin' in under double reefs, — them that *is* a-comin' in. They say two o' them Lackawanna coal-barges went adrift at daylight an' come ashore at Crotch Island. Had two men drownded, I hear."

"Who told you that?" asked Sanford. The news only increased his anxiety.

"The cap'n of the tow line, sir. He 's just telegraphed to New Haven for a big wreckin'-tug."

Sanford told Captain Brandt to wait, ran upstairs two steps at a time, and reappeared in long rubber boots and mackintosh.

"I 'll walk up toward the lighthouse and find

out how they are getting on, Mrs. Bell," he said. "We can see them from the lantern deck. Come, Captain Brandt, I want you with me." A skilled seaman like the skipper might be needed before the day was over.

Betty and Aunty Bell looked after them until they had swung back the garden gate with its clanking ball and chain, and had turned to breast the gale in their walk of a mile or more up the shore road.

"Oh, aunty," said Betty, with a tremor in her voice, all the blood gone from her face, "do you think anything will happen?"

"Not 's long 's Cap'n Joe's aboard, child. He ain't a-takin' no risks he don't know all about. Ye needn't worry a mite. Set down an' finish yer breakfas'. I believe Mr. Sanford ain't done more 'n swallow his coffee," she added, with a pitying look, as she inspected his plate.

The fact that her husband was exposed in an open boat to the fury of a southeaster made no more impression upon her mind than if he had been reported asleep upstairs. She knew there was no storm the captain could not face.

CHAPTER XIX

FROM THE LANTERN DECK

TONY MARVIN, the keeper of Keyport Light, was in his little room next the fog-horn when Sanford and the skipper, wet and glistening as two seals, knocked at the outer door of his quarters.

"Well, I want to know!" broke out Tony in his bluff, hearty way, as he opened the door. "Come in, — come in! Nice weather for ducks, ain't it? Sunthin' 's up, or you fellers would n't be out to-day," leading the way to his room. "Anybody drowned?" he asked facetiously, stopping for a moment on the threshold.

"Not yet, Tony," said Sanford in a serious tone. He had known the keeper for years, — had, in fact, helped him get his appointment at the Light. "But I'm worried about Captain Joe and Caleb." He opened his coat, and walked across the room to a bench set against the whitewashed wall, little streams of water following him as he moved. "Did you see them go by? They're in Captain Potts's Dolly Varden."

"Gosh hang, no! Ye ain't never tellin' me,

be ye, that the cap'n's gone to the Ledge in all this smother? And that fool Caleb with him, too?"

"Yes, and Lonny Bowles," interrupted the skipper. As he spoke he pulled off one of his water-logged boots and poured the contents into a fire-bucket standing against the wall.

"How long since they started?" asked the keeper anxiously, taking down his spyglass from a rack above the buckets.

"Half an hour ago."

"Then they're this side of Crotch Island yit, if they're anywheres. Let's go up to the lantern. Mebbe we can see 'em," he said, unlatching the door of the tower. "Better leave them boots behind, Mr. Sanford, and shed yer coat. A feller's knees git purty tired climbin' these steps, when he ain't used to 't; there's a hundred and ten of 'em. Here, try these slippin's of mine," and he kicked a pair of slippers from under a chair. "Guess they'll fit ye. Seems to me Caleb's been doin' his best to git drownded since that high-flyer of a gal left him. He come by here daylight, one mornin' awhile ago, in a sharpie that you would n't cross a creek in, and it blowin' half a gale. I ain't surprised o' nothin' in Caleb, but Cap'n Joe ought'er have more sense. What's he goin' for, anyhow, to-day?" he grumbled, as Sanford drew on the slippers and placed his foot on the first iron step of the spiral staircase.

"He's taken the new pump with him," said Sanford, as he followed the keeper up the winding steps, the skipper close behind. "They broke the old pump on Saturday, and everything is stopped on the Ledge. Captain knows we're behind, and he does n't want to lose an hour. But it was a foolish venture. He had no business to risk his life in a blow like this, Tony." There was a serious tone in Sanford's voice which quickened the keeper's step.

"What good is the pump to him, if he does get it there? Men can't work to-day," Tony answered. He was now a dozen steps ahead, his voice sounding hollow in the reverberations of the round tower.

"Oh, that ain't a-goin' to stop us!" shouted the skipper from below, resting a moment to get his breath as he spoke. "We've got the masonry clean out o' water; we're all right if Cap'n Joe can git steam on the hoister."

The keeper, whose legs had become as supple as a squirrel's in the five years he had climbed up and down these stairs, reached the lantern deck some minutes ahead of the others. He was wiping the sweat from the lantern glass with a clean white cloth, and drawing back the day curtains so that they might see better, when Sanford's head appeared above the lens deck.

Once upon the iron floor of the deck, the roar of the wind and the dash of the rain, which had been deadened by the thick walls of the structure surrounding the staircase below, burst upon them seemingly with increased fury. A tremulous, swaying motion was plainly felt. A novice would have momentarily expected the structure to measure its length on the rocks below. Above the roar of the storm could be heard, at intervals, the thunder of the surf breaking on Crotch Island beach.

"Gosh A'mighty!" exclaimed the keeper, adjusting the glass, which he had carried up in his hand. "It's a-humpin' things, and no mistake. See them rollers break on Crotch Island," and he swept his glass around. "I see 'em. There they are,—three o' them. There's Cap'n Joe,—ain't no mistakin' him. He's got his cap on, same's he allers wears. And there's Caleb; his beard's a-flyin' straight out. Who's that in the red flannen shirt?"

"Lonny Bowles," said the skipper.

"Yes, that's Bowles. He's a-bailin' for all he's worth. Cap'n Joe's got the tiller and Caleb's a-hangin' on the sheet. Here, Mr. Sanford," and he held out the glass, "ye kin see 'em plain 's day."

Sanford waved the glass away. The keeper's eyes, he said, were better accustomed to scanning a scene like this. He himself could see the Dolly, a mile or more this side of Crotch Island Point, and nearly two miles away from where the three watchers stood. She was hugging the inside shore-line, her sail close-reefed. He could even make out the three figures, which were but so many black dots beaded along her gunwale. All about the staggering boat seethed the gray sea, mottled in wavy lines of foam. Over this circled white gulls, shrieking as they flew.

"He's gittin' ready to go about," continued the keeper, his eye still to the glass. "I see Caleb shiftin' his seat. They know they can't make the P'int on that leg. Jiminy-whiz, but it's soapy out there! See 'er take that roller! Gosh!"

The boat careened, the dots crowded together, and the Dolly bore away from the shore. It was evidently Captain Joe's intention to give Crotch Island Point a wide berth and then lay a straight course for the Ledge, now barely visible through the haze, the derricks and masonry alone showing clear above the fringe of breaking surf tossed white against the dull gray sky.

All eyes were now fixed on the Dolly. Three times she laid a course toward the Ledge, and three times she was forced back behind the island.

"They've got to give it up," said the keeper, laying down his glass. "That tide cuts round that 'ere P'int like a mill-tail, to say nothin' o' them smashers that's rollin' in. How she keeps afloat out there is what beats me."

"She wouldn't if Cap'n Joe wasn't at the tiller," said the skipper, with a laugh. "Ye can't drown him no more 'n a water-rat." He had an abiding faith in Captain Joe almost as great as that of Aunty Bell.

Sanford's face brightened. An overwhelming anxiety for the safety of the endangered men had strangely, almost unaccountably unnerved him. It was some comfort to feel Captain Brandt's confidence in Captain Joe's ability to meet the situation; for that little cockle-shell battling before him as if for its very life — one moment on top of a mountain of water, and the next buried out of sight — held between its frail sides not only two of the best men whom he knew, but really two of the master spirits of their class. One of them, Captain Joe, Sanford admired more than any other man, loving him, too, as he had loved but few.

With a smile to the skipper, he looked off again toward the sea. He saw the struggling boat make a fourth attempt to clear the Point, and in the movement lurch wildly; he saw, too, that her long boom was swaying from side to side. Through the driving spray he made out that two of the dots were trying to steady it. The third dot was standing in the stern.

Here some new movement caught his eye. He strained his neck forward; then taking the glass from the skipper watched the little craft intently.

"There's something the matter," he said nervously, after a moment's pause. "That's Captain Joe waving to one of those two smacks out there scudding in under close reefs. Look yourself; am I right, Tony?" and he passed the glass to the keeper again.

"Looks like it, sir," replied Tony in a low tone, the end of the glass fixed on the tossing boat. "The smack sees 'em now, sir. She's goin' about."

The fishing-smack careened, fluttered in the wind like a baffled pigeon, and bore across to the plunging boat.

"The spray's a-flyin' so ye can't see clear, sir," said the keeper, his eye still at the glass. "She ain't actin' right, somehow; that boom seems to bother 'em. Cap'n Joe's runnin' for'ard. Gosh! that one went clean over 'er. Look out! *Look out!*" in quick crescendo, as if the endangered crew could have heard him. "See 'er take 'em! There's another went clean across. My God, Mr. Sanford! she's over,— capsized!"

Sanford made a rush for the staircase, a rash, unreasonable impulse to help taking possession of him. The keeper caught him firmly by the arm.

"Come back, sir! You're only wastin' yer breath. That smack'll get 'em."

Captain Brandt picked up the glass that the keeper had dropped. His hands shook so he could hardly adjust the lens.

"The boom's broke," he said in a trembling voice; "that's what ails 'em. She's bottom side up. Lord, if she ain't a-wallowin'! I never 'spected to see Cap'n Joe in a hole like that. They're all three in th' water; ain't a man livin' can swim ashore in that sea! Why don't that blamed smack go about? They'll sink 'fore she can get to 'em. Where's the cap'n? He ain't come up yet. There's Lonny and Caleb, but I don't see Cap'n Joe nowhere."

Sanford leaned against the brass rail of the great lens, his eyes on the fishing-smack swooping down to the rescue. The helplessness of his position, his absolute inability to help the drowning men, overwhelmed him: Captain Joe and Caleb perishing before his eyes, and he powerless to lift a hand.

"Do you see the captain anywhere?" he asked, with an effort at self-control. The words seemed to clog his throat.

"Not yet, sir, but there's Lonny, and there's Caleb. You look, Mr. Marvin," he said, turning to the keeper. He could not trust himself any longer. For the first time his faith in Captain Joe had failed him.

Marvin held the glass to his eye and covered the boat. He hardly dared breathe.

"Can't see but two, sir." His voice was broken and husky. "Can't make out the cap'n nowheres. Something must 'a' struck him an' stunned him. My — my — ain't it a shame for him to cut up a caper like this! I allers told Cap'n Joe he'd get hurted in some foolish kick-up. Why in hell don't them other fellers do something? If they don't look out, the Dolly 'll drift so far they'll lose him, — standin' there like two dummies an' lettin' a man drown! Lord! Lord! ain't it too bad!" The keeper's eyes filled. Everything was dim before him.

The skipper sank on the oil-chest and bowed his head. Sanford's hands were over his face. If the end had come, he did not want to see it.

The small, close lantern became as silent as a death-chamber. The keeper, his back against the lens rail, folded his arms across his chest and stared out to sea. His face bore the look of one watching a dying man. Sanford did not move. His thoughts were on Aunty Bell. What should he say to her? Was there not something he could have done? Should he not, after all, have hailed the first tug in the harbor and gone in search of them before it was too late?

The seconds dragged. The silence in its intensity became unbearable. With a deep indrawn sigh, Captain Brandt turned toward Sanford and touched him. "Come away," he said, with the tenderness of one strong man who suffers and is stirred with greater sorrow by another's grief. "This ain't no place for you, Mr. Sanford. Come away."

Sanford raised his eyes and was about to

" Thank God, Tony ! Thank God !"

speak, when the keeper threw up his arms with a joyous shout and seized the glass. "There he is! I see his cap! That's Cap'n Joe! He's holdin' up his hands. Caleb's crawlin' along the bottom; he's reachin' down an' haulin' Cap'n Joe up. Now he's on 'er keel."

Sanford and Captain Brandt sprang to their feet, crowding close to the lantern glass, their eyes fastened on the Dolly. Sanford's hands were trembling. Hot, quick tears rolled down his cheeks and dropped from his chin. The joyful news had unnerved him more than the horror of the previous moments. There was no doubt of its truth; he could see, even with the naked eye, the captain lying flat on the boat's keel. He thought he could follow every line of his body, — never so precious as now.

"He's all right," he said in a dazed way — "all right — all right," repeating it mechanically over and over to himself, as a child would do. Then he turned and laid his hand on the keeper's shoulder.

"Thank God, Tony! Thank God!"

The keeper's hand closed tight in Sanford's. For a moment he did not speak.

"Almighty close shave, sir," he said slowly in a broken whisper, looking into Sanford's. eyes.

Captain Brandt's face was radiant. "Might 'a' knowed he'd come up some'ers, sir. Did n't I tell ye, ye could n't drown him? But where in thunder has he been under water all this time?" he asked, with a laugh that had the unshed tears of a strong man in it, and the exultation of one just recovered from a fright that had almost unnerved him. The laugh not only expressed his joy at the great relief, but carried with it a reminder that he had never seriously doubted the captain's ability to save himself.

All eyes were now fastened on the rescuing smack. As she swept past the capsized boat, her crew leaned far over the side, reached down and caught two of the shipwrecked men, leaving one man still clinging to the keel, the sea breaking over him every moment. Sanford took the glass, and saw that this man was Lonny Bowles, and that Captain Joe, now safe aboard the smack, was waving his cap to the second smack, which hove to in answer. Presently the hailed smack rounded in, lowered her mainsail, and hauled Lonny aboard. She then took the overturned Dolly in tow, and made at once for the harbor. When this was done, the first smack, with Captain Joe and Caleb on board, shook a reef from its mainsail, turned about, and despite the storm laid a straight course back to the Ledge.

This daring and apparently hopeless attempt of Captain Joe to carry out his plan of going to the Ledge awoke a new anxiety in Sanford. There was no longer the question of personal danger to the captain or the men; the fishing-smack was, of course, a better sea boat than the Dolly, but why make the trip at all when the pump had been lost from the overturned boat, and no one could land at the Ledge? Even from where they all stood in the lantern they could see the big rollers flash white as they broke over the enrockment blocks, the spray drenching the tops of the derricks. No small boat could live in such a sea, — not even the life-boat at the Ledge.

As the incoming smack drew near, Sanford, followed by the keeper and Captain Brandt, hurried down the spiral staircase and into the keeper's room below, where they drew on their coats and heavy boots, and made their way to the lighthouse dock.

When she came within hailing distance, Captain Brandt mounted a spile and shouted above the roar of the gale, "Bowles, ahoy! Anybody hurt, Lonny?"

A man in a red shirt detached himself from among the group of men huddled in the smack's bow, stepped on the rail, and, putting his hands to his mouth, trumpeted back, "No!"

"What's the cap'n gone to the Ledge for?"

"Gone to set the pump!"

"Thought the pump was lost overboard!" cried Sanford.

"No, sir; cap'n dived under the Dolly an' found it catched fast, an' Caleb hauled it aboard,

Cap'n tol' me to tell ye that he 'd hev it set all right to-day, blow or no"— The last words were lost in the wind.

"Ain't that jes' like the cap'n?" shouted the keeper, with a loud laugh, slapping his thigh with his hand. "That 's where he was when we thought he was drownded,— he was a-divin' fer that pump. Land o' Moses, ain't he a good un!"

Captain Brandt said nothing, but a smile of happy pride overspread his face. Captain Joe was still his hero.

Sanford spent the afternoon between Aunty Bell's kitchen and the paraphernalia dock, straining his eyes seaward in search of an incoming smack which would bring the captain. The wind had shifted to the northwest, sweeping out the fog and piling the low clouds in heaps. The rain had ceased, and a dash of pale lemon light shone above the blue-gray sea.

About sundown his quick eye detected a tiny sail creeping in behind Crotch Island. As it neared the harbor and he made out the lines of the fishing-smack of the morning, a warm glow tingled through him; it would not be long now before he had his hands on Captain Joe.

When the smack came bowling into the harbor under double reefs, her wind-blown jib a cup, her sail a saucer, and rounded in as graceful as a skater on the outer edge, Sanford's hand was the first that touched the captain's as he sprang from the smack's deck to the dock.

"Captain Joe," he said. His voice broke as he spoke; all his love was in his eyes. "Don't ever do that again. I saw it all from the lighthouse lantern. You have no right to risk your life this way."

"'T ain't nothin', Mr. Sanford." His great hand closed tight over that of the young engineer. "It's all right now, and the pump's screwed fast. Caleb had steam up on the h'ister when I left him on the Ledge. Boom on the Dolly had n't 'a' broke short off out there, we'd 'a' been there sooner."

"We thought you were gone, once," continued Sanford, his voice full of anxiety, still holding to the captain's hand as they walked toward the house.

"Not in the Dolly, sir," the captain answered in an apologetic tone, as if he wanted to atone for the suffering he had caused his friend. "She's got wood enough in 'er to float anywheres. That's what I took 'er out for."

Aunty Bell met them at the kitchen door.

"I hearn ye was overboard," she said quietly, no more stirred over the day's experience than if some child had stepped into a puddle and had come in for a change of shoes. "Ye're wet yet, be n't ye?" patting his big chest to make sure.

"Yes, guess so," he answered carelessly, feeling his own arms as if to satisfy himself as to the reason of his wife's inquiry. "Got a dry shirt?"

"Yes; got everything hangin' there on a chair 'fore the kitchen fire," and she closed the door upon him and Sanford.

"Beats all, Mr. Sanford, don't it?" the captain continued in short sentences, broken by breathless pauses, as he stripped off his wet clothes before the blazing fire, one jerk for the suspenders, another for the trousers, Sanford, jubilant over the captain's safety and eager to do him any service, handing him the dry garments one after another.

"Beats all, I say; don't it, now? There's that Cap'n Potts: been a seaman, man an' boy, all his life,"—here the grizzled wet head was hidden for a moment as a clean flannel shirt was drawn over it,—"yet he ain't got sense 'nough to keep a boom from rottin' 'board a cat-boat,"—the head was up now, and Sanford, fumbling under the chin whisker, was helping the captain with the top button,—"an' snappin' square off in a little gale o' wind like that. There, thank ye, guess that 'll do."

When he had seated himself in his chair, his sturdy legs—stout and tough as two dock-logs —stretched out before the fire, his rough hands spread to the blaze, warming the big, strong body that had been soaking wet for ten consecutive hours, Sanford took a seat beside him, and, laying his hand on his knee, said in a gentle voice, "Why did you risk your life for that pump, Captain Joe?"

"'Cause she acted so durned ornery," he blurted out in an angry tone. "Jes' see what she did: gin out night 'fore last jes' 's we was gittin' ready to h'ist that big stretcher; kep' me an' Caleb up two nights a-castin' an' borin' on 'er out; then all of a sudden she thought she'd upset an' fool us. I tell ye, ye 've got to take hold of a thing like that good an' early, or it 'll git away with ye."

One hand was swung high over his head as if it had been a sledge-hammer.

"Now she 'll stay put till I git through with her. I ain't a-goin' to let no damned pump beat me!"

CHAPTER XX

AT THE PINES

THE Indian summer days had come, — soft, dreamy days of red and gold, with veils of silver mist at sunrise, and skeins of purple clouds at twilight. The air was hazy with the smoke of dull fires smouldering on the hillside. The stems of the bare birches shone white; wreaths of scarlet crowned the low stone walls; dead leaves strewed the lawns, and tall chrysanthemums flamed in the garden-beds. Here and there a belated summer rose, braving the cold, shivered with close-folded lips, or hung head down, pierced by the night-frost.

Sanford had shifted his quarters from the little room over Captain Joe's kitchen to the big east room at The Pines, opening out upon a wide balcony, from which he could see with his glass the feathers of white steam on the Ledge. His apartments in Washington Square had been closed, and Sam ordered to join his master at Keyport, where he found himself promoted from the position of man-of-all-work to that of valet-in-chief, with especial instructions to report daily to Buckles, who grew more reticent and imposing by reason of the added charge.

And with the dreamy days came Helen and Jack; Smearly with a big canvas, which he never afterward touched; and the major, with a nondescript wardrobe, as curious as it was astonishing.

To Helen The Pines was a land of romance and charm. She had been brought up in the country, and loved its quiet, the rest of its shady lanes and cool woods, and the life it brought. The city had charmed her at first. She liked its novelty, its theatres, galleries, and crowded streets, but long before her visit in town was done, she had begun to sigh for green fields, and rose gardens, and the freedom of her young days at home. She had passed the summer with her school friends, Jack spending his Sundays with her whenever he could manage an invitation. But the homes of her friends had been simple ones, with none of the luxury and comfort and the poetry of The Pines.

Mrs. Leroy had begun at once on her arrival to carry out her promise to give the young Maryland girl one more good time before that "Bluebeard Jack bound her hand and foot." She had done this as much from a sincere interest in Helen, as from a sense of duty to Jack and Sanford. She had not, as yet, completely won the girl's confidence. The talk with Smearly, in which Mrs. Leroy had cried out against the marriage relation, still lingered in Helen's mind. Its last impression wore away only when Kate had taken her out on the lawn, on the second morning of her visit, to show her a secluded summer-house smothered in climbing vines and overlooking the water.

"This is for you and Jack," she had said, with a merry twinkle in her eye and a depth of tenderness in her tone. "And for nobody else, dear. Not a soul will be able to find you." Though Helen had laughed and said that she and Jack had been engaged too long to need such retirement, every succeeding morning had found them there, oblivious to the outside world until aroused by a peculiar shuffling sound on the gravel, followed by a warning cough.

"Lunch ready, Marse Jack, — so de waiter-man says."

It was always Sam, — his face as full of smiles as a suddenly disturbed puddle is of ripples.

But if The Pines was an enchanted realm to Helen and Jack, a refreshing retreat to Sanford, and a mine of luxury to Smearly, to the major it was a never ending source of pure delight.

Until that day on which he had stepped within its portals, his experience of Northern hospitality had been confined to Jack's and Sanford's bachelor apartments, for years ideal realms of elegance and ease. These now seemed to him both primitive and meagre. Where Jack had but one room to spare for a friend, and Sanford but two, The Pines had whole suites opening into corridors terminating in vistas of entrancing lounging-places, with marvelous fittings and draperies. Where Sam and Jefferson, in their respective establishments, performed unaided every household duty, from making a cocktail to making a bed, The Pines boasted two extra men, who assisted Buckles at the sideboard, to say nothing of countless maids, gardeners, hostlers, stable-boys, and lesser dependents.

Moreover, the major had come upon a most capacious carriage-house and out-buildings, sheltering a wonderful collection of drags, coupés, and phaetons of patterns never seen by him before, — particularly a most surprising dog-cart with canary-colored wheels; and a stable full of satin-skinned horses with incredible pedigrees, together with countless harnesses mounted in silver, and decorated with monograms. Last, but by no means least, he had discovered, to his infinite joy, a spick-and-span perfectly appointed steam yacht, with sailing-master, engineer, firemen, and crew constantly on board, and all ready, at a moment's notice, to steam off to the uttermost parts of the earth in search of booty or adventure.

The major had found, in fact, all that his wildest flights and his most mendacious imaginings had pictured. The spacious piazzas, velvet lawns, and noble parks of which he had so often boasted as being "upon the estate of a ve'y dear friend of mine up No'th, suh, where I spend so many happy days;" the wonderful cuisine, fragrant Havanas, crusty port and old Hennessy, — the property as well of this diaphanous gentleman, — had at last become actual realities. The women of charming mien and apparel, so long creations of his brain, — "Dianas, suh, clothed one hour in yachtin'-jackets, caps, and dainty yellow shoes, and the next in webs of gossamer, their lovely faces shaded by ravishin' pa'asols and crowned by wonderful hats," — now floated daily along the very gravel walks that his own feet pressed, or were attended nightly by gay gallants in immaculate black and white, whose elbows touched his own.

Of all these luxuries had he dreamed for years, and about all these luxuries had he lied, descanting on their glories by the hour to that silent group of thirsty Pocomokians before the village bar, or to the untraveled neighbors who lightened with their presence the lonely hours at Crab Island. But never until Mrs. Leroy had opened wide to him the portals of The Pines had they been real to his sight and touch.

It is not to be wondered at, therefore, that with the flavor of all this magnificence steeping his soul a gradual change took place in his tone and demeanor. Before a week had passed he had somehow persuaded himself that although the lamp of Aladdin was exclusively the property of Mrs. Leroy, the privilege of rubbing it was unquestionably his own. Gradually, and by the same mental process, he had become convinced that he was not only firmly installed in the Leroy household as High Rubber-in-Chief, the master of the house being temporarily absent, and there being no one else to fill his place, but that the office, if not a life position, at least would last long enough to tide him over until cold weather set in.

At first Mrs. Leroy looked on in amazement, and then, as the humor of the situation dawned upon her, gave him free rein to do as he would. Months ago she had seen through his harmless assumptions, and his present pretensions amused her immensely.

"My dear madam," he would say, "I see the lines of care about yo'r lovely eyes. Let me take you a spin down the shell road in that yaller cyart. It will bring the roses back to your cheeks." Or, "Sanford, my dear fellow, try one of those Reina Victorias; you 'll find them much lighter. Buckles, open a fresh box."

It is worthy of note, too, that when once the

surprise at the novelty of the situation had passed away, his hostess soon realized that no one could have filled the post of major-domo to better satisfaction. The same qualities that served him at Crab Island, making him the best of company when off on an outing with the boys, were displayed in even greater perfection at The Pines. He was courteous, good-humored, unselfish, watchful of everybody's comfort, buoyant as a rubber ball, and ultimately so self-poised that even Buckles began to stand in awe of him, — a victory, by the way, which so delighted Jack Hardy that he rolled over on the grass with shouts of laughter when he discussed it with Sanford and Smearly.

Nor were the greater duties neglected. He was constantly on the lookout for various devices by which his hostess might be relieved in the care of her guests. Tennis tournaments, fishing parties, and tableaux followed in quick succession, each entertainment the result of his ingenious activity and his untiring efforts at making everybody happy.

This daily routine of gayety was interrupted by the important announcement that a committee of engineers, headed by General Barton, would inspect the work at Shark Ledge.

This visit of the engineers meant to Sanford a possible solution of his difficulties. Carleton still withheld the certificate, and the young engineer had had the greatest difficulty in tiding over his payments. A second and last section of the work was nearly completed, thanks to the untiring efforts of Captain Joe and his men and to the stability of the machinery, and there was every probability that now these two sections would be finished before the snow began to fly. This had been the main purpose of Sanford's summer, and the end was in sight. And yet, with all that had been accomplished, Sanford knew that a technical ruling of the Board in sustaining Carleton's unjust report when rejecting the work might delay his payments for months, and if prolonged through the winter might eventually ruin him.

The inspection, then, was all the more important at this time; for while the solidity of the masonry and the care with which it was constructed would speak for themselves, the details must be seen and inspected to be appreciated. If the day, therefore, were fine and the committee able to land on the Ledge, Sanford had no fear of the outcome, — provided, of course, that Carleton could be made to speak the truth.

There was no question that parts of the work as they then stood were in open violation of the plans and specifications of the contract. The concrete base, or disk, was acknowledged by Sanford to be six inches out of level. This error was due to the positive orders of Carleton against the equally positive protest of Sanford and Captain Joe. But the question still remained, whether the Board would sustain Carleton's refusal to give a certificate in view of the error, and whether Carleton could be made to admit that the error was his own, and not Sanford's.

So far as the permanence of the structure was concerned, this six inches' rise over so large an area as the base was immaterial. The point — a vital one — was whether the technical requirements of the contract would be insisted upon. Its final decision lay with the Board.

To Mrs. Leroy the occasion was one of more than usual importance. She sent for the sailing-master, ordered steam up at an early hour, gave Sam — Buckles had assigned Sam to certain duties aboard the yacht — particular directions as to luncheon the following day, and prepared to entertain the whole committee, provided that august body could be induced to accept the invitation she meant to extend. She had already selected General Barton as her especial victim, while Helen was to make herself agreeable to some of the younger members.

The value of linen, glass, cut flowers, dry champagne, and pretty toilettes in settling any of the affairs of life was part of her social training, and while she did not propose to say one word in defense or commendation of Sanford and his work, she fully intended so to soften the rough edges of the chief engineer and his assistants that any adverse ruling would be well-nigh impossible.

If Mrs. Leroy lent a cheerful and willing hand, the presiding genius of the weather was equally considerate. The morning broke clear and bright. The sun silvered the tall grass of the wide marsh crossed by the railroad trestle and draw, and illumined the great clouds of white steam puffed out by the passing trains. The air was balmy and soft, the sky a turquoise flecked with sprays of pearl, the sea a sheet of silver.

When the maid opened her windows, Mrs. Leroy stepped to the balcony and drank in the beauty and freshness of the morning. Even the weather powers, she said to herself, had ceased hostilities, and declared a truce for the day, restraining their turbulent winds until the council of war which was to decide Sanford's fate was over.

As her eye roamed over her perfectly appointed and well-kept lawns, her attention was drawn to a singular-looking figure crossing the grass in the direction of the dock where the yacht was moored. It was that of a man dressed in the jacket and cap of a club commodore. He bore himself with the dignity of a lord high admiral walking the quarter-deck. Closer inspection revealed the manly form of no less distinguished a personage than Major Thomas Slocomb of Pocomoke.

Subsequent inquiries disclosed these facts: Finding in his room the night before a hitherto unsuspected closet door standing partly open, the major had, in harmless curiosity, entered the closet and inspected the contents, and had come upon some attractive garments. That these clothes had evidently been worn by and were then the sole property of his host, Morgan Leroy, Commodore N. Y. Y. C., a man whom he had never seen, only added to the charm of the discovery. Instantly a dozen thoughts crowded through his head, — each more seductive than the other. Evidently this open door and this carefully hung jacket and cap meant something out of the ordinary! It was the first time the door had been left open! It had been done purposely, of course, that he might see its contents! Everything in this wonderful palace of luxury was free, — cigars, brandy, even the stamps on the writing-table before him, — why not, then, these yachting clothes? To-morrow was the great day for the yacht, when the inspection of the engineers was to take place. His age and position naturally made him the absent commodore's rightful successor. Had Leroy been at home, he would, undoubtedly, have worn these clothes himself. The duty of his substitute, therefore, was too plain to admit of a moment's hesitation. He must certainly wear the clothes. One thing, however, touched him deeply,—the delicacy of his hostess in putting them where he could find them, and the exquisite tact with which it had all been done. Even if all other considerations failed, he could not disappoint that queen among women, that Cleopatra of modern times.

As he squeezed his arms into the jacket—Leroy was two thirds his size—and caught the glint of the gilt buttons in the mirror, his last lingering doubt faded.

This, then, was the figure Mrs. Leroy saw from her bedroom window.

When the major boarded the yacht the sailing-master saluted him with marked deference, remembering the uniform, even if he did not the wearer, and the sailors holystoning the decks came up to a half present as he passed them on his way to the saloon to see if Sam had carried out his instructions about certain brews necessary for the comfort of the day.

"Where the devil did you get that rig, major?" roared Smearly, when he and Sanford came down the companionway, half an hour later. "You look like a cross between Dick Deadeye and Little Lord Fauntleroy. It's about two sizes too small for you."

"Do you think so, gentlemen?" twisting his back to the mirrors to get a better view. His face was a study. "It's some time since

I wore 'em; they may be a little tight. I've noticed lately that I am gaining flesh. Will you sit here, gentlemen, or shall I order somethin' coolin' on deck?"— not a quaver in his voice. "Here, Sam," he called, catching sight of that darky's face, "take these gentlemen's orders."

When Helen and Mrs. Leroy appeared, followed by several ladies with Hardy as escort, the major sprang forward to greet them with all the suppressed exuberance of a siphon of Vichy. He greeted Helen first.

"Ah, my dear Helen, you look positively charmin' this mornin'; you are like a tea-rose wet with dew; nothing like these Maryland girls, — unless, my dear madam," he added, turning to Mrs. Leroy, bowing as low to his hostess as the grip of his shoulders would permit, "unless it be yo'r own queenly presence. Sam, put some cushions behind the ladies' backs, or shall I order coffee for you on deck?"

But it was not until the major came up on the return curve of his bow to a perpendicular that his hostess realized in full the effect of Morgan Leroy's nautical outfit. She gave a little gasp, and her face flushed.

"I hope none of these ladies will recognize Morgan's clothes, Henry," she whispered behind her fan to Sanford. "I must say this is going a step too far."

"But didn't you send them to his room,

Kate? He told me this morning he wore them out of deference to your wishes. He found them hanging in his closet." Sanford's face wore a quizzical smile.

"I send them?" Then the whole thing burst upon her. With the keenest appreciation of the humor of the situation in every line of her face, she turned to the major and said, "I must congratulate you, major, on your new outfit, and I must thank you for wearing it to-day. It was very good of you to put it on. It is an important occasion, you know, for Mr. Sanford. Will you give me your arm and take me on deck?"

Helen stared in complete astonishment as she listened to Mrs. Leroy. This last addition to the major's constantly increasing wardrobe — he had a way of borrowing the clothes of any friend with whom he stayed — had for the moment taken her breath away. It was only when Jack whispered an explanation to her that she, too, entered into the spirit of the scene.

Before the yacht had passed through the draw of the railroad trestle on her way to the Ledge, the several guests had settled themselves in the many nooks and corners about the deck or on the more luxurious cushions of the saloon. Mrs. Leroy, now that her guests were happily placed, sat well forward out of immediate hearing, where she could talk over the probable outcome of the day with Sanford, and lay her plans if Carleton's opposition threatened serious trouble. Helen and Jack were as far aft as they could get, watching the gulls dive for scraps thrown from the galley, while Smearly in the saloon below was the centre of a circle of ladies, — guests from the neighboring cottages, — who were laughing at his stories, and who had, thus early in the day, voted him the most entertaining man they had ever met, although a trifle cynical.

As for the major, he was as restless as a newsboy, and everywhere at once: in the galley, giving minute directions to the chef regarding the slicing of the cucumbers and the proper mixing of the salad; up in the pilot-house interviewing the sailing-master on the weather, on the tides, on the points of the wind, on the various beacons, shoals, and currents; and finally down in the pantry, where Sam, in white apron, immaculate waistcoat and tie, was polishing some pipe-stemmed glasses, intended receptacles of cooling appetizers composed of some ingredients of the major's own selection.

"You lookin' mighty fine, major, dis mornin'," said Sam, his mouth stretched in a broad grin. "Dat's de tip-nist, top-nist git-up I done seen fur a coon's age," detecting a certain — to him — cake-walk cut to the coat and white duck trousers. "Did dat come up on de train las' night, sah?" he asked, walking round the major, and wiping a glass as he looked him over admiringly.

"Yes, Sam, and it's the first time I wore 'em. Little tight in the sleeves, ain't they?" the major inquired, holding out his arm.

"Does seem ter pinch leetle mite round de elbows; but you do look good, fur a fac'."

These little confidences were not unusual. Indeed, of all the people about him the major understood Sam the best and enjoyed him the most, — an understanding, by the way, which was mutual. There never was any strain upon the Pocomokian's many resources of high spirits, willingness to please, and general utility, when he was alone with Sam. He never had to make an effort to keep his position; that Sam accorded him. But then, Sam believed in the major.

As the yacht rounded the east end of Crotch Island, Sanford made out quite plainly over the port bow the lighthouse tender steaming along from a point in the direction of Little Gull Light.

"There they come," he said to Mrs. Leroy. "Everything is in our favor to-day, Kate. I was afraid they might be detained. We'll steam about here for a while until the tender lands at the new wharf which we have just finished at the Ledge. The yacht draws a little too much water to risk the wharf, and we had better lie outside of the government boat. It's as still as a mill-pond at the Ledge to-day, and we can all go ashore. If you will permit me, Kate, I'll call to your sailing-master to slow down until the tender reaches the wharf."

At this moment the major's head appeared around the edge of the pilot-house door. He had overheard Sanford's remark. "Allow me, madam," he said in a voice of great dignity, and with a look at Sanford, as if somehow that gentleman had infringed upon his own especial privileges. The next instant the young engineer's suggestion to "slow down" was sent bounding up to the sailing-master, who answered it with a touch of two fingers to his cap, an "Ay, ay, sir," and some sharp, quick pulls on the engine-room gong.

Mrs. Leroy smiled at the major's nautical knowledge and quarter-deck air, and rose to her feet to see the approaching tender. Under Sanford's guiding finger, she followed the course of the long thread of black smoke lying on the still horizon, unwinding slowly from the spool of the tender's funnel.

Everybody was now on deck. Helen and the other younger ladies of the party leaned over the yacht's rail watching the rapidly nearing steamer; the older ladies mounted the deck from the cabin, some of them becoming fully persuaded that the Ledge with its derricks and shanty — a purple-gray mass under the morning glare — was unquestionably the expected boat.

Soon the Ledge loomed up in all its proportions, with its huge rim of circular masonry lying on the water line like a low monitor rigged with derricks for masts. When the rough shanty for the men, and the platforms filled with piles of cement barrels, and the hoisting-engine were distinctly outlined against the sky, everybody crowded forward to see the place of which they had heard so much.

Mrs. Leroy stood one side, that Sanford might explain without interruption the several objects as they came into view.

"Why, Henry," she exclaimed, after everybody had said how wonderful it all was, "how much work you have really done since I saw it in the spring! And there is the engine, is it, to which the pump belonged that nearly drowned Captain Joe and Caleb? And are those the big derricks you had so much trouble over? They don't look very big."

"They are twice the size of your body, Kate," said Sanford, laughing. "They may look to you like knitting-needles from this distance, but that is because everything around them is on so large a scale. You would n't think that shanty which looks like a coal-bin could accommodate twenty men and their stores."

As Sanford ceased speaking, the major

turned quickly, entered the pilot-house, and almost instantly reappeared with the yacht's spyglass. This he carefully adjusted, resting the end on the ratlines. "Victory is ours," he said slowly, closing the glass. "I haven't a doubt about the result."

CHAPTER XXI

THE RECORD OF NICKLES, THE COOK

THE yacht and the lighthouse tender were not the only boats bound for the Ledge. The Screamer, under charge of a tug, — her sails would have been useless in the still air, — was already clear of Keyport Light, and heading for the landing-wharf a mile away. Captain Bob Brandt held the tiller, and Captain Joe and Caleb leaned out of the windows of the pilot-house of the towing tug. They wanted to be there to see if Carleton "played any monkey tricks," to quote Captain Brandt.

None of them had had cause to entertain a friendly spirit toward the superintendent. It had often been difficult for Caleb to keep his hands from Carleton's throat since his experience with him under the willows. As for Captain Brandt, he still remembered the day the level was set, when Carleton had virtually given him the lie.

The Screamer arrived first; she made fast to the now completed dock, and the tug dropped back in the eddy. Then the lighthouse tender came alongside and hooked a line around the Screamer's deck-cleats. The yacht came last, lying outside the others. This made it necessary for the passengers aboard the yacht to cross the deck of the tender, and for those of both the yacht and the tender to cross the deck of the Screamer, before stepping upon the completed masonry of the lighthouse itself.

Nothing could have suited Mrs. Leroy better than this enforced intermingling of guests and visitors. The interchanges of courtesy established at once a cordiality which augured well for the day's outcome and added another touch of sunshine to its happiness, and so she relaxed none of her efforts to propitiate the gods.

It is worthy of note that Carleton played no part in the joyous programme of the day. He sprang ashore as soon as the tender made fast to the Screamer's side (he had met the party of engineers at the railroad depot, and had gone with them to Little Gull Light, — their first stopping-place), and began at once his work of "superintending" with a vigor and alertness never seen in him before, and, to quote Nickles, the cook, who was watching the whole performance from the shanty window, "with more airs than a Noank goat with a hoop-skirt."

The moment the major's foot was firmly planted upon the Ledge a marked change was visible in him. The straight back, head up, rear-admiral manner, which had distinguished him, gave way to one of a thoughtful repose. Engineering problems began to absorb him. Leaving Hardy and Smearly to help the older ladies pick their way over the mortar-incrusted platforms and up and down the rude ladders to the top rim of masonry, he commenced inspecting the work with the eye of a skilled mechanic. He examined carefully the mortar joints of the masonry; squinted his eye along the edges of the cut stones to see if they were true; turned it aloft, taking in the system of derricks, striking one with the palm of his hand and listening for the vibration, to assure himself of its stability. And he asked questions in a way that left no doubt in the minds of the men that he was past grand master in the art of building lighthouses.

All but one man.

This doubter was Lonny Bowles, whom the Pocomokian had cared for in the old warehouse hospital the night of the explosion. Bowles had quietly dogged the major's steps over the work, in the hope of being recognized. At last the good-natured lineaments of the red-shirted quarryman fastened themselves upon the major's remembrance.

"My dear suh!" he broke out, as he jumped down from a huge coping-stone and grasped Lonny's hand. "Of co'se I remember you. I sincerely hope you're all right again," stepping back and looking him over with an expression of real pride and admiration.

"Oh yes, I'm purty hearty, thank ye," said Bowles, laughing as he hitched his sleeves up his arms, bared to the elbow. "How's things gone 'long o' yerself?"

The major expressed his perfect satisfaction with life in its every detail, and was about to compliment Bowles on the wonderful progress of the work so largely due to his efforts, when the man at the hoisting-engine interrupted with, "Don't stand there now lalligaggin', Lonny. Where ye been this half hour? Hurry up with that monkey-wrench. Do you want this drum to come off?" Lonny instantly turned his attention to the work. When he had given the last turn to the endangered nut, the man said, "Who's the duck with the bobtail coat, Lonny?"

"Oh, he's one o' the boss's city gang. Fust time I see him he come inter th' warehouse when we was stove up. I thought he was a sawbones till I see him a-fetchin' water fur th' boys. Then I thought he was a preach till he began to swear. But he ain't neither one; he's an out-an'-out ol' sport, he is, every time, an' a good un. He's struck it rich up here, I guess, from th' way he's boomin' things with them Leroy folks,"— which conviction seemed to be shared by the men around him, now that they were assured of the major's identity. Many of them remembered the nankeen and bombazine suit which the Pocomokian wore on that fatal day, and the generally disheveled appearance that he presented the following morning. The present change in his attire was therefore the more incomprehensible.

During all this time, Sanford, with the assistance of Captain Joe and Caleb, was adjusting his transit, in order that he might measure for the committee the exact difference between the level shown on the plans and the level found in the concrete base. In this adjustment, the major, who had now joined the group, took the deepest interest, discoursing most learnedly, to the officers about him, upon the marvels of modern science, punctuating his remarks every few minutes with pointed allusions to his dear friend Henry, "that Archimedes of the New World," who in this the greatest of all his undertakings had eclipsed all former achievements. The general listened with an amused smile, in which the whole committee joined before long.

Either General Barton's practiced eye forestalled any need of the instrument, or Carleton had already fully posted him as to which side of the circle was some inches too high, for he asked, with some severity: —

"Is n't the top of that concrete base out of level, Mr. Sanford?"

"Yes, sir; some inches too high near the southeast derrick," replied Sanford promptly.

"How did that occur?"

"I should prefer you to ask the superintendent," said Sanford quietly.

Mrs. Leroy, who was standing a short distance away on a dry plank that Sanford had put under her feet, her ears alert, stopped talking to Smearly and turned her head. She did not want to miss a word.

"What have you to say, Mr. Carleton? Did you give any orders to raise that level?" The general looked over his glasses at the superintendent.

Carleton had evidently prepared himself for this ordeal, and had carefully studied his line of answers. As long as he kept the written requirements under the contract he was safe.

"If I understand my instructions, sir, I am not here to give orders. The plans show what is to be done." He spoke in a low, almost gentle voice, and with a certain deference of manner which no one had ever seen in him before, and which Sanford felt was even more to be dreaded than his customary bluster.

Captain Joe stepped closer to Sanford's side, and Caleb and Captain Bob Brandt, who stood on the outside of the circle of officers grouped around the tripod, leaned forward, listening intently. They, too, had noticed the change in Carleton's manner. The other men dropped

THE RECORD OF NICKLES, THE COOK

their shovels and tools, and edged up, not obtrusively, but so as to overhear everything.

"Is this the reason you have withheld the certificate, of which the contractor complains?" asked the general, with a tone in his voice as of a judge interrogating a witness.

Carleton bowed his head meekly in assent. "I can't sign for work that's done wrong, sir."

Captain Joe made a movement as if to speak, when Sanford, checking him with a look, began, "The superintendent is right so far as he goes, general, but there is another clause in the contract which he seems to forget. I'll quote it," drawing an important-looking document from his pocket and spreading it out on the top of a cement barrel: "'Any dispute arising between the United States engineer, or his superintendent, and the contractor, shall be decided by the former, and his decision shall be final.' If the level of this concrete base does not conform to the plans, there is no one to blame but the superintendent himself."

Sanford's flashing eye and rising voice had attracted the attention of the ladies as well as that of their escorts. They ceased talking and played with the points of their parasols, tracing little diagrams in the cement dust, preserving a strict neutrality, like most people overhearing a quarrel in which they have no interest, but who are alert to lose no move in the contest. Sanford would have liked less publicity in the settlement of the matter, and so expressed himself in a quick glance toward the guests. This anxiety was instantly seen by the major, who, with a tact that Sanford had not given him credit for, led the ladies away out of hearing on pretense of showing them some of the heavy masonry.

The engineer-in-chief looked curiously at Carleton, and the awakened light of a new impression gleamed in his eye. Sanford's confident manner and Carleton's momentary agitation over Sanford's statement, upsetting for an instant his lamblike reserve, evidently indicated something hidden behind this dispute which until then had not come to the front.

"I'll take any blame that's coming to me," said Carleton, his meekness merging into a dogged, half-imposed-on tone, "but I can't be responsible for other folks' mistakes. I set that level myself two months ago, and left the bench-marks for 'em to work up to. When I come out next time they'd altered them. I told 'em it would n't do, and they'd have to take up what concrete they'd set and lower the level again. They said they was behind and wanted to catch up, that it made no difference anyhow, and they would n't do it."

General Barton turned to Sanford and was about to speak, when a voice rang out clear and sharp, "That's a lie!"

Everybody looked about for the speaker. If

a bomb had exploded above their heads, the astonishment could not have been greater.

Before any one could speak Captain Bob Brandt forced his way into the middle of the group. His face was flushed with anger, his lower lip was quivering. "I say it again. That's a lie, and you know it," he said calmly, pointing his finger at Carleton, whose cheek paled at this sudden onslaught. "This ain't my job, gentlemen," and he faced General Barton and the committee, "an' it don't make no difference to me whether it gits done 'r not. I'm hired here 'long with my sloop a-layin' there at the wharf, an' I git my pay. But I've been here all summer, an' I stood by when this 'ere galoot you call a superintendent sot this level; and when he says Cap'n Joe did n't do the work as he ordered it he lies like a thief, an' I don't care who hears it. Ask Cap'n Joe Bell and Caleb West, a-standin' right there 'longside o' ye: they'll gin it to ye straight; they're that kind."

Barton was an old man and accustomed to the respectful deference of a government office, but he was also a keen observer of human nature. The expression on the skipper's face and on the faces of the others about him was too fearless to admit of a moment's doubt of their sincerity.

Carleton shrugged his shoulders as if it were to be expected that Sanford's men would stand by him. Then he said, with a half sneer at Captain Brandt, "Five dollars goes a long ways with you fellers." The cat had unconsciously uncovered its claws.

Brandt sprang forward with a wicked look in his eye, when the general raised his hand.

"Come, men, stop this right away." There was a tone in the chief engineer's voice which impelled obedience. "We are here to find out who is responsible for this error. I am surprised, Mr. Sanford," turning almost fiercely upon him, "that a man of your experience did not insist on a written order for this change of plan. While six inches over an area of this size does not materially injure the work, you are too old a contractor to alter a level to one which you admit now was wrong, and which at the time you knew was wrong, without some written order. It violates the contract."

Here Nickles, the cook, who had been craning his neck out of the shanty window so as not to lose a word of the talk, withdrew it so suddenly that one of the men standing by the door hurried into the shanty, thinking something unusual was the matter.

"I have never been able to get a written order from this superintendent for any detail of the work since he has been here," said Sanford in a positive tone, "and he has never raised his hand to help us. What the cause of his enmity is I do not know. We have all of us tried to treat him courteously and follow his orders whenever it was possible to do so. He insisted on this change after both my master diver, Caleb West here, Captain Joe Bell, and others of my best men had protested against it, and we had either to stop work and appeal to the Board, and so lose the summer's work and be liable to the government for non-completion on time, or obey him. I took the latter course, and you can see the result. It was my only way out of the difficulty."

At this instant there came a crash which sounded like breaking china, evidently in the shanty, and a cloud of white dust, the contents of a partly empty flour-barrel, sifted out through the open window. The general turned his head in inquiry, and, seeing nothing unusual, continued : —

"You should have stopped work, sir, and appealed. The government does not want its work done in a careless, unworkmanlike way, and will not pay for it." His voice had a tone in it that sent a pang of anxiety to Mrs. Leroy's heart.

Carleton smiled grimly. He was all right, he said to himself. Nobody believed the Yankee skipper.

Before Sanford could gather his wits in reply the shanty door was flung wide open, and Nickles backed out, carrying in his arms a pine door, higher and wider than himself. He had lifted it from its hinges in the pantry, upsetting everything about it.

"I guess mebbe I ain't been a-watchin' this all summer fur nothin', gents," he said, planting the door squarely before the general. "You kin read it fur yerself, — it's 's plain 's print. If ye want what ye call an 'order,' here it is large as life."

It was the once clean pine door of the shanty, on which Sanford and the men had placed their signatures in blue pencil the day the level was fixed, and Carleton, defying Sanford, had said it should "go that way" or he would stop the work!

General Barton adjusted his eyeglasses and began reading the inscription. A verbatim record of Carleton's instructions was before him. The other members of the Board crowded around, reading it in silence.

General Barton replaced his gold-rimmed eyeglasses carefully in their case, and for a moment looked seaward in an abstracted sort of way. The curiously inscribed door had evidently made a deep impression upon him.

"I had forgotten about that record, general," said Sanford, "but I am very glad it has been preserved. It was made at the time, so we could exactly carry out the superintendent's instructions. As to its truth, I should prefer you to ask the men who signed it. They are all here around you."

The general looked again at Captain Joe and Caleb. There was no questioning their integrity. Theirs were faces that disarmed suspicion at once.

"Are these your signatures?" he asked, pointing to the scrawls in blue lead pencil subscribed under Sanford's.

"They are, sir," said Captain Joe and Caleb almost simultaneously; Caleb answering with a certain tone of solemnity, as if he were still in government service and under oath, lifting his hat as he spoke. Men long in government employ have this sort of unconscious awe in the presence of their superiors.

"Make a copy of it," said the general curtly to the secretary of the Board. Then he turned on his heel, crossed the Screamer's deck, and entered the cabin of the tender, where he was followed by the other members of the committee.

Ten minutes later the steward of the tender called Carleton. The men looked after him as he picked his way over the platforms and across the deck of the sloop. His face was flushed, and a nervous twitching of the muscles of his mouth showed his agitation over the summons. The apparition of the pantry door, they thought, had taken the starch out of him.

Mrs. Leroy crossed to Sanford's side and whispered anxiously, "What do you think, Henry?"

"I don't know yet, Kate. Barton is a gruff, exact man, and a martinet, but he hasn't a dishonest hair on his head. Wait."

The departure of the engineers aboard the tender, followed almost immediately by that of the superintendent, left the opposition, so to speak, unrepresented. Those of the ladies who were on sufficiently intimate terms with Sanford to mention the fact at all, and who, despite the major's efforts to lead them out of range, had heard every word of the discussion, expressed the hope that the affair would come out all right. One, a Mrs. Corson, said in a half-querulous tone that she thought they ought to be ashamed of themselves to find any fault, after all the hard work he had done. Jack and Smearly consulted apart. They were somewhat disturbed, but still believed that Sanford would win his case.

To the major, however, the incident had a far deeper and much more significant meaning.

"It's a part of their infernal system, Henry," he said in a sympathetic voice, now really concerned for his friend's welfare, — "a trick of the damnable oligarchy, suh, that is crushing out the life of the people. It is the first time since the wah that I have come as close as this to any of the representatives of this government, and it will be the last, suh."

Before Sanford could soothe the warlike spirit of his champion, the steward of the ten-

THE RECORD OF NICKLES, THE COOK 333

der again appeared, and, touching his cap, said the committee wished to see Mr. Sanford.

The young engineer excused himself to those about him and followed the steward, Mrs. Leroy looking after him with a glance of anxiety as he crossed the deck of the Screamer, — an anxiety which Sanford tried to relieve by an encouraging wave of his hand.

As Sanford entered the saloon Carleton was just leaving it, hat in hand. He did not raise his eyes. His face was blue-white. Little flecks of saliva were sticking in the corners of his mouth, as if his breath were dry.

General Barton sat at the head of the saloon table. The other members of the Board were seated below him.

"Mr. Sanford," said the general, "we have investigated the differences between yourself and the superintendent with the following result: First, the committee has accepted the work as it stands, believing in the truthfulness of yourself and your men, confirmed by a record which it could not doubt. Second, the withheld certificate will be signed and checks forwarded to you as soon as the necessary papers can be prepared. Third, Superintendent Carleton has been relieved from duty at Shark Ledge Light."

CHAPTER XXII

AFTER THE BATTLE

CARLETON's downfall was known all over the Ledge and on board every boat that lay at its wharf long before either he or Sanford regained the open air. The means of communication was that same old silent current that requires neither pole nor battery to put it into working order. Within thirty seconds of the time the ominous words fell from the general's lips, the single word "Dennis," the universal sobriquet for a discharged man our working world over, was in every man's mouth. Whatever medium was used, the meaning was none the less clear and unmistakable. The steward may have winked to the captain in the pilothouse, or the cook shrugged his shoulders, opening his mouth with the gasping motion of a strangling chicken, and so conveyed the news to the forecastle; or one of the crew, with ears wide open, might have found it necessary to uncoil a rope outside the cabin window at the precise moment the general gave his decision, and have instantly passed the news along to his nearest mate. Of one thing there was no doubt: Carleton had given his last order on Shark Ledge.

An animated discussion followed among the men.

"Ought to give him six months," blurted out Captain Bob Brandt, whose limited experience of government inspecting boards led him to believe that its officers were clothed with certain judicial powers. "Had n't 'a' been for old Hamfats" (Nickles's nickname) "an' his pantry door, he 'd 'a' swore Cap'n Joe's character away."

"Well, I 'm kind'er sorry for him, anyway," said Captain Joe, not noticing the skipper's humorous allusion. "Poor critter, he ain't real responsible. What 's he goin' to do fur a livin', now that the gov'ment ain't a-goin' to support him no more?"

"Ain't nobody cares; he 'll know better 'n to lie nex' time," grunted Lonny Bowles. "Is he comin' ashore here agin, Caleb, er has he dug a hole fur himself 'board the tender in the coal bunkers?"

Caleb smiled grimly, but made no reply. He never liked to think of Carleton, much less to talk of him. Since the night when he had waylaid Betty coming home from Keyport, his name had not passed the diver's lips. He had always avoided him on the work, keeping out of his way, not so much from fear of Carleton as from fear of himself,—fear that in some uncontrollable moment he might fall upon him and throttle him.

If a certain sigh of relief went up from the working force on the Ledge over Carleton's downfall and Sanford's triumph, a much more joyous feeling permeated the yacht. Not only were Jack and Smearly jubilant, but even Sam, with a grin the width of his face, had a little double shuffle of his own in the close quarters of the galley, while the major began forthwith to concoct a brew in which to drink Sanford's health, and of such mighty power that for once Sam disobeyed his instructions, and emptied a pint of Medford spring water instead of an equal amount of old Holland gin into the seductive mixture. "'Fo' God, Mr. Sanford, dey would n't one o' dem ladies knowed deir head from a whirlum-gig if dey 'd drank dat punch," he said afterwards to his master, in palliation of his sin.

Sanford took the situation with a calmness customary to him when things were going well. His principle in life was to do his best every time, and leave the rest to fate. When he worried it was before a crisis. He had not belittled the consequences of a rejection of the work. He knew how serious it might have been. Had the Board become thoroughly convinced that he had openly and without just cause violated both the written contract and the instructions of the superintendent, they might have been forced to make an example of him, and to require all the upper masonry to be torn down and rebuilt on a true level, a result which would have entailed the loss of thousands of dollars.

His own reply to General Barton and the Board was a grim, reserved, " I thank you, gentlemen," with an added hope that the new superintendent might be instructed to give written orders when any departure from the contract was insisted upon, to which the chief engineer agreed.

His greatest satisfaction, though, was really over his men. The vindication of his course was as much their triumph as his. He knew who had been its master spirits; the credit was not due to him, but to Captain Joe, Caleb, and Captain Brandt, whose pluck, skill, and devotion both to himself and the work had made its success possible. He had only inspired them to do their best.

Later, when he called them together on the Ledge and gave them the details of the interview, — he never kept anything of this kind from his working force, — he cautioned one and all of them to exercise the greatest patience and good temper toward the new superintendent, whoever he might be, who was promised in a few days, so that nothing might happen which would incur his ill will; reminding them that it would not do for a second superintendent to be disgruntled, no matter whose fault it was, to which Captain Joe sententiously replied:—

"All right; let 'em send who they like; sooner the better. But one thing I kin tell 'em, an' that is that none on 'em can't stop us now from gittin' through, no matter how ornery they be."

But of all the happy souls that breathed the air of this lovely autumn day Mrs. Leroy was the happiest. She felt, somehow, that the decision of the committee was a triumph for both Sanford and herself: for Sanford because of his constant fight against the elements, for her because of her advice and encouragement. As the words fell from Sanford's lips, telling her of the joyful news,— he had found her aboard the yacht and had told her first of all,— her face flushed, and her eyes lighted with genuine pleasure.

"What did I tell you!" she said, holding out her hand in a hearty, generous way, as a man would have done. "I knew you would do it. Oh, I am so proud of you, you great splendid fellow!"

Then a sudden inspiration seized her. She darted back again to the Ledge in search of Captain Joe, her dainty skirts raised about her tiny boots to keep them from the rough platforms.

"Do come and lunch with us, Captain Bell!" she exclaimed in her joyous way. "I really want you, and the ladies would so love to talk to you." She had not forgotten his tenderness over Betty the morning he came for her; more than that, he had stood by Sanford.

The captain stopped, somewhat surprised, and looked down into her eyes with the kindly expression of a big mastiff diagnosing a kitten.

"Well, that's real nice o' ye, an' I thank ye kindly," he answered, his eyes lighting up at her evident sincerity. "But ye see yer vittles would do me no good. So if ye won't take no offense I'll kind'er grub in with the other men. Cook's jes' give notice to all hands."

As she looked into his eyes her thoughts reverted to that morning in the hospital when the captain's same sense of the fitness of things had saved her from being established as nurse to the wounded men. She was about to press her request again when her glance fell on Caleb standing by himself a little way off. She turned and walked toward him. But it was not to ask him to luncheon.

"I have heard Mr. Sanford speak so often of you that I wanted to know you before I left the work," she said, holding out her little gloved hand. Caleb looked into her face and touched the dainty glove with two of his fingers, — he was afraid to do more, it was so small, — and, with his eyes on hers, listened while she spoke in a tender, sympathetic tone, lowering her voice so that no one could hear but himself, — not even Sanford: "I have heard all about your troubles,

Mr. West, and I am so sorry for you both; she stayed with me one night last summer. She said, poor child, she was very miserable; it's an awful thing to be alone in the world."

Sanford watched her as she flitted over the rough platforms like a bird that sings as it flies. Unaccountable as it was to him even in the happiness of his triumph, a strange feeling of disappointment came over him. He began in an utterly unreasonable way to wonder whether their intimacy would now be as close as before, and whether the daily conferences would end, since he had no longer any anxieties to lay before her.

Something in her delight, and especially in the frank way in which she had held out her hand like a man friend in congratulation, had chilled rather than cheered him. He felt hurt without knowing why. A sense of indefinable personal loss came over him. In the rush of contending emotions suddenly assailing him, he began to doubt whether she had understood his motives that night on the veranda when he had kissed her hand, — whether in fact he had ever understood her. Had she really conquered her feelings as he had his? Or had there been nothing to conquer? Then another feeling rose in his heart, — a vague jealousy of the very work which had bound them so closely together, and which now seemed to claim all her interest.

CHAPTER XXIII

A BROKEN DRAW

THROUGHOUT the luncheon that followed aboard the yacht the major was the life of the party. He had offered no apology either to Sanford or to any member of the committee for his hasty conclusions regarding the "damnable oligarchy." He considered that he had wiped away all bitterness, when, rising to his feet and rapping with the handle of his knife for order, he said with great dignity and suavity of manner:—

"On behalf of this queen among women," turning to Mrs. Leroy, "our lovely hostess, as well as these fair young buds"—a graceful wave of his hand—(some of these buds had grandchildren) "who adorn her table, I rise to thank you, suh,"—semi-military salute to General Barton,—"for the opportunity you have given them of doing honor to a gentleman and a soldier,"—a double-barreled compliment that brought a smile to that gentleman's face, and a suppressed ripple of laughter from the other members of the committee.

In the same generous way he filled his own

and everybody else's bumper for Sanford out of the bowl that Sam had rendered innocuous, addressing his friend as that "young giant, who has lighted up the pathway of the vasty deep." To which bit of grandiloquence Sanford replied that the major was premature, but that he hoped to accomplish it the following year.

In addition to conducting all these functions, the Pocomokian neglected no minor detail of the feast. He insisted upon making the coffee after an especial formula of his own, and cooled in a new way and with his own hands the several cordials banked up on Sam's silver tray. He opened parasols for the ladies and champagne for the men with equal grace and dexterity; was host, waiter, valet, and host again; and throughout the livelong day one unfailing source of enthusiasm, courtesy, and helpfulness. With all this be it said to his credit, he had never overstepped the limits of his position, as High Rubber-in-Chief, — his main purpose having been to get all the fun possible out of the situation, both for himself and for those about him. These praiseworthy efforts were not appreciated by all of the guests. The general and the committee had several times, in their own minds, put him down for a charlatan and a mountebank, especially when they deliberated upon the fit of his clothes, and his bombastic and sometimes fulsome speeches.

All these several vagaries, however, of the

distinguished Pocomokian only endeared him the more to Sanford and his many friends. They saw a little deeper under the veneer, and knew that if the major did smoke his hostess's cigars and drink her cognac, it was always as her guest and in her presence. They knew, too, that, poor and often thirsty as he was, he would as soon have thought of stuffing his carpet-bag with the sheets that covered his temporary bed as of filling his private flask with the contents of the decanter that Buckles brought nightly to his room. It was just this delicate sense of honor that saved him from pure vagabondage.

When coffee and cigars had been served, the general and his party again crossed the gang-plank to the tender, the mooring-lines were thrown off, and the two boats, with many wavings of hands from yacht and Ledge, kept on their respective courses. The tender was to keep on to Keyport, where the committee were to board the train for New York, and the yacht was to idle along until sundown, and so on into Medford harbor. Captain Joe and Caleb were to follow later in the tug that had towed out the Screamer, they being needed in Keyport to load some supplies.

As the tender steamed away the men on the Ledge looked eagerly for Carleton, that they might give him some little leave-taking of their own, — it would have been a characteristic one, — but he was nowhere to be seen.

"Buried up in the coal bunkers, jes' 's I said," laughed Lonny Bowles.

With the final wave to the fast disappearing tender of a red handkerchief, the property of the major, returned by the general standing in the stern of his own boat, Mrs. Leroy's party settled themselves on the forward deck of the yacht to enjoy the afternoon run back to Medford.

The ladies sat under the awnings, where they were made comfortable with cushions from the saloon below, while some of the men threw themselves flat on the deck cushions, or sat Turkish fashion in those several sprawling positions only possible under like conditions, and most difficult for some men to learn to assume properly. Jack Hardy knew to a nicety how to stow his legs away, and so did Sanford. Theirs were always invisible. Smearly never tried the difficult art. He thought it beneath his dignity; and then again there was too much of him in the wrong place. The major wanted to try it, and no doubt would have done so with decorum and grace but for his clothes. It was a straight and narrow way that the major had been walking all day, and he could run no risks.

Everything aboard the yacht had been going as merry as a marriage or any other happy bell of good cheer,— the major at his best, Smearly equally delightful, Helen and Jack happy as two song-birds, and Mrs. Leroy with a joyous word for every one between her confidences to Sanford, when just as the gayety was at its height a quick sharp ring was heard in the engine-room below. Almost at the same instant one of the crew touched Sanford on the shoulder and whispered something in his ear.

Sanford sprang to his feet and looked eagerly toward the shore.

The yacht at the moment was entering the narrow channel of Medford harbor, and the railroad trestle and draw could be plainly seen from its deck. Sanford's quick eye had instantly detected a break in the sky-line. The end of the railroad track placed on the trestle, and crossing within a few hundred feet of Mrs. Leroy's cottage, was evidently twisted out of shape, while across the channel, on its pposite end rested an engine and two cars, the outer one derailed and toppled over. On the water below were crowded small boats of every conceivable kind, hurrying to the scene, while the surrounding banks were black with people watching intently a group of men on board a scow, who were apparently trying to keep above water a large object which looked like a floating house.

Something serious had evidently happened.

A panic of apprehension instantly seized the guests on the yacht. Faces which but a few moments before had been rosy with smiles became suddenly anxious and frightened. Some of the ladies spoke in whispers; could it be possible, every one asked, that the train with General Barton and the committee on board had met with an accident?

Sanford, followed by Mrs. Leroy, hurried into the pilot-house to search the horizon from that elevation and see the better. One moment's survey removed all doubt from his mind. A train had gone through the draw; whether passenger or freight he could not tell. One thing was certain: some lives must be in danger, or the crowd would not watch so intently the group who were working with such energy aboard the rescuing scow. At Sanford's request three quick, short bells sounded in the engine-room below, and the yacht quivered along her entire length as she doubled her speed. When she came within hailing distance of the shore a lobster fisherman pulled out and crossed the yacht's bow.

"What's happened?" shouted Sanford, waving his hat to attract attention.

The fisherman stopped rowing, and the yacht slowed down.

"Train through the draw," came the answer.

"Passenger or freight?"

"'T ain't neither one. It's a repair train from Stonin'ton, with a lot o' dagos an' men. Caboose went clean under, an' two cars piled on top."

Sanford breathed freer; the Board were safe, anyhow.

"Anybody killed?"

"Yes. Some says six; some says more. None in the caboose got out. The dagos was on the dirt-car an' jumped."

The yacht sped on. As she neared the railroad draw Jack took Helen's hand and led her down into the cabin. He did not want her to see any sight that would shock her. Mrs. Leroy stood by Sanford; the yacht was her house, so to speak; some one might need its hospitality and shelter, and she wanted to be the first to offer it. The same idea had crossed Sanford's mind.

"Major," said Sanford, "please tell Sam to get some brandy ready and bring some of the mattresses from the crew's bunks up on deck; they may be useful."

A voice now hailed Sanford. It came from the end of the scow nearest the sunken house, now seen to be one end of a caboose car. "Is there a doctor aboard your yacht?"

"Yes, half a one. Who wants him?" called Smearly, leaning over the rail in the direction of the sound.

"We've got a man here we can't bring to. He's alive, but that's all."

The yacht backed water and moved close to the scow. Sanford jumped down, followed by Smearly carrying the brandy and the major with a mattress, and ran along her deck to where the man lay. The yacht kept on. It was to land the ladies a hundred yards away, and then return.

"Hand me that brandy, quick, major!" exclaimed Smearly, as he dropped on one knee and bent over the sufferer, parting the lips with his fingers and pouring a spoonful between the closed teeth. "Now pull that mattress closer, and some of you fellows make a pillow of your coats, and find something to throw over him when he comes to; it's the cold that's killing him. He'll pull through, I think."

Smearly's early training in the hospital service while making sketches during the war had more than once stood him in good stead.

The major was the first man in his shirt-sleeves; Leroy's commodore coat was beginning to be of some real service. Two of the scow's crew added their own coats, and then ran for an army blanket in the cabin of the scow. The sufferer was lifted up on the mattress and made more comfortable, the coats placed under his head, the army blanket tucked about him.

The injured man gave a convulsive gasp and partly opened his eyes. The brandy was doing its work. Sanford leaned over him to see if he could recognize him, but the ooze and slime clung so thickly to the mustache and closely trimmed beard that he could not make out his features. He seemed to be under thirty years of age, strong and well built. He was dressed in a blue shirt and overalls, and looked like a mechanic.

"How many others?" asked Sanford, looking toward the wreck.

"He's the only one alive," answered the captain of the scow. "We hauled him through the winder of the caboose just as she was a-turnin' over; he's broke something, some'ers, I guess, or he'd 'a' come to quicker. There's two dead men under there," pointing to the sunken caboose, "so the brakeman says. If we had a diver we could git 'em up. The railroad superintendent's been here, an' says he'll send for one; but you know what that means,— he'll send for a diver after they git this caboose up; by that time they'd be smashed into pulp."

The yacht had now steamed back to the wreck with word from Mrs. Leroy to send for whatever would be needed to make the injured man comfortable. Sam delivered the message, standing in the bow of the yacht. He had not liked the idea of leaving Sanford, when the yacht moved off from the scow, and had so expressed himself to the sailing-master. He was Sanford's servant, not Mrs. Leroy's, he had said, and when people were getting blown up and his master had to stay and attend to them, his place was beside him, not "waitin' on de ladies."

With the approach of the yacht Sanford looked at his watch thoughtfully, and raising his voice to the sailing-master, who was standing in the pilot-house, his hand on the wheel, said: "Captain, I want you to tow this scow to Mrs. Leroy's dock, so a doctor can get at this wounded man. He needs hot blankets at once. Then crowd on everything you've got and run to Keyport. Find Captain Joe Bell, and tell him to put my big air-pump aboard and bring Caleb West and his diving-dress. There are two dead men down here who must be got at before the wrecking train begins on the caboose. My colored boy, Sam, will go with you and help you find the captain's house, — he knows where he lives. If you are quick you can make Keyport and back in an hour"

CHAPTER XXIV

THE SWINGING GATE

WHEN the tug landed Caleb at Keyport this same afternoon, he hurried through his duties and went straight to his cabin. Mrs. Leroy's sympathetic words were still in his ears. He could hear the very tones of her voice and recall the pleading look in her eyes. He wished he had told her the whole truth then and there, and how he felt toward Betty; and he might have done so had not the other ladies been there, expecting her aboard the yacht. He did not feel hurt or angry; he never was with those who spoke well of his wife. Her words had only deepened the conviction that had lately taken possession of his own mind, — that he alone, of all who knew Betty, had shut his heart against her. Even this woman, — a total stranger, — who had taken her out of the streets and befriended her still pleaded for her. When would his own heart ever be softened? What did he want her to do for him? Crawl back on her hands and knees and lie outside his door until he took her in? And if she never came, — what then?

How long would she be able to endure her present life? He had saved her from Carleton. So far no one except Betty, Carleton, and himself had known of the night attack; not even Captain Joe. It was best not to talk about it; it might injure her. But who else would try to waylay and insult her? Maybe his holding out so long against her would force her into other temptations, and so ruin her. What if it was already too late? Lacey had been seen round Keyport lately,— once at night. He knew he wrote to her; Bert Simmons, the letter-carrier, had shown him other letters with the Stonington postmark. Was Lacey hanging round Keyport because she had sent for him? And if she went back to him after all,— whose fault was it?

At the thought of Lacey the beads of sweat stood on his forehead. Various conflicting emotions took possession of him, bringing the hot blood to his cheek and setting his finger-nails deep into the palms of his hands. It was only at rare intervals, when he had run into Stonington aboard the Screamer, or on one of the tugs short of coal or water, that he had seen the man who had ruined his home, and then only at a distance. The young rigger was at work around the cars on the dock. Caleb had never known whether Lacey had seen him. He thought not. The men said the young fellow always moved away when any of the Keyport boats came in. Then his mind reverted to Captain Joe and to the night he pleaded for her, and to the way he said over and over again, "She ain't nothin' but a child, Caleb, an' all of us is liable to go astray." These words seemed to burn themselves into his brain.

As the twilight came on he went upstairs on tiptoe, treading as lightly as if he knew she was asleep and he feared to waken her. Standing by the bed, he looked about him in an aimless, helpless way, his eyes resting finally on the counterpane, and the pillow he had placed every night for her on her side of the bed. It was yellow and soiled now. In the same half-dazed, dreamy way he stepped to the closet, opened the door cautiously, and laid his hand upon her dresses, which hung where she had left them, smoothing them softly with his rough fingers. He could easily have persuaded himself (had she been dead) that her spirit was near him, whispering to him, leading him about, her hand in his.

As he stood handling the dresses, with their little sleeves and skirts, all the paternal seemed suddenly to come out in him. She was no longer his wife, no longer the keeper of his house, no longer the custodian of his good name. She was his child, his daughter, his own flesh and blood, — one who had gone astray, one who had pleaded for forgiveness, and who was now alone in the world, with every door closed against her but Captain Joe's.

In the brightness of this new light of pity in him a great weight seemed lifted from his heart. His own sorrow and loneliness seemed trivial and selfish beside hers. He big and strong, fearless to go and come, able to look every man in the face; and she a timid girl, shrinking, frightened, insulted, hiding even from those who loved her. What sort of man was he to shut his door in her face and send her shuddering down the road?

With these new thoughts there came a sudden desire to help, to reach out his arms toward her, to stand up and defend her, — defend her, out in the open, before all the people.

Catching up his hat, he hurried from the house and walked briskly down the road. It was Betty's hour for coming home. Since her encounter with Carleton there had been few evenings in the week he had not, with one excuse or another, loitered along the road, hiding behind the fish-house until she passed, watching her until she reached the swinging gate. Soon the residents up and down the road began to time his movements. "Here comes Caleb," they would say; "Betty ain't far off. Ain't nothin' goin' to touch her as long as Caleb's round."

This watchful care had had its effect. Not only had Captain Joe and Aunty Bell taken her part, but Caleb was looking after her too. When this became common talk the little remaining tattle ceased. Better not talk about Betty, the gossips said among themselves; Caleb might hear it.

When the diver reached the top of the hill overlooking Captain Joe's cottage, his eye fell upon Betty's slight figure stepping briskly up the hill, her shawl drawn tightly about her shoulders, her hat low down on her face. She had passed the willows and was halfway to the swinging gate. Caleb quickened his pace and walked straight toward her.

She saw him coming, and stopped in sudden fright. For an instant she wavered, undecided whether she would turn and run, or brave it out and pass him. If she could only get inside the garden before he reached her! As she neared the gate she heard his footsteps on the road, and could see from under the rim of her hat the rough shoes and coarse trousers cement-stained up as far as his knees. Only once since she had gone off with Lacey had she been so close to him.

Gathering all her strength she sprang forward, her hand on the swinging gate.

"I'll hold it back, child," came a low, sweet voice, and an arm was stretched out before her. "It shan't slam to and hurt ye."

He was so close she could have touched him. She saw, even in her agony, the gray, fluffy beard and the wrinkled, weather-stained throat with the unbuttoned collar of the flannel shirt.

She saw, too, the big brown hand, as it rested on the gate.

She did not see his eyes. She dared not look so high.

As she entered the kitchen door she gave a hurried glance behind. He was following her slowly, as if in deep thought; his hands behind his back, his eyes on the ground.

Aunty Bell was bending over the stove when Betty dashed in.

"It's Caleb! He's coming in! Oh, aunty, don't let him see me — please — please!"

The little woman turned quickly, startled at the sudden interruption.

"He don't want ye, child." The girl's appearance alarmed her. She is not often this way, she thought.

"He does — he does. He spoke to me — Oh, where shall I go?" she moaned, wringing her hands, her whole body trembling like one with an ague.

"Go nowhere," answered Aunty Bell in decided tones. "Stay where ye be. I'll go see him. 'T ain't nothin', child, only somethin' for the cap'n." She had long since given up all hope of Caleb's softening.

As she spoke the diver's slow and measured step could be heard sounding along the plank walk.

Aunty Bell let down her apron and stepped to the door. Betty crept behind the panels, watching him through the crack, stifling her breath lest she should miss his first word. Oh, the music of his voice at the gate! Not his words, but the way he spoke, — the gentleness, the pity, the compassion of it all! As this thought surged through her mind she grew calmer; a sudden impulse to rush out and throw herself at his feet took possession of her. He surely could not repel her when his voice carried such tenderness to her heart. A great sob rose in her throat. The measured, slow step came closer.

At this instant she heard the outer gate swing to a second time with a resounding bang, and Captain Joe's voice calling, "Git yer dress, Caleb, quick as God 'll let ye! Train through the Medford draw an' two men drownded. I've been lookin' fur ye everywhere."

"Who says so?" answered Caleb calmly without moving.

"Mr. Sanford's sent the yacht. His nigger's outside now. Hurry, I tell ye; we ain't got a minute."

Betty waited, her heart throbbing. Caleb paused for an instant and looked earnestly and hesitatingly toward the house. Then he turned quickly and followed Captain Joe.

Aunty Bell waited until she saw both men cross the road on their way to the dock. Then she went in to find Betty.

She was still crouched behind the door, her

limbs trembling beneath her. On her face was the dazed look of one who had missed, without knowing why, some great crisis.

"Don't cry, child," said the little woman, patting her cheek. "It's all right. I knowed he did n't come for ye."

"But, Aunty Bell, Aunty Bell," she sobbed, as she threw her arms about her neck, "I wanted him so."

CHAPTER XXV

UNDER THE PITILESS STARS

The purple twilight had already settled over Medford harbor when the yacht with Captain Joe and Caleb on board glided beneath the wrecked trestle with its toppling cars, and made fast to one of the outlying spiles of the draw. As the yacht's stern swung in toward the sunken caboose which coffined the bodies of the drowned men, a small boat put off from the shore and Sanford sprang aboard. He had succeeded in persuading the section boss in charge of the wrecking gang to delay wrecking operations until Caleb could get the bodies, insisting that it was inhuman to disturb the wreck until they were recovered. As the yacht was expected every moment and the services of the diver would be free, the argument carried weight.

"Everything is ready, sir," said Captain Joe, as Sanford walked aft to meet him. "We've 'iled up the cylinders, an' the pump can git to work in a minute. I'll tend Caleb; I know how he likes his air. Come, Caleb, git inter yer dress; this tide's on the turn."

The three men walked along the yacht's deck to where the captain had been oiling the air-pump. It had been lifted clear of its wooden case and stood near the rail, its polished brasses glistening in the light of a ship's lantern slung to the ratlines. Sprawled over a deck settee lay the rubber diving-dress, — body, arms, and legs in one piece, like a suit of seamless underwear, — and beside it the copper helmet, a trunkless head with a single staring eye. The air-hose and life-line, together with the back-plate and breast-plate of lead and the iron-shod shoes, lay on the deck.

Caleb placed his folded coat on a camp-stool, drew off his shoes, tucked his trousers into his stocking legs, and began twisting himself into his rubber dress, Sanford helping him with the arms and neckpiece. Captain Joe, meanwhile, overhauled the plates and loosened the fastenings of the weighted shoes.

With the screwing on of Caleb's helmet and the tightening of his face-plate, the crowd increased. The news of the coming diver had preceded the arrival of the yacht, and the trestle and shores were lined with people.

When Caleb, completely equipped, stepped on the top round of the ladder fastened to the yacht's side, the crowd climbed hurriedly over the wrecked cars to the stringers of the trestle to get a better view of the huge man-fish with its distorted head and single eye, and its long antennæ of hose and life-line. Such a sight would be uncanny even when the blazing sun burnished the diver's polished helmet and the one eye of the face-plate glared ominously; but at night, under the wide sky, with only a single swinging lamp to illumine the gloomy shadows, the man-fish became a thing of dread, — a ghoulish spectre who prowled over foul and loathsome things, and who rose from the slime of deep bottoms only to breathe and sink again.

Caleb slowly descended the yacht's ladder, one iron-shod foot at a time, until the water reached his armpits. Then he swung himself clear, and the black, oily ooze closed over him.

Captain Joe leaned over the yacht's rail, the life-line wound about his wrist, his sensitive hand alert for the slightest nibble of the man-fish. These nibbles are the unspoken words of the diver below to his "tender" above. His life often depends on these being instantly understood and answered.

For the diver is more than amphibious; he is twice-bodied, — one man under water, one man above, with two heads and four hands. The connecting links between these two bodies — these Siamese twins — are the life-line and signal-cord through which they speak to each other, and the air-hose carrying their life-breath.

As Caleb dropped out of sight the crew crowded to the yacht's rail, straining their eyes in the gloom. In the steady light of the lantern they could see the cord tighten and slacken as the diver felt his way among the wreckage, or sank to the bottom. They could follow, too, the circle of air bubbles floating on the water above where he worked. No one spoke; no one moved. An almost deathly stillness prevailed. The only sounds were the wheezing of the air-pump turned by the sailor, and the swish of the life-line cutting through the water as the diver talked to his tender. With these were mingled the unheeded sounds of the night and of the sea, — the soft purring of the tall grasses moving gently to and fro in the night-wind, and the murmuring of the sluggish water stirred by the rising tide and gurgling along the yacht's side on its way to the stern.

"Has he found them yet, Captain Joe?" Sanford asked, after some moments, under his breath.

"Not yet, sir. He's been through one car, an' is now crawlin' through t'other. He says they're badly broke up. Run that air-hose overboard, sir; let it all go; he wants it all. Thank ye. He says the men are in their bunks at t'other end, if anywheres; that's it, sir."

There came a quick double jerk, answered by one long pull.

"More air, sir, — *more air!*" Captain Joe cried in a quick, rising voice. "So-o, that'll do."

The crew looked on in astonishment. The

talk of the man-fish was like the telephone talk of a denizen from another world.

A quarter of an hour passed. Not a single tremor had been felt along the life-line, nor had Captain Joe moved from his position on the rail. His eye was still on the circle of bubbles that rose and were lost in the current. Sanford grew uneasy.

"What's he doing now, captain?" he asked in an anxious voice.

"Don't know, sir; ain't heard from him in some time."

"Ask him."

"No, sir; better let him alone. He might be crawlin' through somewheres; might tangle him up if I moved the line. He's got to feel his way, sir. It's black as mud down there. If the men warn't in the caboose he wouldn't never find 'em at night."

A quick, sharp jerk from under the surface now swished through the water, followed by a series of strong, rapid pulls, — seesaw pulls, as if some great fish were struggling with the line.

"He's got one of 'em, sir," said the captain, with sudden animation. "Says that's all. He's been through two cars an' felt along every inch o' the way. If there's another, he's got washed out o' the door."

As he spoke the air-hose slackened and the life-line began to sag.

Captain Joe turned quickly to Sanford. "Pull in that hose, Mr. Sanford," hauling in the slack of the life-line himself. "He's a-comin' up; he'll bring him with him."

These varied movements on the yacht stirred the overhanging crowd into action. They hoped the diver was coming up; they hoped, too, he would bring the dead man. His appearing with his awful burden would be less terrible than not knowing what the man-fish was doing. The crew of the yacht crowded still closer to the rail; this fishing at night for the dead had a fascination they could not resist. Some of them even mounted the ratlines, and others ran aft to see the diver rise from the deep sea.

In a moment more the black water heaved in widening circles, and Caleb's head and shoulders were thrust up within an oar's length of the yacht. The light of the lantern fell upon his wet helmet and extended arm.

The hand clutched a man's boot.

Attached to the boot were a pair of blue overalls and a jacket. The head of the drowned man hung down in the water. The face was hidden.

Captain Joe leaned forward, lowered the lantern that Caleb might see the ladder, reeled in the life-line hand over hand, and dragged the diver and his burden to the foot of the ladder. Sanford seized a boat-hook, and, reaching down, held the foot close to the yacht's side; then a sailor threw a noose of marline twine around the boot. The body was now safe from the treacherous tide.

Caleb raised himself slowly until his helmet was just above the level of the deck. Captain Joe removed the lead plates from his breast and back, and unscrewed his glass face-plate, letting out his big beard and letting in the cool night-air.

"Any more down there?" he cried, his mouth close to Caleb's face as he spoke.

Caleb shook his head inside the copper helmet. "No; don't think so. Guess ye thought I was a-goin' to stay all night, did n't ye? I had ter crawl through two cars 'fore I got him; when I found him he was under a tool-chest. One o' them lower cars, I see, has got its end stove out."

"Jes' 's I told ye, Mr. Sanford," said Captain Joe in a positive tone; "t'other body went out with the tide."

The yacht, with the rescued dead man laid on the deck and covered with a sheet, steamed across the narrow channel, reversed her screw, and touched the fender spiles of her wharf as gently as one would tap an egg. Sanford, who, now that the body was found, had gone ahead in the small boat in search of the section boss, was waiting on the wharf for the arrival of the yacht.

"There's more trouble, Captain Joe," he called. "There's a man here that the scow saved from the wreck. Mr. Smearly thought he would pull through, but the doctor who's with him says he can't live an hour. His spine is injured. Major Slocomb and Mr. Smearly are now in Stonington in search of a surgeon. The section boss tells me his name is Williams, and that he works in the machine shops. Better look at him and see if you know him."

Captain Joe and Caleb walked toward the scow. She was moored close to the grassy slope of the shore. On her deck stood half a dozen men,—one a diver sent by the manager of the road, and who had arrived with his dress and equipment too late to be of service.

The injured man lay in the centre. Beside him, seated on one of Mrs. Leroy's piazza chairs, was the village doctor; his hand was on the patient's pulse. One of Mrs. Leroy's maids knelt at the wounded man's feet, wringing out cloths that had been dipped in buckets of boiling water brought by the men servants. Mrs. Leroy and Helen and one or two guests sat a short distance away on the lawn. Over by the stables swinging lights could be seen glimmering here and there, as if men were hurrying. There were lights, too, on the dock and on the scow's deck; one hung back of the sufferer's head, where it could not shine on his eyes.

The wounded man, who had been stripped of his wet clothes, lay on a clean mattress. Over him was thrown a soft white blanket. His head was propped up on a pillow taken from one of Mrs. Leroy's beds. She had begged to have him moved to the house, but the doctor would not consent until the surgeon arrived. So he kept him out in the warm night-air, under the stars.

Dying and dead men were no new sight to Captain Joe and Caleb. The captain had sat by too many wounded men knocked breathless by falling derricks, and seen their life-blood ooze away, and Caleb had dragged too many sailors from sunken cabins. This accident was not serious; only three killed and one wounded out of twenty. In the morning their home people would come and take them away,—in cloth-covered boxes, or in plain pine. That was all.

With these thoughts in his mind, and in obedience to Sanford's request, Captain Joe walked toward the sufferer, nodded to the Medford doctor sitting beside him, picked up the lantern which hung behind the man's head, and turned the light full on the pale face. Caleb stood at one side talking with the captain of the scow.

"He ain't no dago," said Captain Joe, as he turned to the doctor. "Looks to me like one o' them young fellers what's"— He stopped abruptly. Something about the injured man attracted him.

He dropped on one knee beside the bed, pushed back the matted hair from the man's forehead, and examined the skin carefully.

For some moments he remained silent, scanning every line in the face. Then he rose to his feet, folded his arms across his chest, his eyes still fastened on the sufferer, and said slowly and thoughtfully to himself, —

"Well, I'm damned!"

The doctor bent his head in expectation, eager to hear the captain's next words, but the captain was too absorbed to notice the gesture. For some minutes he continued looking at the dying man.

"Come here, Caleb!" he called, beckoning to the diver. "Hold the lantern close. Who's that?" His voice sank almost to a whisper. "Look in his face."

"I don't know, cap'n; I never see him afore."

At the sound of the voices the head on the pillow turned, and the man half opened his eyes, and groaned heavily. He was evidently in great pain, — too great for the opiates wholly to deaden.

"Look agin, Caleb; see that scar on his cheek; that's where the Screamer hit 'im. That's Bill Lacey."

Caleb caught up the lantern as Captain Joe had done, and turned the light full on the dying man's face. Slowly and carefully he examined every feature, — the broad forehead, deep-sunk eyes, short, curly hair about the temples, and the mustache and close-trimmed beard, which had been worn as a disguise, no doubt, along with his new name of Williams. In the same searching way his eye passed over the broad shoulders and slender, supple body outlined under the clinging blanket, and so on down to the small, well-shaped feet that the kneeling maid was warming.

"It's him," he said quietly, stepping back to the mast, and folding his arms behind his back, while his eyes were fixed on the drawn face.

During this exhaustive search Captain Joe followed every expression that swept over the diver's face. How would the death of this man affect Betty?

With an absorbed air, the captain picked up an empty nail-keg, and crossing the deck sat down beside the mattress, his hands on his knees, watching the sufferer. As he looked at the twitching muscles of the face and the fading color, the bitterness cherished for months against this man faded away. He saw only the punishment that had come, its swiftness and its sureness. Then another face came before him, — a smaller one, with large and pleading eyes.

"Ain't no chance for him, I s'pose?" he said to the doctor in a low tone.

The only answer was an ominous shake of the head and a significant rubbing of the edge of the doctor's hand across the waist-line of the captain's back. Captain Joe nodded his head; he knew, — the spine was broken.

The passing of a spirit is a sacred and momentous thing, an impressive spectacle even to rough men who have seen it so often.

One by one the watchers on the scow withdrew. Captain Joe and the doctor remained beside the bed; Caleb stood a few feet away, leaning against the mast, the full glow of the lantern shedding a warm light over his big frame and throwing his face into shadow. What wild, turbulent thoughts surged through his brain no one knew but himself. Beads of sweat had trickled down his face, and he loosened his collar to breathe the better.

Presently the captain sank on his knee again beside the mattress. His face had the firm, determined expression of one whose mind has been made up on some line of action that has engrossed his thoughts. He put his mouth close to the sufferer's ear.

"It's me, Billy, — Cap'n Joe. Do ye know me?"

The eyes opened slowly and fastened themselves for an instant upon the captain's face. A dull gleam of recognition stirred in their glassy depths; then the lids closed wearily. The glimpse of Lacey's mind was but momentary, yet to the captain it was unmistakable. The brain was still alert.

He leaned back and beckoned to Caleb.

"Come over 'ere," he said in a low whisper, "an' git down close to 'im. He ain't got long ter live. Don't think o' what he done to you; git that out o' yer head; think o' where he's a-goin'. Don't let him go with that on yer mind; it ain't decent, an' it'll haunt ye. Git down close to 'im, an' tell 'im ye ain't got nothin' agin 'im; do it for me, Caleb. Ye won't never regret it."

The diver knelt in a passive, listless way, as one kneels in a church to the sound of an altar bell. The flame of the lantern fell on his face and shaggy beard, lighting up the earnest, thoughtful eyes and tightly pressed lips.

"Pull yerself together, Billy, jes' once fur me," said Captain Joe in a half-coaxing voice. "It's Caleb bendin' over ye; he wants to tell ye somethin'."

The sunken, shriveled lids parted quickly, and the eyes rested for a moment on the diver's face. The lips moved, as if the man were about to speak. But no words came.

Over the cheeks and nose there passed a convulsive twitching, — the neck stiffened, the head straightened back upon the pillow.

Then the jaw fell.

"He's dead," said the doctor, laying his hand over the man's heart.

Captain Joe drew the blanket over the dead face, rose from his knees, and, with his arm in Caleb's, left the scow and walked slowly toward the yacht. The doctor gathered up his remedies, gave some directions to the watchman, and joined Mrs. Leroy and the ladies on the lawn.

Only the watchman on the scow was left, and the silent stars,—stern, unflinching, pitiless, like the eyes of many judges.

CHAPTER XXVI

CALEB TRIMS HIS LIGHTS

CALEB and Captain Joe sat on the yacht's deck on their way back to Keyport. The air-pump had been lifted into its case, and the dress and equipment had been made ready to be put ashore at the paraphernalia dock.

The moon had risen, flooding the yacht with white light and striping the deck with the clear-cut, black shadows of the stanchions. On the starboard bow burned Keyport Light, and beyond flashed Little Gull, a tiny star on the far-off horizon.

Caleb leaned back on a settee, his eyes fixed on the glistening sea. He had not spoken a word since his eyes rested on Lacey's face.

"Caleb," said Captain Joe, laying his hand on the diver's knee, "mebbe ye don't feel right to me fur sayin' what I did, but I did n't want ye to let 'im go an' not tell 'im ye had n't no hatred in yer heart toward 'im. It'd come back to plague ye, and ye've had sufferin' enough already 'long o' him. He won't worry you nor her no more. He's lived a mean, stinkin' life, an' he's died 's I allus knowed he would,—with nobody's hand ter help 'im. Caleb,"—he paused for an instant and looked into the diver's face,—"you 'n me 's knowed each other by an' large a many a year; ye know what I want ye to do; ye know what hurts me an' has ever sence the child come back. He's out o' yer hands now. God's punished him. Be good to yerself an' to her, an' forgive her. Take Betty back."

The old man turned and slipped his hand over Captain Joe's,—a hard, horny hand, with a heart-throb in every finger-tip.

"Cap'n Joe, I know how ye feel. There ain't nothin' between us; but yer wrong about *him*. As I stood over him to-night I fit it all out with myself. If he'd 'a' lived long 'nough I'd 'a' told him, jes' 's ye wanted me to. But yer ain't never had this thing right; I ain't a-blamin' her."

"Then take 'er home, an' quit this foolish life ye're leadin', an' her heart a-breakin' every day for love o' ye. Ain't ye lonely 'nough without her? God knows she is without you."

Caleb slowly withdrew his hand from Captain Joe's and put his arms behind his head, making a rest of his interlocked fingers.

"When ye say she's a-breakin' her heart for me, Cap'n Joe, ye don't know it all." His eyes looked up at the sky as he spoke. "'Tain't that I ain't willin' to take 'er back. I allus wanted to help her, an' I allus wanted to take

care of her, — not to have her take care o' me.
I made up my mind this mornin', when I see
how folks was a-treatin' 'er, to ask 'er to come
home. If I'd treat 'er right, they'd treat 'er
right; I know it. But I warn't the man for
her, an' she don't love me now no more 'n
she did. That's what hurts me an' makes
me afraid. Now I'll tell ye why I know she
don't love me; tell ye something ye don't know
at all," — he turned his head as he spoke, and
looked the captain full in the eyes, his voice
shaking, — "an' when I tell ye I want to say
I ain't a-blamin' her." The words that followed
came like the slow ticking of a clock. "He's
— been — a-writin' — to 'er — ever since — she
left 'im. Bert Simmons — showed me the letters."

"You found that out, did ye?" said Captain
Joe, a sudden angry tremor in his voice. "Ye're
right; he has! Been a-writin' to her ever sence
she left him, — sometimes once a month, sometimes once a week, an' lately about every day."

Caleb raised his head. This last was news
to him.

"And that ain't all. Every one o' them letters she's brought to me, jes' 's fast as she
got 'em, an' I locked 'em in my sea-chest along
o' the money ye gin her every week, an' the
money and letters are there now An' there's
more to it yet. *There ain't nary seal broke on
any one of Lacey's.* Whoever's been a-lyin' to

ye, Caleb, ain't told ye one half o' what he ought to know."

Captain Joe swung back his garden gate and walked quickly up the plank walk, his big, burly body swaying as he moved. The house was dark, except for a light in the kitchen window, and another in Betty's room. He saw Aunty Bell in a chair by the table, but he hurried by, on his way upstairs, without a word. Caleb followed with slow and measured step. When he reached the porch, Aunty Bell had left her seat and was standing on the mat.

"Why, Caleb, be ye comin' in too?" she said. "I'll git supper for both o' ye. Guess ye're tuckered out."

"I don't want no supper," he answered gravely, without looking at her. "I'll go into the settin'-room an' wait, if ye'll let me."

She opened the door silently for him, wondering if he was in one of his moods. The only light in the room came from the street-lamp, stenciling the vines on the drawn shades.

"I'll fetch a light for ye, Caleb," she said quietly, and turned toward the kitchen. In the hall she paused, her knees shaking, a prayer in her heart. Captain Joe and Betty were coming down the stairs, Betty's face hidden on his shoulder, her trembling fingers clinging to his coat.

"Ain't nothin' to skeer ye, child," the cap-

" Ain't nothin' to skeer ye, child"

tain said, patting the girl's cheek as he stopped at the threshold. "It's all right. He's in there waitin'," and he closed the door upon them.

Then he walked straight toward Aunty Bell, two big tears rolling down his cheeks, and, laying his hand upon her shoulder, said, "Caleb's got his lights trimmed, an' Betty's found harbor. The little gal's home."

In another room, some miles away, before a window that looked upon the sea, sat a woman, with cheeks tight pressed between her hands. The low-lying drowsy moon shed a white light on her thoughtful face and silvered the fluff of loosened hair that fell about her shoulders. She had sat there for hours — long after the house was silent. Outside the world was still: only the lapping of little wave-tongues along the shore was heard; the croaking of frogs in the marsh, and the cry of the night-hawk circling as he flew.

On the desk beside her lay an open letter with a Paris postmark. It had come by the late mail.

Once in a while her eyes would rest on the shimmer of silver framing the Ledge. Then some remembrance of the day would rush over her: the anxious waiting for the verdict; Sanford's upraised hand as he entered the cabin;

the gaunt outline of the wrecked trestle and the ghostly lantern that burned above the head of the dying man. From out the turmoil of these contending memories one face shone clear and strong, with fixed and questioning eyes.

In that one look she had read his inmost depth. She had caught the sudden uplifting of the lids, the wondering glance at her joyous words of praise, and the shadow that followed.

"It is best so," she whispered to herself at last. "It is the only way. I did not mean to hurt him, — only to help. Help him — and me."

With a tired, listless air, she rose from her seat, folded the letter slowly, and locked it in her desk.

THE END.

www.ingramcontent.com/pod-product-compliance
Lightning Source LLC
Chambersburg PA
CBHW032027220426
43664CB00006B/391